FEELING POWER

FEELING POWER

Emotions and Education

MEGAN BOLER

Routledge

NEW YORK LONDON

Published in 1999 by
Routledge
29 West 35th Street
New York, NY 10001

Published in Great Britain by
Routledge
11 New Fetter Lane
London EC4P 4EE

Printed in the United States of America on acid-free paper.

Permissions Acknowledgments:
Boler, Megan. "The Risk of Empathy: Interrogating Multiculturalism's Gaze." Reprinted from Cultural Studies Vol. 11 no. 2 pp. 253–273 Copyright © 1997 by Routledge. Reprinted with permission of publisher.
Boler, Megan. "License to Feel: Teaching in the Context of War." From *Articulating the Global and the Local* by Ann Cvetkovich and Douglas Kellner. Copyright © 1996 by Westview Press. Reprinted by Permission of Perseus Books LLC.

10 9 8 7 6 5 4 3 2 1

Library of Congress Catalogue-in-Publication Data

Boler, Megan.
Feeling Power : emotions and education / Megan Boler ;
foreword by Maxine Greene.
p. cm.
Includes bibliographical references.
ISBN 0-415-92103-1 hb. — ISBN 0-415-92104 X pb
1. Critical pedagogy. 2. Affective education. 3. Emotions and cognition
4. Feminism and education. I. Title.
LC196.B65 1999
370.15'3 — dc21 98-27448
CIP

for my mother Deetje B.
in honor of her rebel spirit, poet's soul,
and relentless and inspiring struggle for a just world

FEELING POWER

Emotions and Education

MEGAN BOLER

PART I

Emotions as a Site of Social Control

PART II

Emotions as a Site of Political Resistance

Foreword

by Maxine Greene

TONI MORRISON, writing in *The New Yorker*, tells of coming upon an old fisherwoman fishing off the seawall at the end of a neighbor's garden. They talk; the woman says she will be coming back; but the writer never sees or hears of her again. She begins to tell about the difficulty of dealing with the stranger, of the "resources available to us for benign access to each other, for vaulting the mere blue air that separates us. . . ." At the end she concludes that there are no strangers; rather, we are likely to be seeking some missing aspect of ourselves. "For the stranger is not foreign, she is random, not alien but remembered; and it is the randomness of the encounter with our already known—although unacknowledged—selves that summons a ripple of alarm. That makes us reject the figure and the emotions it provokes—especially when these emotions are profound. It is also what makes us want to own, govern, administrate the Other. To romance her, if we can, back into our own mirrors. In either instance (of alarm or false reverence), we deny her personhood, the specific individuality we insist on for ourselves."[1] In many senses Megan Boler's book moves us to confront the mystery of the stranger, "to close the distance," to rediscover "the singularity, the community, the inextinguishable sacredness of the human race."[1] She does this by provoking her readers to explore the "gendered rules of emotional conduct" and the "politics of emotion," to recognize what a rediscovery of the place of emotion in education can signify. She takes us on a remarkable journey through landscapes frequently invisible—landscapes on which the place of social control and of resistance to such control show themselves. Because emotion plays such an important role in both, as this book makes so clear, we may find in ourselves a numbness or passivity due to our denials, to our *not* reading the landscapes Boler brings within our sight.

Surely women and girls have suffered most frequently from the subordination of emotion to formal conceptions of rationality. Megan Boler not only points to the ways in which they have been embarrassed and demeaned by being thought of as "emotional" beings, incapable of the kinds of conceptual-

---

[1] Toni Morrison, "Strangers." *The New Yorker*, 12 October, 1998, p. 70.

ization, logical thinking, and controlled behavior assumed to make men and boys more effective citizens, producers, or administrators. She points as well to the role of feminist theory and feminist thinking in reconceptions of critical thinking and pedagogy. Few scholars have taken heed, as Boler does, of the influence of the consciousness-raising movement on such pedagogies as Paulo Freire's, or the kinship of feminist theorists to the great thinkers in the civil rights movement. Nor (not surprisingly) have our best known workers in the domains of critical literacy named the explorations and articulations of emergent feminist scholars as contributory to poststructuralist, postmodern, and neo-Marxist modes of thought.

Probing the importance of emotion (and its unquestionable neglect) Boler does not try to reconstitute old dualisms. At once she is wholly aware of what is called "binary opposition." Her argument for the recognition of emotion in discourse and praxis makes more understandable the claim that, in patriarchal society, "man" is the founding principle and "woman" the excluded, the opposite, the other. The critical operations intended to undermine such oppositions must include, according to the text that follows, attentiveness to the exclusion of emotion from the Enlightenment conception of the human being in addition to the discoveries stemming from consciousness-raising, an opening between the public and the private spaces that may allow for new modes of collaboration, particularly where emotion is concerned.

It is difficult not to refer to poetry in pondering the bringing of the life of emotion into the open, fresh air, instead of confining it to enclosed rooms. Adrienne Rich, most particularly, has grasped what is involved. In a poem called "Mother-Right," she writes:

> The man is walking boundaries
> measuring   He believes in what is his
> the grass   the waters underneath   the air
> the air   through which child and mother
> are running   the boy singing
> the woman   eyes sharpened in the light
> heart stumbling   making for the open [2]

Megan Boler's work suggests images of break through, suggestions of what the woman released by the power of emotion (no longer apologized for) can do. Her goal is not guaranteed; but she is "making for the open"; and that seems to be the end in view that Megan Boler and the women who are and have been her colleagues and sisters have in mind in educational settings.

---

[2] Adrienne Rich, *The Dream of a Common Language.* New York: W.W. Norton & Co., 1978.

Reading this book, one scents a kind of wonderful incompleteness along with a consciousness of unrealized possibility. This is the consciousness of resistance, resistance in the name of some new coherence, some new wholeness. Just as the being of many men is dependent on their exclusions and subordinations, on images of what they are not, so may an acknowledgment of the "power of emotion"—not to speak of an integration of emotion into education—make such negation less and less necessary.

Megan Boler speaks of violence and the various efforts being made to find ways of controlling it. She speaks of the shortcomings of approaches founded on a concept of ideology or a concept of the unconscious; and, in doing these things she goes beyond the empirical and the rhetorical. Her work lurches readers into what may be a new concern for transforming praxis, even in the face of others' protests. Appropriately, Megan Boler speaks about the importance of "testimonial reading," of challenges to passive and self-indulgent empathy. As she sets before us her "pedagogy of discomfort," the fundamental notion is ethical; since education for her is a deeply ethical project. We are asked to take responsibility we could not take if it were not for the recognition of the importance of connection, the meanings of power, the necessity of an affirmation of the place of emotion in a fully lived life. Again, this book takes its readers on a journey. The tracks inevitably need repair; but even the discomfort is empowering. We may look out at the landscapes with more and more self-awareness, more and more commitment to "the inextinguishable sacredness of the human race."

Maxine Greene
Teachers College, Columbia University

Preface

Feeling Power: Emotions and Education

Until the philosophy that holds one race superior and another
Inferior, is finally and permanently discredited and abandoned...
Until basic human rights are equally guaranteed to all,
Until that day
the dream of lasting peace...
will remain but a fleeting illusion to be pursued,
and never attained

— Bob Marley [1]

"Your people contain incredible potential, but they die
without using much of it." (an alien's words to an earthling woman saved
after the destruction of the earth)

— Octavia Butler [2]

A STUDY OF emotions requires acute attention to differences in culture, social class, race, and gender. The dominant culture applies inconsistent norms and rules to different communities; likewise, each culture reflects their own internal norms and values with respect to emotional rules and expression, and variable modes of resistance to the dominant cultural values. Yet I have learned as I have lectured in different communities on the politics of emotion, in New Zealand and in the United States, that women and men from diverse cultural and ethnic backgrounds recognize similar patterns of gendered rules of emotion.

Within Western patriarchal culture, emotions are a primary site of social control; emotions are also a site of political resistance and can mobilize social movements of liberation; and feminist theories and practices, in the last three decades, have developed pioneering studies of emotion, gender, and power. As in this book, these are the three main points of a lecture on the "Feminist Politics of Emotions" I have delivered to audiences of students in New Zealand and the United States.[3]

In response to this lecture, students express engaged recognition of how the "politics of emotion" shape their lives. The terrain of gendered rules of emotional conduct is intimately familiar to them yet, they say, rarely named. The analysis of how emotional rules can be challenged and how emotions can be "reclaimed" as part of our cognitive and ethical inquiry seems to provide the students hope for changing the quality of their lives and taking action towards freedom and social justice. In their written responses to the lecture, dozens addressed experiences in which their emotions had been pathologized; further, most had been taught to view emotions as their private problem rather than as a sign that something is wrong with the outside world. Less familiar to them but greatly appreciated were the strategies, developed particularly by feminist theorists and pedagogies, to challenge and resist this privatization and pathologizing of emotions.

One student writes in response:

> I found myself relating (though not able to recognize until suggested by others in class) to a lot of the "rules of emotions." The rule that "women don't get angry" for instance. I never found myself letting my emotions out by getting angry at those who hurt me. The rule of not showing emotions in public resulted in me waiting until I was alone and just crying and crying until I was almost sick. . . . When I went to a doctor, he set me up for a counseling appointment and an appointment with a psychiatrist, and lots of medication, I really thought I'd lost it. . . . To prevent situations like this, I believe there needs to be some kind of awareness program in schools to establish the understanding that physical illness is not the only way people can be sick. . . . Kids also need to be aware that overpowering emotions are a result of circumstance rather than character. . . . It is something that I *will* address in my classroom, be it part of the curriculum or not.

As though a floodgate had been released, the journals revealed in sum dozens and dozens of pages of students' analyses and interpretations of the politics of emotion.

One student left a note at my office in which she described how her actions were affected after thinking about the politics of emotions:

> [The] lecture . . . extended my thinking beyond the time taking notes. . . . I was angry [with a friend] over something they had done. The next time I spoke to that person was after your lecture, and I know that I handled the situation differently by letting my anger be known. As normally I would reduce it to having a bad day, etc., which is not the reason. . . . Your words have altered my outlook, after thought on how to deal with the emotion of anger.

I open *Feeling Power* with these examples to make the point that the "risky" business of addressing emotions within our classrooms is a productive and necessary direction for the exploration of social justice and education. The social control of emotions, and emotions as a site of resistance to oppression, are underexplored areas of study in most scholarly disciplines as well as within pedagogical practices. "When people cannot name alternatives, imagine a better state of things, share with others a project of change, they are likely to remain anchored or submerged, even as they proudly assert their autonomy" (Greene 1988: 9). In order to name, imagine and materialize a better world, we need an account of how Western discourses of emotion shape our scholarly work, as well as pedagogical recognition of how emotions shape our classroom interactions.

AN ORIGIN STORY OF FEELING POWER

I FIRST BECAME interested in emotion's *absent-presence* as a student of philosophy. Theories of subjectivity (accounts of our identities, our sense of relation to others and to the world) and epistemology (the study of knowledge, how we know and perceive) were undergoing radical change as philosophies of science had begun to question the relationship of the scientist to his production of knowledge.[4] Positivism, science committed to the possibility of objective, neutral inquiry and universal truths, was being increasingly challenged — for example, by theories of relativism. Yet even these challenges rarely explored emotion. Why didn't these new theorists of knowledge explore the role emotions play in shaping our perceptions, our selection of what we pay attention to, and our values that in turn determine what seems important to explore? In the many years since that awakening to emotion's absence, I have searched countless indexes and tables of contents in texts where emotion would seem to be undeniably a relevant or central area of inquiry; I have read text upon text; I have even read "between the lines" to find mention of emotion. With important and invaluable exceptions, I have come up empty-handed.

It began to dawn on me that emotion's exclusion from philosophy and science was not a coincidence. I discovered that the exclusion was part of an ancient historical tradition. The boundary — the division between "truth" and reason on the one side, and "subjective bias" and emotion on the other — was not a neutral division. The two sides of this binary pair were not equal: Emotion had been positioned on the "negative" side of the binary division. And emotion was not alone on the "bad" side of the fence — women were there too. When I raised the question of emotion with my predominantly male colleagues, I discovered that not only was emotion not considered a worthy topic for their agenda, but also my mention of emotion was a faux pas. I had stepped directly into an ancient trap, a trap in part set precisely for me. As a woman, I was already marginalized as a philosopher; I did not qualify as a man of reason[5], perhaps most particularly in the philosophy of science. By raising the specter of emotion publicly, I confirmed my disqualification from their club. And I fulfilled the common cultural stereotype of it being only the "unreasonable" woman who speaks, inappropriately, about emotion in the hallowed halls of academe.

In the bigger picture, their masculine, rational inquiry into subjectivity *required* my "hysterical" voice as the feminine repository of emotion.[6] Emotion — best kept silent — is nonetheless required as a foundational presence, the crucial counterbalance and reflective mirror-opposite to reason's superiority. The denigration of emotion and women is what enables reason and masculine intellectual mastery to appear as the winner in the contest for truth.

I realized that given my scholarly interests I could not pursue my investigation of subjectivities and emotion within the disciplinary confines of philosophy. I turned to an interdisciplinary graduate program, History of Consciousness, where I was able to pursue more broadly the history of ideas — for example, how the disciplinary boundaries and divisions, which I had encountered in terms of reason and emotion, had come to be instituted in Western patriarchal thought. Cultural studies, semiotics, and feminist theories provided approaches that take into account many disciplines — philosophy, sociology, psychology, psychoanalysis, literature, anthropology, history — and how they overlap. I was taught to read not only as an activity for absorbing information and ideas but simultaneously to question texts as representations of far more than a unidimensional transmission of "truths." I learned to investigate how meanings, truths, and authority are produced: Who is the intended audience? How was the book itself, as a material product, being marketed? What does its cover, blurbs, picture, categorization, price, publishing location tell us? What is the author assuming? What contradictory agendas and ideologies shape the text itself? How do countless cultural values, teachings, assumptions, and ideologies mediate our interpretations of the text? Exposed to interdisciplinary approaches, I began to acquire the tools I needed to pursue emotion's absent-presence.

As someone deeply aware of the injustices that define our world, I began also to consider how my scholarship might be applied to reshape our social and political experience. Indeed my interest in emotion was by no means purely theoretical. By rethinking the absence of emotion, how emotion shapes how we treat other people and informs our moral assumptions and judgments, I believe we have the potential to radically change our cultural values and violent practices of cruelty and injustice, which are often rooted in unspoken "emotional" investments in unexamined ideological beliefs. In short, what is the effect of affect in the classroom?[7]

How could I productively apply my study of emotion to a social or political site of struggle? The family had been theorized by psychoanalysis; the workplace by Marxists; but what about education? Most in the United States undergo twelve compulsory years of schooling. Each of us can recount at least one if not many horror stories about our schooling experience which exemplify humiliation, shame, cruelty, fear, and anger — and sometimes joy, pleasure, and desire. I myself had attended eighteen public schools as I grew up. As soon as I began teaching in 1985, I discovered these explorations of emotion made sense in my own teaching work. I care deeply about my students, and I consider teaching a profoundly ethical undertaking with aims and effects that require ongoing scrutiny. I was able to expose students to new modes of social inquiry, critical thinking, and self-reflection, and to help them discover ways of approaching their education with passionate engagement. Thus I arrived to the study of emotions and education.

EDUCATION AS THE SOCIAL CONTROL OF EMOTIONS

THE FIRST PREMISE of *Feeling Power* is that within education, as in the wider culture, emotions are a site of social control. Education is by no means merely "instruction" and transmission of information. Education shapes our values, beliefs, and who and what we become. Education is a social institution that serves the interests of the nation-state and functions to maintain the status quo and social order. It is therefore a primary mode of enforcing social control of the nation's citizens. Total social control is referred to as *hegemony* — control achieved not only through explicit force, violence, and coercion but by engineering our "consent" to this control.

I argue that the social control of emotions is a central and underexplored aspect of education in relation to hegemony. Contradictory rules of emotional conduct and expressio n function to uphold the dominant culture's hierarchies and values — for example, women are excluded from education on the grounds of their "irrationality"; and women are also assigned to teach the young because they are naturally caring and nurturing. In this book I seek to show how students and teachers have been controlled and shaped by dominant discourses of emotion, which I identify as the moral/religious, scientific/medical, and rational discourses of emotion.

Education is also a potential site of critical inquiry and transformation, both of the self and of the culture. Education offers us the opportunity to reinterpret and become reflective "if education is conceived as a process of futuring, or releasing persons to become different, of provoking persons to repair lacks and to take action to create themselves" (Greene 1988: 22). Education aims in part to help us understand our values and priorities, how we have come to believe what we do, and how we can define ethical ways of living with others. Emotions function in part as moral and ethical evaluations; they give us information about what we care about and why. Thus a primary and underexplored source for this transformation and resistance is our emotional experience as it informs both our cognitive and moral perceptions. Our emotions help us to envision future horizons of possibilities and who we want to become.[8] Thus the second thesis of *Feeling Power* is that emotions are a mode of resistance — to dominant cultural norms, for example, or to the imposition of authority. Given these aims of critical inquiry, educators and students require systematic accounts of how emotions shape the selectivity of our cognitive and ethical attention and vision.

My project thus has multiple agendas. I envision *Feeling Power* as a theoretical intervention as well as a set of directions for further inquiry into this underexplored terrain of emotion and power. As a theoretical intervention, I explore how and why scholarly disciplines omit, erase, denigrate, and devalue emotions particularly within the cognitive and moral domain. I hope that scholars will examine how emotions shape our inquiries and analyses, how and why we are taught to strive to leave emotions out of our scholarship, and why emotions so rarely are the subject of our studies. In terms of educational practices and theories, I hope that educators can consider how their pedagogies are informed by their own emotions, moods, and values; how the inexplicit subtexts of emotion impact students; how curricula that neglect emotion (for example, teaching students never to use the word "I" in writing as it is "too personal" — a phobia in part reflecting the fear of emotion in higher education) deny students possibilities of passionate engagement. I hope students can recognize how, for example, the competitive individualism that so often defines education fosters fear and isolation, and that these traumas are *not* a necessary part of education.

I am not arguing that a pedagogy of emotions requires confession, that we must all bare our souls. I am arguing that we consider the reasons emotions have been systematically discounted, and develop more creative alternatives for emotions' roles in educational practices.

DEFINING EMOTIONS

Emotions are notoriously difficult to define. One finds little agreement, across disciplines, or even within a given discipline, on how to define emotion. Philosophical psychology and philosophies of education often examine emotion's role in relation to three different *domains*: cognitive, moral, and aesthetic. Different schools of thought consider different kinds of questions, including:[9]

- Do we analyze specific occasions of emotional response, or generalized moods? How do we identify an emotion's presence: Are emotions a measurable, physiological sensation? A behavior or action or verbal articulation? A report from one's own private introspection? A necessary component of belief and perception? A form of moral judgment?
- Are there universal emotions, or do we only feel what we have been given the language to describe?
- To what extent do emotions "exceed" language, exist beyond any possible description? Why do we so often use metaphors to describe emotional experiences?
- To what extent does culture or personal idiosyncrasy shape emotions? How does "individual personality" (e.g., "I'm just naturally shy"); our particular family upbringing; our culture and religious beliefs; our social class, gender, and ethnic positions shape what we learn to express, how we interpret emotions, and how we assign value and meaning to different emotions?

Philosophers, and some educators, have debated these questions for centuries.[10] In *Feeling Power* I examine emotions not in terms of any one of these isolated questions or schools of thought. Rather, I set out to explore how scholarly disciplines and cultural rules have taught us to think about and experience whatever it is we call "emotions."

Very few of the theories I draw upon define emotion in terms of the classical, philosophical, psychological definitions. Because I am interested to understand emotions as they are embedded in culture and ideology, as "embodied and situated,"[11] an inclusive definition is useful as a launching point. Emotions are in part sensational, or physiological: consisting of the actual feeling — increased heartbeat, adrenaline, etc. Emotions are also "cognitive," or "conceptual": shaped by our beliefs and perceptions. There is, as well, a powerful linguistic dimension to our emotional awareness, attributions of meanings, and interpretations. My own philosophical conception of emotions, if it must be categorized, resonates with cognitive accounts of emotion that understand emotions and cognition as inextricably linked. My view is also resonant with "evaluative" theories of emotion, which understand emotions as moral evaluations or judgments and thus central to our ethical reasoning.[12]

From the countless, varied, and inconsistent definitions of emotions across the interdisciplinary literatures I study, I have elected to use the term *emotion*, rather than *feeling*, *affect*, or *passion*. My reason is primarily that *emotion* is a term found frequently in our common language. Arguably, *feeling* is also commonly used in our everyday language, but in scholarly definitions *feeling* is often reserved to refer to the "sensational" experience of an emotion. In the book title I adopt *feeling* in part because it functions as both a noun and a verb; *Emotional Power* would not have the dual meanings.

The book is structured to identify distinct Western cultural discourses that shape different disciplinary conceptions of emotion. Each chapter offers a different perspective on the terrain of emotion and power. My purpose is to investigate both how different scholarly disciplines have shaped what we commonly "experience" as emotions, and how these disciplines do or do not legitimize emotions as a worthy object of inquiry.

I emphasize throughout that emotions need to be brought out of the private and into the public sphere; that emotions are a site of oppression as well as a source of radical social and political resistance; and that feminists have developed largely unrecognized, grassroots analyses of the politics of emotion, which cultural studies and social theorists continue to neglect. As a result of Western cultural discourses, which on the whole do not value emotions, even the most radical social theories tend to overlook this most silenced terrain of social control and resistance.

FEELING POWER

To address the contradictions embedded in our views of emotion, I organize this book into two parts. Part 1 focuses on "Emotions as a Site of Social Control." "Feeling *power*" refers in the first instance to how we learn to internalize and enact roles and rules assigned to us within the dominant culture. We "feel *power*" in the sense that we understand and enact our appropriate roles of subordination and domination significantly through learned emotional expressions and silences. For example, the clichés that "boys don't cry" and "girls shouldn't get angry" reflect gendered roles, which have far-reaching implications as a way of organizing access to power in our culture. These emotional expressions and silences are arbitrary, in the sense that they are culturally specific rather than universal. For example, there are cultures in which the rule is not "boys shouldn't cry." In patriarchal and capitalist culture, we learn emotional rules that help to maintain our society's particular hierarchies of gender, race, and class. In this sense the emotional rules we learn are not arbitrary; they are systematically designed to enforce our acceptance of gendered divisions of "private" and "public," of women as emotional and men as rational. These divisions justify social stratifications and maintaining power in the hands of an elite few. The first four chapters offer a theoretical framework, historical accounts, and close analysis of contemporary modes of the social control of emotions.

Part 2, chapters 5 to 8, focuses on "Emotions as a Site of Political Resistance." "*Feeling* power" refers in a second sense to the power of *feeling* as a basis of collective and individual social resistance to injustices. In the United States, the second wave of feminism and the civil rights movement "politicized" anger, for example — and this anger formed the basis for the collective social movement's resistance to injustice. I credit the women's liberation movement (which drew from the civil rights movement) and feminist pedagogy with developing the first collectively articulated feminist "politics of emotion," particularly through the practices of consciousness-raising. Feminist theories developed in the last three decades have systematically worked to challenge the divisions of emotions and reason, private and public, in contemporary discourse usually argued through analyses of "situated" or embodied knowledges.[13] In the last three chapters I explore specific ethical dilemmas faced in higher education classrooms and attempt to outline pedagogies that engage both critical inquiry and collective, historical analysis of emotions as part of this inquiry process.

Chapter 1, "Feeling Power: Theorizing Emotions and Social Control in Education," provides an overview of theories that help to understand emotions as embedded in culture, ideology, and power relations. Drawing on diverse feminist theories, I understand emotions as neither entirely "public" nor entirely "private," but rather representative of a socially and collaboratively constructed psychic terrain. Feminist theories are especially helpful to a study of emotions and power for two reasons. First, feminist theories have challenged divisions of "private" vs. "public," and in so doing have offered us new approaches to considering how emotions — long considered solely "private" experience — are public and political terrain. Second, the division of public/private has historically been mapped onto a parallel division of masculine/feminine. Feminist political movements and theoretical analyses of gender have reconceptualized emotions as a public object of inquiry. By examining how historical, political, and cultural forces and differences shape emotions, feminist approaches challenge the view of emotions as individualized, "natural," or universal. Drawing as well on poststructuralist theories, I suggest "economies of mind" as a framework for understanding emotions, a "mutual transaction" between larger social forces, and the "internal" psychic terrain of the subject/person. Michel Foucault's studies of the subject and power offer concepts (which he did not apply to a study of emotions per se nor to women's oppression) useful to a historicized approach to the study of emotions and discipline in education.

In Chapter 2, "Disciplined Emotions: Locating Emotions in Gendered Educational Histories," I attempt to "locate" emotions in educational histories. I examine emotion's visible and less visible traces in educational history as represented in historical examples from the period of the mid-1800s to the 1930s. Emotions are a feature always present in educational environments, yet rarely do we find educational histories that systematically explore, or even mention, the significant role of emotions as a feature of the daily lives of teachers and students. I argue that within educational practices, emotion most often is visible as something to be "controlled." The control of emotions in education occurs through two primary ideological forces: explicit rules of morality, strongly influenced by Protestant values; and explicit values of utility and skills measured through the "neutral" gaze of social sciences which frames the virtuous student in terms of efficiency and mental health. I examine instances of the explicit social control of emotion in nineteenth-century curricula. I analyze how emotional rules function to uphold gendered divisions and roles, here focusing on women's association as the virtuous mother/schoolteacher, and the simultaneous absence of emotion in "masculinized" representations of educational histories. I conclude with an analysis of the "mental-hygiene movement" and its targeting of the "overemotional" student as the major cause of social ills.

Chapter 3, "Capitalizing on Emotional 'Skills': 'Emotional Intelligence' and Scientific Morality," examines the contemporary discourse of "emotional intelligence," introduced by popular science and psychology as "emotional quotient" or the new version of "IQ." I examine the overlap of the early-twentieth-century mental-hygiene movement with the contemporary popularity of emotional intelligence. Through the increasing authority of cognitive science and the applied use of behavioral psychology we are faced with a new conception of the moral individual: a self premised as biologically predisposed to make the "right" moral choices if properly educated. I argue that "emotional intelligence" reflects a contemporary example of pastoral power: the individual seduced to police his or her emotions in the interest of neoliberal, globalized capitalism.

The study of "emotional intelligence" provides a backdrop for Chapter 4, "Taming the Labile Student: Emotional Literacy Curricula," in which I analyze contemporary emotional literacy curricula, which I have studied and observed in K–12 schools in the United States and Australia. Emotional literacy curricula offer both promise and cause for alarm. In this chapter, I analyze the social and legislative climate that supports the emergence of these curricula. I outline the historical roots of emotional literacy programs. I evaluate emotional literacy curricula programs in terms of the risk of "individualizing" emotions on the one hand, and the promise of expanding our capacities to analyze the sociocultural context of emotions on the other.

Chapter 5 explores how practices of consciousness-raising and feminist pedagogy represent a historical first in the form of a collectively articulated "political" discourse of emotions. In "A Feminist Politics of Emotion," I analyze emotions both as a site of women's oppression as well as a basis for catalyzing political change. I explore the phenomenon that feminist invocations of emotions are denigrated as "touchy-feelie," and ask why similar invocations of consciousness-raising by radical and critical theorists are not denigrated or dismissed as in the same way. Given that critical, feminist, and poststructuralist educational theories tend to distance themselves from analyses of emotion, I suggest how educational theory and feminist philosophies of emotion might productively cross-fertilize to expand our pedagogical theories of emotion.

Chapter 6, "License to Feel: Teaching in the Context of Wars," explores the challenge of developing pedagogies that effectively invite critical inquiry in the midst of social crises. I analyze my experience of teaching during the Persian Gulf War: Do we simply proceed with "business as usual," or do we consider the effects of U.S. military aggressions and our campus's own debates and protests against the war? I examine how students' expressions of "powerlessness and numbness" evoked by the crisis of war contribute to an absent sense of "community" in our classroom. I investigate how powerlessness and numbness reflect in part a response to mass media representations of the war. I explore the impossible challenge of engaging in critical inquiry when faced with our collective numbness and lack of community ethos. I conclude with an analysis of how the differential power relations between educator and students prohibits community, and how students' primary mode of agency when feeling powerless is to resist the educator's attempts to engage critical inquiry.

Chapter 7, "The Risks of Empathy: Interrogating Multiculturalism's Gaze," explores the shortcomings of empathy, embraced since Aristotle as a means of cultivating virtuous behavior and "social imagination." Engendered particularly through the use of literature, educators have hoped to resolve social conflicts and xenophobia, fear of the other, through empathy. I argue that "passive empathy," as traditionally conceived, does not contribute to social change but encourages a passive form of "pity." I contrast what I call "confessional" vs. "testimonial" reading, and outline a mode of reading which calls upon us instead to "bear witness" and to actively engage in an examination of ethical responsibilities through our own emotional self-reflection.

In the final chapter, "A Pedagogy of Discomfort: Witnessing and the Politics of Anger and Fear," I outline a pedagogy that explores the emotional dimensions of our cognitive and moral perception. Focusing on controversial issues of race and sexual orientation as addressed in some curricula, I explore what both educators and students stand to gain by engaging in the discomforting process of questioning our learned values and assumptions. A pedagogy of discomfort invites us to examine how our modes of seeing have been specifically shaped by the dominant culture of our historical moment. I suggest the strategy of learning to recognize when we "spectate" vs. when we "bear witness" as a guiding framework for understanding the selectivity of our vision and emotional attention. I explore the predictable emotions of "defensive anger" and fears of losing our cultural and personal identity encountered as we learn to inhabit a more ambiguous sense of self and recognize the complexity of ethical relations.

The "fate" of emotions in education has, so far, been largely one of discipline and subjugation. I have hope that this fate is not a determined destiny but a historically specific confluence of social forces which is being altered. But education — specifically, relations between educator and student, relations between peers, and the creative expression within our work — also engenders passion, creativity, and joy. I choose to think of the millennium as marking a turning point with respect to emotions and education. We may, collectively, be in a position to "recuperate" emotions from their shunned status, and reclaim them in new ways through embodied and ethical practices located in the mutual interrogation of emotions as a site of control and resistance.

---

1 "War," from recording *Natural Mystic* Island Records, (1995).

2 *Dawn*, NY: Warner Books ([1987] 1997).

3 Most recently I have delivered this lecture to students in women's studies and education at the Virginia Polytechnic Institute and State University, and to an audience of one hundred students enrolled in Feminist Perspectives in Education at the University of Auckland, New Zealand.

4 In 1983, I was reading the work of Karl Popper, Paul Goodman, Thomas Kuhn, Richard Rorty, Richard Bernstein, and Alastair MacIntyre. I had not yet been directed towards feminist epistemologies of science such as Donna Haraway (1991), Sandra Harding (1986), or Evelyn Fox Keller (1985).

5 See Genevieve Lloyd (1984).

6 See Elaine Showalter (1997).

7 I am grateful to Deetje B. for this pithy sentence.

8 Maxine Greene, a preeminent philosopher of education of our time, should be credited with most consistently pursuing the question of how education invites us to explore what it means to seek freedom — as she says, not merely freedom from "negative restraints" but freedom towards who and what we want to become. These questions are pursued throughout her work; see Greene (1973, 1986, 1988).

9 See Calhoun and Solomon for a valuable overview of the questions addressed in philosophical psychology, and excerpts from philosophers' work on emotion from Aristotle to the present.

10 Calhoun and Solomon (1984) list "ten problems in the analysis of emotion." These are: what counts as an emotion; which emotions are basic; what are emotions about (intentionality); explaining emotions; the rationality of emotions; emotions and ethics; emotions and culture; emotions and expression; emotions and responsibility; emotions and knowledge (23–40).

11 "Situated knowledges," the embodied qualities of epistemology and knowing, has been a central focus of feminist theories and philosophies. Particularly following Donna Haraway's articulation (1991), this concept has been explored by countless feminist writers. For my own project, such feminist analyses of subjectivity have been both inspiring and frustrating. Frustrating, because more often than not these articulations do not systematically explore emotions, although emotion is frequently mentioned in passing. In philosophy of education, Greene also articulates "partiality" and "multiplicity" of our vision (1988, 21 and throughout). I explore feminist theories on these questions further in the next chapter.

12 I am also strongly compelled by theories of affect, developed in Spinoza's philosophy, and in the work of Gilles Deleuze (1987), and the overlap of these accounts with psychoanalytic object relations theory (Stern, 1985). Particularly useful for this direction is the contemporary work of Massumi (1996) and Gatens (1996b). However, I do not fully explore these accounts in *Feeling Power* but have left this for my next project. I explore the implications of some of these philosophies in Leach and Boler (1998); and in an essay titled "Affecting Assemblages: Towards a Feminist Theory of Emotion," Deleuze: A Symposium, The University of Western Australia, 6 December, 1996.

13 I refer here to Haraway (1990) and the vast adoption of her concept "situated knowledges" throughout feminist and cultural studies.

Acknowledgments

THE JOURNEY OF *Feeling Power* has been a long one, and there are many whose support and conversations have inspired and shaped my work. My thanks go to the many students I've been fortunate to work with over the years, whose insights and experience have shaped mine and informed my project.

My explorations of philosophy began at Mills College in late-night conversations with my friend Candace Vogler. At the University of California, Santa Cruz, my colleagues in History of Consciousness and other departments provided a rich intellectual community. I acknowledge these friends, colleagues, and writing-group members: Gloria Anzaldúa, Marcy Darnovsky, Giovanna DiChiro, Edna Escamill, Susan Gevirtz, Mary John, Katie King, Nathalie Magnan, Lynda Marín, Brinda Rao, Chela Sandoval, Zoe Sofoulis, Marita Sturken, Sarah Williams, and Magdalena Zchokke.

I am especially grateful for the support and many close readings of my dissertation committee, Donna Haraway, Helene Moglen, and Deborah Britzman, whose brilliant insights and guidance continue to shape my intellectual work. Thanks also go to Don Rothman and Elizabeth Grosz, who served on my qualifying exam committee. The community of scholars thinking about pedagogy provided a foundation for my work in education: Don Rothman, Roz Spafford, Virginia Draper, Amanda Konradi, Leslie Bow, Ellen Hart, and Sarah-Hope Parmeter. For all I learned in influential seminars taught by Hayden White, Carolyn Burke, Stephen Heath, Barbara Epstein, and Jim Clifford, I am appreciative. I am grateful as well for the ongoing support of Wendy Brown.

The intellectual community of the Philosophy of Education Society continues to provide a home, and I thank Deanne Bogdan for introducing me. I acknowledge the encouragement and support of Nicholas Burbules, Ann Diller, Maureen Ford, Zelia Gregoriou, Michael Katz, Wendy Kholi, Susan Laird, Mary Leach, Natasha Levinson, Cris Mayo, Emily Robertson, Lynda Stone, and Barbara Thayer Bacon as well as many others.

I was fortunate to work with an astonishing and diverse intellectual community in the School of Education at the University of Auckland, New Zealand. These people provided warm collegiality and a rich exchange of ideas: Alison Jones, Eve Coxon, Roger Dale, Kuni Jenkins, Kay Morris Matthews, Leonie Pihama, Peter Roberts, Susan Robertson, Judith Simon, Linda Smith, Graham Smith, and Lonise Tanielu. I owe a special thanks to Steve Appel, Jim Marshall, and Michael Peters for thoughtful comments on various essays, and to Linda Smith for the opportunity to engage in a collaborative research project. I am grateful for the intellectual collegiality of the faculty of the Center for Film and Television Studies at Auckland University.

The support, encouragement, and insights of friends and family have been greatly appreciated: Ann Marie Bley, Leslie Cohen, Antoinette Falco, Nancy Faulstich, Adee Horn, Miki Kashtan, Michele Lloyd, Karyn Mlodnosky, Eda Regan, and Mel Stapper, who was a source of fabulous support during the final stretch. A heartfelt appreciation to my family, my grandmother, Jane Forstner, to Kathy, Molly, Sarah, and Olivia Boler, and to my father, Robert. I honor the enormous inspiration of my great-uncle Phil Roeber, whose irreverance, artistic talent in abstract expressionism, socialist politics, and daunting knowledge of literature continue to inspire me. A special thanks to Nancy Gonchar, who provided me a place and space to write when I most needed it. I am immensely grateful to the canine and feline companies who provided levity.

My heartful gratitude goes to Jim Garrison, Barbara Houston, and Kate Rousmaniere, who painstakingly and graciously read chapters at the twelfth hour; and I greatly appreciate comments generously provided by Deetje B., Doreen Drury, Gretchen Givens, Martha McCaughey, Kathryn Pauly Morgan, Sara Sethi, and Jane Sooby. I appreciate ongoing conversations with colleagues Bill Green, Karen Jones, and Roger Simon.

I wish to acknowledge and thank Maxine Greene, whose passion, inspirational intellectual work, and vibrant presence pioneers a path so that women scholars like myself might find our way.

To Jennie McKnight no appreciation will suffice for her infinite willingness to engage in intellectual exploration and debate and her enormous investment of time in reading, revising and editing. Jennie's insights and succinct articulations are reflected throughout my work, and for her patience and creative intelligence I am immensely grateful.

Finally, my deep appreciation to my mother, Deetje B., whose wisdom, intellectual and political insight, encouragement and love have enabled me to come this far.

To the many other friends I haven't named, to the strangers with whom I've conversed at bus stops, in cabs, at academic conferences, and along the wild path of life, your stories, experiences, and insights regarding emotions have given me the strength to go on.

Thanks go to the support of Sheila Peuse and Billie Harris. My thanks as well to my editor, Heidi Freund, and the staff at Routledge.

I wish to acknowledge the History of Consciousness, UCSC Graduate Studies and Research, Phi Beta Kappa of Northern California, UCSC Feminist Studies FRA, the UCSC Center for Cultural Studies, and University of Auckland Faculty Research Awards for their research support.

CHAPTER ONE

FEELING POWER

Theorizing Emotions and Social Control in Education

We refuse to be
what you wanted us to be
we are what we are
and that's the way it's goin' to be.
You can't educate us, with no equal opportunity
(Talkin' bout my freedom, people's freedom and liberty.)
—Bob Marley[1]

INTRODUCTION

TWO EXAMPLES OF resistance to education from popular culture evidence how emotion and power are intertwined. Bob Marley's popular songs consistently express his passionate protests against injustice. In this song, "Babylon System," he expresses on behalf of the colonized people of the African Diaspora a collective refusal and resistance to the rhetoric of "equal opportunity education," which he recognizes has not, in fact, led to his people's freedom and liberty. Marley's call for revolution is conveyed through strong emotions — anger, empathy, hope, and joy, as he envisions a better world. Marley expresses what have been called "outlaw emotions"— emotions such as anger that are perceived as threatening by the dominant culture.

In a different popular representation of refusal, a *Calvin and Hobbes* cartoon, Calvin hands a book back to his mother and says, "I read this library book you got me." She responds, "What did you think of it?" Scratching his head, he answers, "It really made me see things differently. It's given me a lot to think about." In the last frame, Calvin's mother says, "I'm glad you enjoyed it," and Calvin, walking away, says, "It's complicating my life. Don't get me any more." Calvin's refusal is meant to be humorous: We may identify with Calvin's desire not to "complicate his life" by reading books; we may identify with his mother in our role as parent, educator, or friend who wants to encourage others to engage in critical inquiry about how they "see their world."

How is Calvin's resistance to "seeing the world differently" shaped by his emotional investments? Is his resistance "political," like Marley's? Social theorists such as Paolo Freire, Frantz Fanon, and Albert Memmi would likely answer yes: Calvin's resistance can be interpreted as his "fear of freedom,"[2] but unlike Marley's expresses the desire to remain within the "comfort-zone" of unquestioned beliefs. Calvin's refusal is the mirror-side of Marley's call for revolution: Calvin likes things the way they are.[3]

Some may say, "Give Calvin a break! It's not that he's afraid of changing his comfortable worldview. He just doesn't like books, doesn't like to think, or is resisting his mother like any normal child does!" But why might we see Calvin's resistance as simply his "individual preference," as a "normal" child's behavior, when we see Marley's resistance as angry and political? Calvin's resistance to change represents an invisible conformity to the status quo, though it is nonetheless an expression of resisting education. In contrast Marley's resistance to education is seen as angry, visible, and potentially threatening.

These introductory examples are meant to evidence that the relationship between a person and their educational experience is fraught with different emotions and histories. Certain emotions are culturally classified as "natural," benign, and normal, while others are seen as outlaw forms of political resistance. The determination of the normalcy and deviance of emotions can be generalized to some extent according to social class, gender, race, and culture, but are also highly determined by particular social contexts and power dynamics between given subjects in a situation. This highlights the impossibility of generalizing about emotional expressions: Resisting education, for example, means different things in different contexts.

Throughout this book, I question the Western philosophical and psychological tendencies to think of emotions as "natural," "universal" responses, located solely within the individual. Rather, in each case an emotion reflects the complex dynamics of one's lived situation. The two resistant responses above each reflect particular reasons and perceptions; and we understand the significance of the two different situations by understanding the different "histories" of resistance (anger, passion, fear, rigidity) that shape the emotional expressions. Emotions are inseparable from actions and relations, from lived experience. On the whole, education is impoverished in both theory and practice in accounting for the particularities of emotions in relation to lived power relations.

Resistance to change is only one example of the complicated emotional terrain of educational work. One can think of myriad other examples, including the following:

- The inevitable fears of judgment that occur in a competitive climate of grades and evaluation.
- The joy and Eros that are part of inquiry and interaction with others.
- Self-doubt and shame, common especially to women's experience within higher education: women with Ph.D.s who experience the "imposter" syndrome and continue to be plagued with doubts regarding their intellectual authority.
- Anger, alienation, and hopelessness experienced by those who don't "conform" and who thus emerge as "losers" in the education game.
- The "emotional baggage" we all carry into the classroom, stemming from our different cultural, religious, gendered, racialized, and social class backgrounds.

While one might want to speak in generalized terms about how emotion and education intersect, each of these examples would need to be examined in its culturally and historically specific context, which would include accounting for the idiosyncratic differences of each person. Emotions are slippery and unpredictable, as educators have long recognized.[4] In the early decades of this century, social scientists and educators crusaded the "mental-hygiene movement," in which they targeted the "labile" student (she or he who did not emotionally conform) as the cause of society's troubles. Despite their efforts, they didn't succeed with a prescription for the social control of emotions. It is perhaps this slipperiness which in part contributes to education often evading the subject of emotion.

In this chapter, I begin by stating my approach to understanding emotions in relation to power relations. I summarize why a theory of emotions and power is needed for theorizing education and developing effective pedagogies. I then turn to feminist theories from different disciplines that contribute to a theory of emotions and power. I summarize why it is particularly difficult to develop "histories of emotion." Finally, I outline concepts borrowed from poststructuralist thought which inform my approach to the study of emotions and education.

"FEELING POWER"

A PROMISING AND underexplored approach to this muddy undertaking is a study of how emotions are a site of social control. *Feeling power* means at least two things: Feeling *power* refers to the ways in which our emotions, which reflect our complex identities situated within social hierarchies, "embody" and "act out" relations of power. *Feeling* power on the other hand also refers to the *power of feeling* — a power largely untapped in Western cultures in which we learn to fear and control emotions.

Feeling *power* suggests an approach to the question of social control. Behavioral and expressive conduct is developed according to socially enforced rules of power. How does one learn not to express anger at one's boss, or that doing so is a very risky business? How are people taught to internalize guilt, shame, and fear as ways of guiding "appropriate" social conduct?

Feeling power, on the other hand, directs us to explore how people resist our oppression and subjugation. For example, what gives women the courage to publicly challenge sexual harassment? If we choose to resist the social control of emotions as part of the fight for freedom and justice, we are challenged to understand when and how that resistance and courage arise. But resistance, as a version of *feeling* power, takes many forms. Education is an environment governed by rules of power and authority. Ironically, one may discover that students (like Calvin) may resist the educator's suggestions, no matter what that suggestion is. The parental cliché "Do what I say because I know what's best for you" is in part an invitation for the young person to rebel and say "No, *I'll* decide what's best for me!" In education, then, resistance is complicated as young people find themselves in a climate where one of their few spaces of power available to them is to resist authority.[5] Thus however well-meaning or liberatory one's educational directive, sometimes the most creative option for students is to resist. To analyze the emotional dimensions of resistance in education thus poses an exceptionally complicated question.

A challenge within education is to provide creative spaces to develop flexible and creative modes of resistance involving emotional breadth and exploration that are not prescriptive. In *Feeling Power* I call for collectively self-reflective, historically-traced understandings of our emotions as part of a public process — a project that involves the educator as well as the student undertaking the risky process of change.

Approaching the Labile Terrain

An interdisciplinary approach to emotions and education serves a particular purpose. It helps to illuminate how emotions are visibly and invisibly addressed within education, and how emotions reflect particular historical, cultural, and social arrangements. Thus rather than exhaustively studying one view of emotions and education,[6] I am interested in how different views of emotion and education reflect distinct social and political agendas, related to the language and discourses available at any given historical moment.

In the philosophy of education we find emotions most consistently addressed in the aesthetic realm,[7] sometimes addressed in the moral realm, and less frequently addressed in the cognitive realm. In my interdisciplinary map, the approaches to emotions through moral or aesthetic education each represent different philosophical discourses and historical moments. While my work is strongly shaped by these philosophies of education, I am interested in how different educational schools of thought conceptualize emotion.[8] What conception of emotion underlies any given educational agenda?[9]

The specific focus of my study is how affect occurs in the specific site of the classroom, as mediated by ideologies and capitalist values and its entailed gendered forms. What I contribute that has not been offered before is a detailing of the specific historical logic of this education of emotions, as it has met the needs of Western capitalist cultures over the last century.

I am specifically interested in a theory of emotions and education that begins from an examination of power relations: how structures and experiences of race, class, and gender, for example, are shaped by the social control of emotion, and how political movements have resisted injustice by drawing on the power of emotions. Rather than attempt to summarize the traditions of philosophy and emotion, I begin from analyses of power. Analyses of power that bear most directly on theorizing emotion are found in feminist theories developed over the last three decades, and most systematically from the 1980s to the present.

TENSIONS BETWEEN "POWER" AND "EMOTIONS"

Emotion has most often been theorized as a "private," "natural," and individual experience that is "essentially" located in the individual.[10] Despite the increasing embrace of emotions over the last two decades as "socially constructed," the view of emotion as individualized is deeply embedded in our language and conceptual frameworks. As a result, I fear we still do not have a theory of emotions that adequately understands them as collaboratively constructed terrain.

The primary objects of study throughout *Feeling Power* are "discourses." Rather than assuming that utterances and language are transparent or self-explanatory, "discourse" refers to the culturally and historically specific status of a particular form of speech, and to the variable authority and legitimacy of different kinds of languages or utterances. I analyze specific discourses on emotions, and how they are *contested.*

> These range from *media* discourses like television and news, to *institutionalized* discourses like medicine, literature, and science. Discourses are structured and interrelated; some are more prestigious, legitimated, and hence more "obvious" than others, while there are discourses that have an uphill struggle to win any recognition at all [such as feminism, civil rights, etc]. Thus discourses are *power* relations. (O'Sullivan et al. 1994: 94)

For example, I examine texts, or classroom incidents, in terms of *which contesting discourses* of emotion inform the assumptions or interactions. I focus on discourse because I want to understand how emotions are not simply located in the individual, are not simply biological or privately experienced phenomena, but rather reflect linguistically-embedded cultural values and rules and are thus a site of power and resistance.

In attempting to understand emotions in relation to power and culture, we are immediately confronted with an unresolved tension embedded in our everyday language and scholarly discourses. This is a tension between studies of "structures" and forces of power (economic, political, and legislative), on the one hand; and accounts of individualized, "intrapsychic" experience, on the other. If we adopt, for example, a Marxist perspective that emphasizes how capitalism shapes who we are, it becomes challenging to account for how and when individuals resist capitalism, and how people choose to act on their own will and resist dominant social forces. If on the other hand one focuses on the agent, or the person, there is a tendency to explain people's choices without accounting for how choices are powerfully influenced by social forces.[10]

Feminist theories offer some of the most pioneering approaches to understanding emotions as collective and collaborative terrain. The success of feminist approaches has to do with challenges to the divisions of "public" and "private" spheres. Both "women" and "emotions" have historically been relegated to the private and domestic spheres of the home, of caring for others — spheres outside the province of the politically governed, public spaces constructed and inhabited by men.

These theories assist in rethinking emotions as collaboratively constructed and historically situated, rather than simply as individualized phenomenon located in the interior self. This approach requires analysis of Western "binary oppositions" — such as emotion vs. reason, private vs. public, bad vs. good— as well as simultaneously understanding the gendered dimensions of these divisions. Feminists have had a particular interest in critiquing binary divisions, because "women" and everything associated with women falls on the "bad" side of the binary.

The shift in thinking about emotion as public rather than simply private allows us to glimpse the relationship between social control, hegemony,[12] and emotions. Examples of material force include enforcing gender roles that keep women in the domestic sphere; requiring that people work full-time, which exhausts them and prevents them from creatively challenging the status quo or having the energy for revolution; keeping people in poverty, which breeds hopelessness. This social control is achieved as well though "shaping" or "winning" the consent of the oppressed.

Ideologies, necessary to achieving hegemony, consist of accepted ideas which appear as "natural," outside history. By appearing natural, these ideas, which profit capitalism and patriarchy for example, do not seem to reflect the interests of an outside group. Instead, what are in fact deeply social and historically specific, value-laden rules appear as "natural" and "universal."

Hegemony refers to "total social control" obtained through material and economic force — but obtained as well by "shaping" and "winning" the consent of the oppressed. The success of hegemony, particularly patriarchal and capitalist hegemony, requires that divisions between public and private spheres be upheld. The work of feminist theorists is particularly useful to demonstrate how hegemony and emotion overlap. Public and private divisions, mapped onto gendered roles and emotional rules, requires in turn that women internalize ideologies and "enact" their inferiority on a daily basis — to comply with their own subjugation.

Feminist theorists — philosophers, political theorists, sociologists, and poststructuralists, among others — recognize emotions as not only informing our ethical lives and cognitive perceptions, but as a political terrain. Emotions are "political" in several senses: Within Western cultures, for example, it has served the interests of patriarchy and capitalism to view women as naturally nurturing and caring, and also as tending towards an overemotionality that justifies their exclusion from the rational polis. Emotions are also political in the sense that emotions can catalyze social and political movements. The civil rights movement can be analyzed as significantly shaped by the moral revolution offered by anger: Those who fought for civil rights were angry about the disenfranchisement, segregation, and systematic violence towards African-Americans.

Feminist theories thus help us examine hegemony, and forms of political and social control, not simply in abstract terms and as large social forces but as lived out in our daily interactions — in our emotions, for example. Perhaps more than any other scholarly approach, feminist theories interrogate the embodied, material, and particularized experience of our daily lives.[13]

The emphasis on the "particular" turns out to be especially helpful in analyzing emotions. Because of their particularity, in fact their unpredictability, emotions have defied theorizing of any sort and may always elude a full theoretical account. To theorize emotions is a slippery business, which does not lend to quick prescriptions and generalized rules applicable to all educational instances and all students and teachers. For example, why are women on the whole more prone to self-doubt and shame than are men? Yet even this generality masks important particularities. A female student may feel shame only in some contexts, dependent on her relationship to the teacher, to other classmates, to her family upbringing, etc.

A theory of emotions concerned with their historical specificity[14] must account for significant differences in how a culture assigns different emotional rules to men and women, or to people of different social class or cultural backgrounds. The importance of the emotional "particulars" in educational transactions requires a theory that is able to analyze emotions in their cultural and historical specificity.

FEMINIST CHALLENGES TO THE VIEW OF EMOTIONS AS "INDIVIDUALIZED"

OUR COMMON LANGUAGE and scholarly discourses tend to characterize emotions as

- Located in the individual.
- "Natural" phenomenon we must learn to "control."
- "Private" experiences many of which we are taught not to express publicly.

There is some truth to each of these common conceptions. When one feels an emotion, it does seem to be uniquely located in one's individual body/mind/psyche. Many emotions seem to occur without our willing them: "Anger swelled within me," "I exploded with joy," "Grief washed over me." We then *choose* what to express of these naturally occurring emotions; we are expected to learn to control our expressions and emotional reactions. Finally, emotions are private in the sense that often we cannot "see" another's emotion (and sometimes we ourselves may experience an emotion we don't notice or choose not to recognize).

The common conceptions of emotion are linked to what I call the dominant discourses of emotions: the pathological, rooted in medicine and science; the rational, rooted in the Enlightenment philosophy of the Man of Reason; and the religious, rooted in conceptions of "channeling" passions in an appropriate manner.[15] I discuss these discourses in greater detail in the next chapter.

An example of how they overlap is found in the common idea that we must "control" our emotions and, if we don't, our "inappropriate" emotional behavior may be pathologized and medicated. Similarly, in the history of Western philosophy, women have more often than not been seen as "naturally" incapable of reason and thus justifiably excluded from sharing in public power.

It is tempting to think that eugenics and other extreme characterizations of biological differences in men and women are a thing of the past. But common language, popular culture, mass media, and science frequently refers to gendered differences in emotion as rooted in biology. This view, widely contested by feminist studies over the last two decades, is fueled by contemporary studies in neurobiology which readily capture popular attention. In a newspaper article titled "Gender Differences in Jealousy," evolutionary psychologists claim genes as the rationale for such differences in jealousy: Men are more upset by women's "sexual" rather than her "emotional" infidelity, ostensibly because her "monogamous womb" is the safeguard for his genetic destiny; women, on the other hand, are less distressed by a man's "sexual" infidelity, because what she needs is his emotional bonding to her and the family to keep him bringing home the bacon. The article goes on to voice concern over biological explanation of gendered differences:

> there is also a debate over the social consequences of the two jealousy theories. Critics of the evolutionary theory say it is dangerous to call the jealousy gender gap a product of our genes. "This theory holds profound implications for legal and social policy," says psychologist David DeSteno, of Ohio State University. "Men could get away with murder [of a sexually unfaithful spouse] by attributing it to their biology and saying they had no control over themselves." (*New Zealand Herald*, January, 1997: 62)

With the growing popularity of cognitive and neurobiological sciences, narratives which explain emotions as 'natural' and 'universal' are proliferating. More than ever we need analyses of emotion that counterbalance the dubious political agendas of scientific authority.[16]

FEMINIST CHALLENGES TO WESTERN THOUGHT: *Dismantling the Binaries of Male/Female, Public/Private, Reason/Emotion*

TO DEVELOP A HISTORICIZED approach to theorizing emotions and education is challenging because, in Western culture, emotion has been most often excluded from the Enlightenment project of truth, reason, and the pursuit of knowledge.[17] In 1984, philosopher Genevieve Lloyd published *The Man of Reason*, in which she argues that to

> bring to the surface the implicit maleness of our ideals of Reason is not necessarily to adopt a "sexual relativism" about rational belief and truth; but . . . it means, for example, that there are not only practical reasons, but also conceptual ones, for the conflicts many women experience between reason and femininity. The obstacles to female cultivation of Reason spring to a large extent from the fact that our ideals of Reason have historically incorporated an exclusion of the feminine, and that femininity itself has been partly constructed through such processes of exclusion. (1984: x)

Women's exclusion from the ideal of reason has rested on her association with emotion, nature, and passive subordination. Lloyd traces women's exclusion from reason throughout Western philosophy, from Plato to Descartes, Hume to Rousseau, Kant and Hegel to Sartre. In short, to "recover" a place for women within Western philosophical traditions[18] and to also maintain a view that values emotions in cognition and moral knowledge is to challenge ancient, deep-seated oppositions that continue to shape women's experience in education.[19]

In her influential analysis of the historical emergence of Western hypervaluation of objectivity, Susan Bordo confirms the association of femininity and subjectivity, and masculinity with objectivity. However, Bordo qualifies Lloyd's philosophical and historical account. Bordo argues that the "flight to objectivity" dates not back to Greek philosophy but is a specifically Seventeenth-century "masculinization of thought." The Greeks, she argues, as well as philosophers since, have in fact not evaded femininity until the emergence of Cartesian rationality. Cartesian anxiety results in part, she argues, from the effects of the Copernican and scientific revolution and ensuing sense of "separation" between self and world, the breakdown of "symbiosis and cosmic unity" (1987: 58). (Bordo further analyzes Descartes' anxiety as a mirroring of a wider cultural anxiety in psychoanalytic terms, the separation from the maternal.) At this juncture one finds the powerful Western confluence of femininity and subjectivity as a corruption to be transcended. Bordo argues that the flight to objectivity is significantly fueled by masculine anxieties and fears, largely fear of femininity.

The accounts provided by such philosophers as Lloyd and Bordo have pioneered feminist critiques of Western thought. However, even in these influential texts specific histories of emotions are fairly marginalized in the production of feminist deconstruction of Western rationality.

In her "Introduction" to an issue on emotions in *Discourse: Journal for*

Theoretical Studies in Media and Culture, interdisciplinary scholar Kathleen Woodward writes:

> If we can write histories of rationality, so too can we write histories of the emotions. It is necessary to underline the *s*, to call attention to the plural, so that we do not find ourselves only engaged in deconstructing the antinomy of reason and emotion, which is to say, making explicit what we already know. . . . Our vocabularies for the emotions are impoverished, and if our language is so bizarrely truncated, what of our experience both in and out of the academy? (1990 – 91: 3)

Woodward calls for "histories of emotion" that parallel feminist histories of rationality. In addition to understanding how rationality has framed our educational values and practices, we also require histories of how emotions enlist subordination and enable resistances.

FEMINIST THEORIES OF EMOTION

Feminist studies across the disciplines have developed a fourth primary discourse of emotions, the political. The politics of emotion emerge within the women's liberation movement to challenge the three dominant discourses of emotions (the pathological, rational, and religious).[20] Feminist practices and theories explore the social construction of emotion, and systematically contest emotions as natural, universal, or biological. I offer here a synopsis of examples of feminist theorists who have developed a politics of emotion within such fields as anthropology, sociology, political theory, and philosophy.

In a rare study dedicated to interdisciplinary, crosscultural ethnographies[21] of the discourses of emotion, Catherine Lutz and Lila Abu-Lughod open their 1990 edited collection as follows:

> Emotions are one of those taken-for-granted objects of both specialized knowledge and everyday discourse now becoming part of the domain in anthropological inquiry. Although still primarily the preserve of philosophy and psychology within the academic disciplines, emotions are also ordinary concerns of a popular American cultural discourse whose relationship to such professional discourses is complex and only partially charted. Tied to tropes of interiority and granted ultimate facticity by being located in the natural body, emotions stubbornly retain their place, even in all but the most recent anthropological discussions, as the aspect of human experience least subject to control, least constructed or learned (hence most universal), least public, and therefore least amenable to sociocultural analysis. (1)

Emotions, they argue, are taken for granted and are understood largely through "common sense" within both specialized academic knowledges as well as within everyday language. The commonsense level at which emotions function (as opposed to being brought into self-reflective or public attention, e.g., through therapy or meta-narratives about emotion) is grounded in pervasive conceptions of emotion as:

- *universal* ("All cultures feel joy and fear and anger");
- *natural* ("It's natural to be angry when someone offends you!");
- *private* or "interior": "Only I experience what I am feeling";[22] many ideologies assign emotions to the private sphere, which prevents emotions being publicly expressed.

Ethnographers like Lutz and Abu-Lughod emphasize that the primary Western narratives about emotions portray them as an "internal," interior space tied to the "natural" body and functioning as a universal "fact" of biological existence.

In philosophy,[23] two influential essays published in 1989 represent feminist analyses of emotions as socially constructed. In an essay called "Anger and Insubordination," Elizabeth Spelman begins with Aristotle's maxim that "anyone who does not get angry when there is reason to be angry, or does not get angry in the right way at the right time and with the right people, is a dolt" (quoted in Spelman 1989: 263). Spelman begins by pointing out that the "person who should get angry" was not, in Aristotle's world, women or slaves but the Greek men. Spelman persuasively argues that women are not in fact permitted to express anger. This prohibition functions to maintain women in her subordinate status. When women are prevented from expressing anger at injustice, transgression, or violence, they are forced to submit without expressing resistance.[24] Further, women's silence is interpreted as willing agreement to their subordination.

Philosopher Alison Jaggar analyzes what she calls "outlaw" emotions — emotions that have historically been prohibited to women but which, when expressed, empower women and challenge their subordinate status. Developing the feminist social constructionist view of emotions, Jaggar speaks of "emotional hegemony" and "emotional subversion," and argues that by

> forming our emotional constitution in particular ways, our society helps to ensure its own perpetuation. The dominant values are implicit in responses taken to be pre-cultural or a-cultural, our so-called gut responses. Not only do these conservative responses hamper and disrupt our attempts to live in or prefigure alternative social forms but . . . they limit our vision theoretically. (1989: 143)

Jaggar's comments echo Maxine Greene's articulations. Greene explores how "obstacles or blocks" to "freedom" are "artifacts, human creations, not 'natural' or objectively existent necessities. When oppression or exploitation or segregation or neglect is perceived as 'natural' or a 'given,' there is little stirring in the name of freedom" (1988: 9). Without the ability to envision alternatives and transformational possibilities, we "are likely to remain anchored or submerged" (ibid.: 59). One can see the resonance between feminist philosophies of "outlaw" emotions and a vision of radical education for freedom.

The work of two other feminist philosophers expands an account of emotions as collaboratively constructed. Emotions cannot be understood as simply "rational" or "irrational."

Sandra Bartky (1990) analyzes "psychological domination," drawing on the work of Frantz Fanon and Jean-Paul Sartre, and offers a gendered account of "psychic alienation." One of her central theses is that "[I]t is itself psychologically oppressive both to believe and at the same time not to believe that one is inferior — in other words, to believe a contradiction" (30). She challenges Marxist accounts of false consciousness, by emphasizing instances in which women hold contradictory beliefs about their inferiority. In other words, it does not suffice to say "women believe they are inferior as a result of internalizing patriarchal ideologies." She discovered a discrepancy between what women actually believe, and how they feel. She describes how, as women students in her class hand in their written work, they consistently apologized and/or expressed shame about their work. Yet, these women would not say that they "believed" they were actually inferior to their male counterparts — yet, they "felt" they were inferior. Bartky stresses that this discrepancy reveals a problem with analyzing such phenomenon in terms of ideologies. How do we explain that discrepancy?

To study emotions allows us to explore the revealed "space" between ideology and internalized feeling. In making this distinction I am not saying that emotions offer an "unmediated, raw data" which are outside of ideology.[25] Rather, I suggest that neither the framework of ideology and consciousness nor of desire and the unconscious offer us adequate entries into this terrain of emotions and power.

Sue Campbell develops promising directions for what I call an "expressivist" theory of emotions. Her emphasis on how emotions are collaboratively formed importantly suggests how emotions are neither private, nor merely an internalized effect of ideology.

Campbell's essay "Being Dismissed: The Politics of Emotional Expression" (1994), builds on recent feminist philosophical analyses of bitterness. Bitterness is usually viewed as an "undesirable" emotion that should be avoided. Some feminists have reclaimed bitterness as a "legitimate and rational" response to injustice or oppression.[26] Campbell critiques this rationalist language, and points out that to argue that the bitter person has "legitimate and rational reasons" for her feeling thrusts the "burden of justification" onto the bitter individual. As an alternative to this reinscription of the rational individual, Campbell demonstrates how bitterness is *collaboratively* formed. It's not that you knew you felt bitter, and then happened to decide to express it. Rather, you expressed your anger and then were told, "You're just bitter." Once accused of bitterness, you must justify your reasons. Further, she argues, to be told "you're bitter" is a dismissal and a silencing. Even if you then articulate your reasons for being bitter, the other is no longer listening. If, instead, we recognize that bitterness is collaboratively and publicly formed, it does not make sense to require the bitter individual to justify her reasons. Rather, what is called for is a *full social accountability on everyone's part for the interpretive context.*

Building on Marilyn Frye's concept of "social uptake" (1983), Campbell discusses the "blocking" or "dismissal" of emotions. These are instances in which those with greater power enforce the culturally condoned habits of inattention. " 'Social uptake' is defined as necessary to the *success* of emotions" (1994: 480). Social uptake refers for example to a woman who gets angry watching her mechanic mess up the successful adjustment she herself had made to her carburetor. When she expresses her anger he calls her a "crazy bitch" and changes the subject. Not only does he refuse to "uptake" her anger, but he displaces it and frames her as crazy. Her emotional expression is successfully "blocked" through this social interaction.

Feminist Sociology and Political Philosophies

I BRIEFLY EXAMINE feminist contributions that draw on Marxist and psychoanalytic analyses to theorize emotions. The work of social and political theorists resonates with my interest in "economies of mind," which I discuss in the last section of this chapter. In 1983, feminist sociologist Arlie Hochschild published *The Managed Heart: The Commercialization of Human Feeling.* Hochschild developed a groundbreaking concept of "emotional labor." Marxists had previously analyzed labor without reference to the "private" worlds of women's work and labor.[27] Hochschild studies the airline industry and the work of stewardesses, examining how women's emotion is "commodified" into a product. The concept of emotional labor represents a significant shift: Emotion is viewed not simply as the private, "caring" act of a mother, for example, but as a "product" that profits corporate business.[28]

Political philosopher Ann Ferguson elaborates the notion of "sex/affective production". Elaborating the pioneering work of Gayle Rubin on the "sex/gender" system,[29] Ferguson accounts for both economic production as well as the "production and reproduction of people" through "parenting and kinship, sexual structures, and economic modes of production." Thus the "modes" though which people are produced will vary a great deal in different historical, cultural, regional, and familial contexts. She continues, "each mode of sex/affective production will have its own *distinctive logic of exchange of the human services of sexuality, nurturance, and affection*, and will therefore differently constitute the human nature of its social product: human children" (1991: 68, emphasis added). She states that this production is by no means limited to family/kinship networks. Her socialist-feminist perspective emphasizes the specificity of how capitalism and gender shape affective production especially by creating "problematic and contradictory gender identities in both boys and girls in childhood, identities which then make subsequent experiences in peer interaction in schools and communities, and later in workplaces, very important in determining sexual preference, sexual practices, and the ultimate content of one's gender identity"(ibid.).

The sex/affective production paradigm is extremely useful to providing a missing history of the education of emotions. Central to Ferguson's argument is her challenge to the division of public and private spheres:

> The separation between the public and private, the realm of economic production and the realm of domestic life specific to capitalist society, should not lead us to the error of conceptualizing sex/affective production, or the production of people, as a process occurring in a place or realm different from that where the production of things take place. The sexual division of wage labor . . . male decision making and female obedience roles, and high-status male work vs. low-status female work are all specific aspects of the capitalist production process. (ibid.)

This point is key to my project: Affective production and the production of people do not occur "in a place or realm different from that where the production of things [and knowledge] takes place." In education, for example, affective production occurs even in the most sterile and rational classrooms.

Feminist Psychoanalysis and Emotions

FEMINIST PSYCHOANALYTIC theorist Jessica Benjamin opens her book *The Bonds of Love* noting: "Since Thomas Hobbes, in his justification of authority, first analyzed the passions, domination has been understood a psychological problem" (1988: 3). Benjamin looks to Freud's theories for explanation of this psychological conundrum. In her explanation, "the injunction to love our neighbor is not a reflection of abiding concern for others," but instead reflects our "propensity for aggression" (4). In short, love is one of the ways we "tame" our aggression, one of the ways we become civilized. "Obedience to the laws of civilization is first inspired, not by fear or prudence . . . but by love, love for those early powerful figures who first demand obedience" (5). Domination thus powerfully structures the relationship between our "psyche" and our "social life." Benjamin's book explores "domination as a two-way process, a system involving the participation of those who submit to power as well as those who exercise it." This is what she calls the "bonds of love."[30]

Object relations theory, a version of psychoanalysis rooted in the work of Jacques Lacan, represents a valuable direction for exploring emotions and social relations. One of the most slippery features of emotions is that they seem at times to exceed or defy language. Psychoanalysis, and object relations theories, attempt to explain the relationship between what we can and cannot say, what is conscious and what seems to be inaccessible to our consciousness and thus to our language.

However, in this book I have elected not to use psychoanalysis as an overriding mode of inquiry. Elsewhere, I do explore psychoanalysis and theories of affective intersubjective communication.[31] But alternatively I suggest a focus on what I term "inscribed habits of inattention," in part as an alternative to the concept of the "unconscious." Inscribed habits of inattention describe the selectivity of our attention. For example, how do we choose/learn which emotions in ourselves and others to notice and attend to?[32] I am particularly interested in how these inscribed habits of inattention are embedded in discourses and in educational practices and philosophies.

Political philosopher Iris Marion Young writes, "I think psychoanalysis is indispensable to feminist social theory, because this is the only framework that theorizes desire and the unconscious" (1990: 3). It may be that psychoanalysis is the "only framework that theorizes desire and the unconscious." However, I would argue we need additional or complementary theories of emotions as they shape our material experience, both as a matter of sheer principle (we should not have only one such theory, although, of course, psychoanalysis consists of many theories and variations) and because we may not wish to explain our emotional world solely through the lens of desire and the unconscious. Calling for histories of emotions, Kathleen Woodward writes:

> Such histories would offer us breathing room for the now banal rhetoric of post-structuralism and Lacanian analysis as it is summed up by the word "desire." In its ubiquity and virtual solitude, in the deployment of the discourse of desire everywhere, desire has assumed the status of a master category (it is the agent of

narrative, it is the hallowed sign of subjectivity). *But it is also a curiously empty category.* (1990–91: 3–4, emphasis added)

Having spent many years searching educational theories for systematic accounts of emotions, I share Woodward's frustration with the relatively "empty" categories not only of "desire" but of the "unconscious." One finds consistently that across critical, feminist, and poststructural theories of education, authors repeatedly come up to the emotionally sticky subject but seem to evade this murky terrain by quickly invoking the umbrella categories of "desire" and the "unconscious."[33] Perhaps my frustration would be lessened if these authors were to develop fuller explications of how psychoanalysis helps us to understand pedagogies.[34]

Although indeed some aspects of our psychic life may be relegated to the "unconscious," I am more interested in how we might explain these "inaccessible" parts of our psyche as a result of socially determined "habits of inscribed inattention." It may be that in the process of becoming civilized, and obtaining language, we come to "repress" many of our feelings. However, I would argue that we might interrogate such phenomena as "repression" through a close examination of specific historical and cultural rules, as they are applied to different classes and persons.[35] I am interested in exploring how culturally patterned, inscribed habits of inattention account for these silences.

A related objection to analyzing emotions and education in terms of psychoanalysis is that "education is not therapy."[36] While in fact, educators are not trained as therapists, the dynamics between teacher and student can parallel the therapist/client relation. Whether we like the analogy or not, and whether we agree that teachers are in fact sometimes like therapists, emotions are a significant feature of the educational transaction and process.[37] In an interview regarding "Cultural Strangeness and the Subject in Crisis," Julia Kristeva speaks about (European) culture and subject as in a permanent crisis. She notes that the "power of the therapist . . . of the educator . . . of a certain familiar authority" is both a "provisional and stabilizing apparatus," as well as being "relative and flexible" (1990–91: 161). She sees this role of the therapist as a necessary model for pedagogy, but one which "will require a great deal of money. . . . There must be many more professors. But this also requires a certain personal devotion, a certain moral, pedagogical attention on the part of teachers, who are not necessarily prepared by their studies to do this" (ibid.).

In addition to the logistical problem of setting up pedagogy as a therapeutic relation, to view education simply as a therapeutic relation overlooks a key difference between education and therapy. Education involves a mediating third term: the text, or curricula. The relations between persons are powerfully mediated by this "physical" object of knowledge represented by the text. To examine and discuss emotions in a classroom is structurally different than to do so in a "private" therapeutic relationship. Leaving aside our individual meetings between student and teacher, I suggest that the direction for a pedagogy of emotions is genealogy: not confession, not therapy or spectating and voyeurism, but witnessing.

In the next chapter I seek to contribute to this absence of histories of emotion in education. Here I briefly outline some issues intrinsic to the discipline of history which inform my interdisciplinary approach.

HISTORIES OF EMOTION

The challenge of "mapping" a history of emotions has to do not only with the slippery nature of emotions, but the slippery nature of history as a discipline. What is a historian's evidence of the past? "To articulate the past historically does not mean to recognize it — the way it really was"(Ranke). "It means to seize hold of a memory as it flashes up at a moment of danger" (Benjamin [1959] 1969: 255). Since historians cannot recreate the actual event in question, they must always rely on some mediated form: A written account or document is the most common evidence for the historian. What would count as the evidence of emotional education?

The two most explicit forms of evidence include curricula that outline how to discipline emotions, and public debates about what kind of emotional character is desirable for social harmony. Transcripts of interactions between students, and between teachers and students, provide another source of the "unofficial" education of emotions.

> Often the stories that we remember and tell about our own schooling are not so much about what we learned, but how we learned and with whom. There are stories about teachers we loved, teachers we hated and those we feared. . . . There were good days and others full of tears and broken hearts, and many, many days of boredom, monotony, and endless repetition. (Rousmaniere et al. 1997: 4)

But because disciplines are notoriously divided territories, the analysis of what actually occurs in a classroom is seen to be the province of sociology or psychology.

The definition of any discipline is not simply a matter of an arbitrary boundary. "Boundaries are not simply lines on a map. Rather . . . 'they denote territorial possessions that can be encroached upon, colonized, and reallocated. Some are so strongly defended as to be virtually impenetrable; others are weakly guarded and open to incoming and outgoing traffic'" (Tony Becher, quoted in Klein 1993: 186). In large part as a result of how historians have defined the boundaries of their methods and evidence, emotions have fallen through the cracks of educational histories.

The persistent interventions of feminist scholarship and work by scholars of color have radically challenged the boundary of "public vs. private." Histories traditionally document what occurs within the "public sphere." The public sphere has been defined largely in terms of male activities.[38] Existing histories tend to focus on the public debates of education, or focus on larger social forces or trends. Most of what is documented and taught to us highlights traditionally "public" aspects of education such as the legacy of Horace Mann, who crusaded for the common schools in the U.S.; legislature drafted by male politicians; and curricula debated by male-populated boards of education. Over the last two decades, feminists and scholars of color have reshaped what counts as history, and the discipline has begun for example to consider oral histories, diaries, and other less traditional forms of representation as "legitimate" historical evidence.[39]

But the reasons why emotions appear absent from educational histories lie even deeper. Assigned to the "private" sphere, emotions have not been considered "noteworthy" within the male-defined perimeters of historical scholarship. The relegation of emotions to the private sphere is inextricably intertwined with the simultaneous consignment of women to the private sphere, and the related neglect of women's histories. Women's work, which includes "emotional labor," is also consigned to the private sphere. Rarely do educational histories examine, for example, the daily lives and practices of the female majority of schoolteachers, or the experience of students subjected to educational discipline.[40] Examples of emotion's present-absence, the daily dynamics of teachers' and students' lives, and the myriad ways in which emotions constitute interpersonal dynamics and learning processes, are largely absent from historical representations.

Madeleine Grumet addresses the questions of absence and presence eloquently, exploring curriculum as the "presence of an absence" (1988: xiii). In the 1970s, she recounts, the "absences" were discovered in terms of "hidden curricula." She explores as well how the binary oppositions between the "public" and the "domestic" play out through women's presence as schoolteachers, and how the female schoolteacher embodies deceptive divisions between "economy" and the more "privatized" sphere of the family and the school. She argues that in order to recognize the schools' "dynamic function in mediating the public and domestic oppositions," and in order to permit women to have the power of transformative agents, we must examine the "motives that we bring into our work as educators" particularly as related to our "genderization and reproductive projects" (xiv–xv). Emotions are an underexplored site of educational histories that allows us to understand these gendered relations.

In *Feeling Power* I seek not simply to provide a philosophy or psychology of emotions and education, but to argue for pedagogies that invoke emotions in a historicized sense. I turn now to some concepts from poststructural[41] theory which offer approaches to studying emotions in both their "local" and "global" historical context. These poststructural concepts help me to argue that emotions are not simply located in an individual or a personality, but in a subject who is shaped by dominant discourses and ideologies and who also resists those ideologies through emotional knowledge and critical inquiry.

Perhaps not surprisingly, the most recent feminist theories of education that (albeit obliquely) address emotions situate themselves in poststructuralist theory. They do not, for example, align themselves with the early practices of feminist pedagogy and consciousness raising but tend to work with Marxist and psychoanalytical theories, particularly as these have been reformulated by Michel Foucault and others in cultural studies and critical theory.[42]

ECONOMIES OF MIND: *Archaeology and Genealogy*

TO COMPLEMENT MY focus on "inscribed habits of inattention" as a description of how emotions are a site of social control, I suggest "economies of mind" to describe how the effects of power are made visible through a historical analysis of emotion. Raymond Williams's discussion of what he calls "structures of feeling" most closely resonates with how economies of mind function within the fertile terrain of emotion.[43] *Archaeology* describes a way to analyze the discourses that subject individuals to the internalization of capitalist and patriarchal power, values, and ideologies (Foucault, 1980: 85). *Genealogy* describes how we can glimpse resistances to this subjectification: At the same time as discourses of discipline and control emerge, the subjects of power also are able to develop "subjugated knowledges" and thus resist and transform power. Power is not monolithic, but is a dynamic flux that thrives within social relations. What we least understand is how these lived relations of power manifest in terms of emotions and structures of feeling.

In one of his few passages that reference emotion, Michel Foucault notes that "genealogy retrieves an indispensable restraint; *it must record the singularity of events outside of any monstrous finality; it must seek them in the most unpromising places, in what we tend to feel is without history — in sentiments, love, conscience, instincts*; it must be sensitive to their recurrence, not in order to trace the gradual curve of their evolution, but to isolate the different scenes where they engage in different roles. Finally, genealogy must define even those instances where they are absent, the moment where they remained unrealized . . ." (Foucault in Rabinow, 1984: 76, emphasis added). Emotions in education promise a rich site for genealogical study, as they are most present within "hidden curricula."

Economies of mind refers both to the subject produced by a knowledge and the knowledge produced by a self; economy implies here "exchange," and currency or commodity. Economies of mind describes an analysis of the infinitesimal (emotions), which in turn reveals the more dispersed and "global" effects of power that these discourses of emotion serve.[44] This emphasis on the "global" pushes us to think of emotions, and "choices," not as residing within the individual but as a mediating space: Emotions are a medium, a space in which differences and ethics are communicated, negotiated, and shaped.

Concluding this central directive for archaeology, Foucault says, "above all what must be shown is the manner in which [the techniques and procedures of power] are invested and annexed by more global phenomena and the subtle fashion in which more general powers or economic interests are able to engage with these technologies that are at once both relatively autonomous of power and act as its infinitesimal elements" (1980: 99). Applied to the question of emotion, archaeology allows us to examine the "infinitesimal" and supposedly "private" instances of our feelings, as experiences in which economic power and dominant culture are deeply invested. Rarely, if ever, do we feel something "naturally," in a vacuum removed from outside forces and structures and relations. Even sitting all alone in the wilderness feeling joy is related to other experiences of suffering, and what counts as suffering and joy is powerfully shaped by language, social customs and values.

Pastoral Power

Modern and secularized society has increasingly become a government of "individualization." Within Western democratic and capitalist patriarchies, individuals are policed and disciplined through modes of internalized control. These modes of self-control do away with the need for a singular sovereign ruler, and instead disperse governance among social relations of everyday lives. This form of individualized governance can be called "pastoral power." We are taught to "internalize" rules of self-control and discipline, which I argue occurs fundamentally through structures of feeling. With respect to education, *pastoral power* describes modern methods of maintaining discipline and control. These methods include:

- surveillance, or *fear of being surveilled,* which forces individuals to "internalize" the sense of being watched and thus police themselves. Surveillance capitalizes on *internalized fear* and relies on confession and self-blame.
- recruiting peers into the work of policing one another. *Peer policing capitalizes on such structures of feeling as shame, humiliation, and desire for conformity.*
- an increased governance of the relations between individuals. Successful governance of relations between individuals relies on hierarchies, norms, and differentiations. For example, instilling competition within schools creates particular relations *governed by jealousy and feelings of inferiority, superiority, and shame.* Relations between teacher and student depend on shared obedience to authority, governing who can express anger to whom, and *a climate of fear and respect of authority.*
- an increase in the number of officials of pastoral power — the number of teachers, social workers, etc. continues to proliferate. It is no longer only the priest who solicits "confessions." Within educational history, a key example I discuss later, is *women constructed as caring nurturers.* Through child-centered pedagogies and a *"pedagogy of love,"* for example, women become the *"caring police."*

Each of these modes of pastoral power reveal emotions as a site of social control, although Foucault doesn't explicitly address either emotions or gender.

Pastoral power thus offers a framework to analyze how emotions are an invisible presence in education, and how emotions are disciplined to maintain social control through these individualizing techniques. In her chapter titled "Pedagogy for Patriarchy," Grumet notes that the "doctrine of self-control and denial of emotions [is] extended into those traits listed as desirable," the example she gives being "in the 1928 *Commonwealth Teacher-Training Study*" (1988: 53). These traits of self-control and denial of emotions characterize the gendered relations to education in different and complex ways, embedded in presences and absences that must be painstakingly sought out within the annals of history.

In this book I emphasize two key modes of disciplined control still present in contemporary educational discourses. In *Discipline and Punish,* Foucault offers a detailed study of how power becomes embodied within the subjects of pastoral power's governance. He identifies two primary discourses which shape the disciplining of bodies, and which are useful in understanding historical shifts and discourses or morality in educational histories. Foucault argues that "[d]iscipline increases the force of the body (in economic terms of *utility*) and diminishes these same forces (in political terms of *obedience*)" (1979: 138, emphasis added).

In educational histories, we find these two discourses of morality — *obedi-*

ence/rules, and *utility*/skills — powerfully reflected in religious discourses on the one hand and the growth of scientific authority on the other. In the next three chapters, I will show how the social control of emotions in education relies on various combinations of rules-based and utility-based morality.

In sum, emotions are a prime site for developing pastoral power, as emotions are already discursively constructed as "private," "individualized," and "natural," exceeding language and thus sometimes beyond the reach of our articulation. Until we develop pegdagogies that invite emotions as part of critical and ethical inquiry, our resistance to the pervasive Western discourses of emotions may well remain "embryonic" (Williams 1977). In what follows, I attempt to show that pastoral power and its strategies are indidious, subtle, and frequently "invisible," existing in internalized space, a kind of third space:[45] neither private nor public, the terrain of feeling power.

---

1 "Babylon System," *Survival* (1979).

2 Marxists have classically explained this phenomenon in terms of "false consciousness." One of the effects of ideology is to put "blinders" on the worker, for example, in order to exploit his labor. While theories of hegemony and ideology go a long ways in explaining why we act against our own interests (I am here begging the tricky question of who gets to decide what counts as our own "best" interests), feminist theorists like Bartky (1990) challenge this explanation. Part of what I argue in this book is that our existing theories don't adequately explain the complexity of how we comply with our own subjugation. Fanon (1967) drew on psychoanalysis and existential philosophies to explain how the colonized internalize their oppression; but Fanon also ingeniously critiques the limits of these explanatory frameworks for their own racist assumptions. Psychoanalysis introduces yet another paradigm to explain why and how we comply with our oppression; see for example Benjamin (1988). Some philosophers approach this question in terms of "self-deception," for a wide range of essays on this topic, see *Perspectives on Self-Deception*, Brian McLaughlin and Amelie Rorty, eds. (1988).

3 For discussion of the difference between perspectives of the colonizer and colonized, see for example Freire (1973); Fanon (1967); Memmi (1965); Linda Smith (1998); and Graham Smith (1997).

4 A landmark collection was published in 1984 titled *Changing the Subject: Psychology, Social Regulation, and Subjectivity* (Henriques et al). These essays offer critical and poststructural analyses of the development of psychology and the social sciences as disciplines that powerfully regulate our subjectivity. While they use Marxism and psychoanalysis as frameworks for their analysis, they also maintain critical reflection on the limits of these frameworks and examine how these discourses themselves discursively shape how we are able to think about the "individual's" psychological experiences. Though emotion is not their specific focus, their approach represents exceptionally promising, interdisciplinary directions for educational studies and new theories of emotion and power. I remain enormously grateful to Helene Moglen for introducing me to this text as well as to Jessica Benjamin's and for numerous

other directions that continue to inform my study of emotions, power, and gender.

5 A well-known study of British working-class youth argues that these boys who "blew off" school, failed, and didn't attend class had developed powerful ways of resisting authority (Willis 1977). One question posed to these studies has been: Should we call such actions "resistance" if there is no well-formulated goal, if one is simply resisting for the sake of resisting?

6 In subsequent chapters I do examine, for example, Aristotelian and Deweyan philosophies relevant to emotions and education and take up specific philosophical dilemmas concerning emotions.

7 Greene (for example, 1973, 1988) has consistently analyzed emotions, sometimes explicitly and often as a subtext, in her moral and aesthetic approach to the philosophy of education, which centrally engages literature. See also the edited collection examining the influence of Greene's work (Ayers and Miller 1998). One of the earliest essays published in *Educational Theory,* which placed emotions at the center of issues of educational philosophy, is Schrag's "Learning What One Feels and Enlarging the Range of One's Feelings" (1972). See also Boler (1997b).

8 In addition to Greene, I am thinking here of the work of Noddings (for example, 1984) and Martin (1985a, 1985b, 1994). An interesting project would be to examine the different conceptions of emotion in the work of three major women philosophers of education, Maxine Greene, Nel Noddings, and Jane Roland Martin. Each works within distinctive philosophical backgrounds, and emotions play different roles with respect to the cognitive and moral domain for each philosopher. I explore Greene's early analyses of "private vs. public" in the existentialist tradition with respect to discourses of emotion in Boler (1997b). Other collections and essays on gender in the philosophy of education contribute more and less directly to issues of emotion and education: See for example Houston (1996); Diller et al. (1996); Kohli (1995); Stone, ed. (1994).

9 A central approach to studying how education shapes students' worldviews and values is traced in curricula studies. See Pinar (1975); Greene (1965, 1988).

10 The field of psychology has particularly reinforced the individualized view of emotions. Increasingly one finds in psychology redefinitions of intelligence to include "social intelligence." Yet a recent anthology on this topic, *Personality and Intelligence* Robert Sternberg and Patricia Ruzgis, eds. (1994) has a final chapter on emotions tacked on almost as an addendum, which critiques all of the previous essays for neglecting the topic of emotion. In any exhaustive search of databases, one will find thousands of entries on emotion. However, one will find only a handful that address emotions in relation to power relations or interethnic conflict, for example. ERIC, the Educational Resources Information Center, is a database used in libraries to cover education and related fields. One search I conducted in 1995, using an ERIC listing 1966–present, revealed the following classification of entries. The term with the greatest number of references is self-esteem with 7920 entries; self-control, 7122; desire, 3131; fear, 3020; aggression, 2531; empathy, 1944; anger, 1019; pleasure, 712; guilt, 544; optimism, 444; joy, 375; shame, 163; envy, 26.

11 Within the field of cultural studies, for example, Stuart Hall expresses a tension between "structuralists" and "culturalists." The culturalists, like Raymond Williams, are primarily interested in the lived experience of culture, the particular instances of how individuals and communities play out and manifest the larger structural forces and ideologies. The structuralists, on the other hand, are much more interested in the forces of ideology, in the nation state or economy, or in language as political determinants of what counts as meaningful. Each side faces its own version of the problematic question of how agency and structure, or individual and society are interrelated. Hall credits a few thinkers for bridging agency and structure. Following his tribute to Althusser, Gramsci, and Laclau, Levi-Strauss is named as Hall's big hero, for having introduced semiotics and psychoanalysis. Levi-Strauss fills the gap

in structuralism: "By way of the Freudian concepts of the unconscious and the Lacanian concepts of how subjects are constituted in language . . . restores the decentered subject, the contradictory subject, as a set of positions in language and knowledge, from which culture can appear to be enunciated." (Hall [(1980)] in Dirks et al., 1994: 536).

Cultural studies generally provide us with the language to speak basically from one of two directions. Either we adopt the Marxist language of ideology, consciousness, and false consciousness, or we adopt the psychoanalytic language of desires and the unconscious. Even Foucault, in his early work *Mental Illness and Psychology* (1976), waffled between the two accounts: existential psychology, which mutates into Marxist humanist psychology; or psychoanalysis. Yet despite these two dominant accounts of subjectivity we still have dozens of radical social theorists perplexed by the problem of agency versus structural determination.

12 See Gramsci (1971); Hebdige (1979); Fiske (1987, 1989); Althusser (1971).

13 Western philosophy has been criticized not only by feminist but by other recent social theorists and French philosophies for its subscription to "metanarratives," to absolutes or transcendental definitions of "truth." It is worth noting that Aristotle's concept of "practical wisdom" requires an emphasis on particulars, a view he develops with great attention to the role of emotions in the process of practical reasoning. See Sherman (1989, 1997); Ross (1964); Nussbaum (1995).

14 Offering another framework for articulating the interplay of ideology and affect, Lawrence Grossberg describes two concepts: "mattering maps" and "affective epidemics." Determined by particular ideologies, mattering maps "represent a coherent system of values . . . [and] organize and prioritize people's investments" (1992, 282). Grossberg analyzes the new conservative ideologies as they "mobilize ideology (ibid). Why do we feel "trapped" by these ideologies, even if we disagree with them? He speaks of the power of ideologies as "magnetic sites," sites that are not created through one simple monolithic "pull." Rather, the power of ideologies functions like "'transit lines' which control the trajectories and define the spaces of everyday life. They direct people's movements, constructing lines of flight across the space of their mattering maps" (283–4). Affective epidemics describe these ideological sites: The "most powerful affective epidemic in the contemporary U.S. is organized around and across the family" (285). He argues that both the ideals of the nuclear family as well as discourses of the family increasingly are invoked, within Reaganomics, as the lightning rod for most moral and ideological debates. The family is heralded as the savior of the moral fabric of the nation, as well as blamed for the nation's failures. Thus the family is a predominant "mattering map," surrounded with affective discourses of pathology and crises.

Grossberg's reference to mattering maps as defined through "lines of flight" refers to the work of philosopher Gilles Deleuze and Felix Guattari. Elsewhere, I explore how Deleuze (1990; 1995; 1987; 1983) offers directions for educational theories and practices. Several theorists have developed the work of Deleuze in promising directions for both feminist theories and for analyzing affect. In an essay titled "The Autonomy of Affect" (1996), Brian Massumi (translator of Deleuze's work) draws on Deleuze and Spinoza to argue a distinction between affect and emotion which provocatively suggests that affects are "less containable" than emotions. Massumi's theorizations provide directions for developing theories of emotional resistance which I have used in an essay examining the feminist independent video work of Martha Rosler (Boler 1996). A growing number of feminist theorists, including Rosi Braidotti (1994) and Moira Gatens (1996), draw on Deleuze to offer directions for a theory of embodied subjectivity which undertake close analysis of emotions.

15 See Boler (1997a, 1997b).

16 For many years feminist theorists have argued against the ideology that women are 'naturally' more emotional than men, and instead focused on how this view effec-

tively keeps women from the boy's club of rationality and public power. However, in the 1980s, due largely to the work of Gilligan (1982) and Belenky et al (1986), and in a different but related vein Noddings (1984) some feminists articulated a 'celebratory' approach to women's emotionality. Rather than repudiate it as a negative patriarchal stereotype, this position embraces emotion as an essential gendered difference that women should use to their advantage.

Rather than review these debates in detail, I examine the nature/nurture controversy in terms of different discourses of emotion that emerge at particular historical and political moments. I am more interested in when and why the scientific community, for example, proliferates arguments on the biological basis of gendered differences, rather than whether or not such differences are 'real.' My hope is for a feminist account of emotions that need not subscribe to either a simply essentialist, nor simply social-constructionist, view, but an historical account of the genealogies of emotion in all their complexities.

17 Critiques of rationality, which emerge strongly within feminist and poststructuralist contexts, are articulated in response to different philosophical legacies and frequently directed at concepts of Cartesian ego or Kantian reason. The narratives that empower this thinking self are critiqued as disembodied, universal, and autonomous, falsely divorced from social or political influence. See for example, Linda Alcoff and Elizabeth Potter, eds., *Feminist Epistemologies* (1993); Jane Flax, *Disputed Subjects: Essays on Psychoanalysis, Politics, and Philosophy* (1993); Nancy Fraser, *Unruly Practices: Power, Discourse, and Gender in Contemporary Social Theory* (1989); Alison Jaggar and Susan Bordo, eds., *Gender/Body/Knowledge*, (1989); Genevieve Lloyd, *The Man of Reason: "Male" and "Female" in Western Philosophy*, (1984); Sandra Harding and Merrill Hintikka, eds., *Discovering Reality: Feminist Perspectives on Epistemology, Metaphysics, Methodology, and Philosophy of Science* (1983). In political philosophy, see Carol Pateman, *The Disorder of Women* (1989); in poststructural philosophy, Gilles Deleuze and Felix Guattari, *A Thousand Plateaus*, Brian Massumi, ed. and trans., (1987); in postcolonial studies, Gayatri Spivak, *Outside in the Teaching Machine*, (1993). For feminist poststructural treatments of education, see for example: Elizabeth Ellsworth, "Why Doesn't This Feel Empowering? Working Through the Repressive Myths of Critical Pedagogy," *Harvard Educational Review* (1989); Patti Lather, *Getting Smart: Feminist Research and Pedagogy With/in the Postmodern* (1991); Mary Leach and Megan Boler, "Gilles Deleuze: Practicing Education Through Flight and Gossip," in *Naming the Multiple: Poststructuralism and Education*, Michael Peters, ed. (1998). *Feminisms and Critical Pedagogy*, Luke and Gore (1992).

18 Many women philosophers approach emotions within the analytic tradition, less informed by feminist theories of difference, and elect (or, because of the strict views of "what counts as philosophy," are explicitly told by their departments not to publish in such journals as *Hypatia*) to publish less under the rubric of "feminist" philosophy (e.g., *Hypatia: Journal of Women and Philosophy*, and collections such as *Feminist Ethics*, op. cit.). The work of women philosophers in the analytic tradition has been influential in putting emotions back on philosophy's map in provocative ways. See for example in *Identity, Character, and Morality*, Owen Flanagan and Amelie Rorty, eds. (1990): Barbara Herman on Kant; Annette Baier on Hume; Patricia Greenspan, *Emotions and Reasons: An Inquiry into Emotional Justification* (1988); Amelie Rorty, "Explaining Emotions," in *Explaining Emotions*, A. Rorty, ed. (1980); Lorraine Code, "What Is Natural About Epistemology Naturalized?" *American Philosophical Quarterly*, (1996);. Karen Jones, "Trust as an Affective Attitude," in *Ethics* (1996).

19 In the next chapter I explore more specifically women's contradictory relation to education.

20 I discuss these dominant discourses at length in Boler (1997b).

21 The work of Michelle Rosaldo (1984) also marks a central contribution to feminist

anthropology of emotion.

22 Scheman (1996) offers an invaluable analysis of what she calls the " individual psychologizing of emotions."

23 Feminist who have also been influential in shaping philosophical conceptions of emotion and gender include Scheman (1996, 1993); Helen Longino, "To See Feelingly: Reason, Passion, and Dialogue in Feminist Philosophy, in *Feminisms in the Academy*, Domna Stanton and Abigail Stewart , eds. (1995); Morwenna Griffiths, *Feminisms and the Self: The Web of Identity* (1995).

24 See also Frye (1983), "Some Notes on Anger."

25 Moira Gatens suggests that feminists and Marxists have been polarized over this binary distinction(1996).

26 See Lynne McFall, "What's Wrong with Bitterness?" (1991). For further discussions see Boler (1997c).

27 Another approach to explaining how it is that we comply with our own subjugation (not unrelated to Benjamin's analysis of domination, but with a different emphases) has come from a radical, Marxist tradition which analyzes the relationship of consciousness to "ideology" and hegemony." See Appel (1996), Althusser (1971), Hebdige (1979), Apple (1990).

28 For an introduction to sociological feminist challenges to these dualisms, see for example Dorothy Smith, *The Everyday World as Problematic: A Feminist Sociology* (1987); Barbara Laslett, "Unfeeling Knowledge: Emotion and Objectivity in the History of Sociology," *Sociological Forum* (1990); Ann Game and Andrew Metcalfe, *Passionate Sociology* (1996). Hochschild (1983) analyzes the strange status of emotion as a product: It is intangible, elusive, unlike the production of material goods. Garrison interestingly notes similar phenomena in teaching and caring (1997).

29 Gayle Rubin's essay "The Traffic in Women" (1979) represents a phenomenal landmark critique of how Marxism, Freudian psychoanalysis, and structural anthropology have overlooked gender.

30 The psychoanalytic model relies on a paradigm in which human nature is understood in terms of impulses, drives and instincts which we must civilized — how "aggressive" desires become buried in the "unconscious" through psychic processes. While Freud's work focuses less explicitly on emotions per se (though attending to anxieties, etc.), later object relations theories following the work of Jacques Lacan look more attentively at emotions, as well as at the role of language and the symbolic relations that construct our sense of self in relation to others. See Sofoulis (1996); Stern (1985).

31 See Boler, "Taming the Labile Other" (Philosophy of Education Society Proceedings 1997).

32 I explore this in chapter 8. The question of the "selectivity of our attention" is an issue explored by Aristotle, Dewey, and Greene (for example, 1988). Sherman (1989, 1997) offers helpful study of Aristotle on this. On Dewey, see especially Garrison (1997).

33 I explore this further in chapter 5, "A Feminist Politics of Emotion." I am thinking here of random examples that might include the nonetheless invaluable work of Lankshear and McLaren (1993); Ellsworth (1989); essays in Luke and Gore (1992). This is not meant as a critique of what such authors do explore, but simply to point out that our language seems impoverished when we hit the rocky terrain of emotions in the classroom.

34 On this count, Britzman (1998) represents a significant contribution.

35 Some psychoanalytic theorists might argue that this is in fact what such a theory does. However, with respect to accounting for how emotions are educated, I'm not aware of literatures that explore the specifically historical and cultural dynamics of power and emotion through a psychoanalytic lens.

36 See Schrag (1972).

37 See Stern (1985); Higgins (*Philosophy of Education Society*, 1998); Alston (1991);

Britzman (1998).

38 See the 1997 special issue of *Harvard Educational Review* on women and educational history.

39 See Scott (1991); Gluck and Patai (1991); Smith (1992); Christian(1988); *Harvard Educational Review* 1997 special issue on women and educational history.

40 Feminist sociologies of education offer invaluable studies of the social, institutionalized, and lived dynamics of relations. See Jones (1998), Fine et al. (1997).

41 Poststructuralism refers to theories developed particularly by French theorists such as Foucault (1972, 1980); Bourdieu (1984). The "post" means in part that these theories historically follow what are called "structuralist" theories, which refer to the work of Marx, Freud, and Levi-Strauss among others. Structural theories are so-called because of their emphasis on how "structures" shape the subject or person within society: e.g., how the worker is "determined" by the forces of capitalism's structures. Poststructuralism seeks to develop theories of power that are "two-way," that can account for how the worker, for example, can "resist" the forces of domination. All of these are in contrast to what might be called "individualized" or psychological theories that focus on the individual as if divorced from social forces altogether. Yet another field of approach is cultural studies, which was in its early stages marked by two strands, the culturalists and the structuralists (see footnote 10).

42 In chapter 5 I explore the reasons feminist theories of education distance themselves from the tradition of consciousness-raising and feminist pedagogy.

43 Some Marxist analyses of consciousness provide social theory with tools for analyzing how ideology becomes embodied, and how dominant cultural values becomes part of our material, everyday experience. This internalization of ideology occurs through various processes: in the simplest example, through language. One of the few Marxist theorists to explore this terrain is Raymond Williams, considered one of the fathers of "cultural studies," who coined the concept "structures of feeling." Structures of feeling name the simultaneously cultural and discursive dimension of our experience, but do not neglect that these experiences are embodied and felt.

Williams points out that theorists tend to describe and analyze "culture and society . . . in a habitual past tense" (1977: 128). This results in "fixing" them, creating them though our language as if they are unchanging and rigid. In so doing, we end up bifurcating the "social" from the "personal." The personal is how we then refer to the temporal experience, the emotional and embodied experience, of our daily life. When our analysis creates and analyzes a fixed form, we fail to adequately account for the "complexities, the experienced tensions, shifts, and uncertainties, the intricate forms of unevenness and confusion"(1977: 129). Our analyses have created the abstract categories of fixed social forms, such as the "'human psyche,' 'the unconscious,' with their 'functions' in art and in myth and in dream" (1977, 130). These forms "become social consciousness only when they are lived, actively, in real relationships, and moreover in relationships which are more than systematic exchanges between fixed units. Indeed just because all consciousness is social, its processes occur not only between but within the relationship and the related" (ibid.). Williams is describing the subterranean economy of emotions and feeling. Our daily interactions, with the world, with others, even with ourselves, are defined through relational consciousness that is rarely fixed but rather is fluid, unpredictable, slippery, and "labile" ("overemotional"; see chapter 2 "Disciplined Emotions").

Emotions offer important insights into social control because emotion, "practical consciousness," "is almost always different from official consciousness. . . . For practical consciousness is what is actually being lived, and not only what is thought is being lived. Yet the actual alternative to the received and produced fixed forms is not silence: not the absence, the unconscious, which bourgeois culture has mythicized. It is a kind of feeling and thinking which is indeed social and material, but in an embryonic phase before it can become fully articulate and defined exchange" (131).

The articulation and exchange, the forms in which we must produce the "embryonic" emotions for example, require language. Thus in neo-Marxist analyses of culture, language and discourses are a central site of study.

44 See the collection *Articulating the Local in the Global*, eds. Kellner and Cvetkovich (1996). I explore these questions further in chapter 6.

45 See Soja (1996) for intriguing analyses of "third space."

CHAPTER TWO

DISCIPLINED EMOTIONS

Locating Emotions in Gendered Educational Histories

Hygienists placed their hopes in the psychological counterpart of social control, the outcome of personality development. Here was a form of social control without coercion of laws, rules, and legal prohibitions . . . .The mental hygiene movement arose contemporaneously with the era of mass immigration just ending. The omnipresent problem of the immigrants . . . heightened hygienist sensitivity to the need for defining standards for wholesome personality throughout the school.

— Sol Cohen[1]

[O]ne of the persistent stories of moral regulation is its failure. Wherever there is moral regulation there is resistance; wherever social forms are imposed there is human capacity to subvert and exceed their constraints.

— Rousmaniere et al[2]

Four hundred years (four hundred years)
Education, the same philosophy
{we} build your penitentiary, we build your schools
Brainwash education to make us the fools
Hate is your reward for our love
Telling us of your God above . . .
We gonna chase those crazy
Chase those crazy baldheads out of town

—Bob Marley[3]

HISTORIES OF EDUCATION have largely neglected a vast and untold story: the subterranean disciplining of emotions.[4] A primary goal of education is to discipline young people's social and moral values and behaviors. This moral conduct is inextricably tied to emotional control. Although social control is directed at all who participate in education — teachers, administrators, and students—discourses of emotion in education are most consistently present and visible in relation to women. Women are the repository of emotion in Western culture, while in their role as schoolteacher they are simultaneously assigned to prepare moral citizens and expected to be the "guardian against the irrational." Yet overall, explicit attention to the subject of emotion appears only rarely in educational histories and theories — in chronicles of character and moral education, for example, and in handbooks for teachers on pedagogy and discipline.

Despite the rare appearances of explicit discussions of emotion, emotions have been consistently educated, whether explicitly or inexplicitly, in every classroom throughout the centuries. How do we begin to map the visible and less visible traces of emotion in educational histories?[5] How do we offer an account that begins to explain emotions, both in their absence and presence, as a key site of social control?

As a result of the disciplinary and evidential limitations, my approach runs the risk of a "retroactive analysis": I could say there weren't explicit discourses of emotion or when there were, the predominantly male historians didn't address emotions or women's work. However, to demonstrate my thesis by showing the absence of emotion seems largely unsatisfying. In order to map a history of the emotions, it is necessary to cast our gaze slightly away from emotions. Thus, I draw upon "evidence" that by and large doesn't call itself emotion. I examine emotion's "displaced" historical presence in terms of two lenses: the notion of *utility, or skills-based discipline* and *obedience, or rules-based discipline.* The former is framed largely through the authority of *science*, and the latter through *religious or moral* values. Further, I don't limit my investigation to sites of explicit discourses of emotion because I want to understand why and how certain things are silenced. What is spoken/visible and not spoken/invisible offers a primary focus of my inquiry.

In this chapter, I argue that pastoral power — teaching students and teachers to self-police — manifests through a combination of religious, scientific, and rational discourses. These three Western discourses are the foundation of Western educational values. Through schooling, these ideologies in turn shape gendered representations and internalized norms of emotions and their expression. I first provide two gendered examples from the turn of the century, which illustrate the combination of rules- and skills-based authority of science and (increasingly covert) religious values. I then begin this narrative within the framework of the common school movement in the United States, which dates from the mid-1800s. To understand the common school movement, I examine how religious, scientific, and rational discourses have "controlled" women's emotions and relation to knowledge as a strategy to maintain her subordinate status within patriarchal culture. I conclude the chapter with a discussion of the mental-hygiene movement, which dates to the turn of the century and flourished until after World War II. A "modern" version of pastoral power, the mental-hygiene movement targeted children's "emotions" as the causes of all social ills.[6]

The ultimate aims of schools are widely recognized as social control. Schools produce students of "moral character."[7] What counts as "moral" changes over time, depending on authoritative discourses (religious vs. scientific), social and economic needs (when and in what form is women's labor required in the workforce), and historically specific hierarchies of gender, race, and social class.[8] In the history of United States education, assimilation and "Americanization" are two primary forms of educational shaping of citizens.[9] Revisionist accounts emphasize how economic and political interests define morality and social values, which translate into rules of conduct taught in schools.[10] Feminist accounts, which may also be revisionist, emphasize how morality is also tied to maintaining male privilege.[11] What I contribute to this previously explained terrain of education and moral control is a map of how emotions function as site of social control.

Protestant and other religious values have framed the "good student" through more and less explicit moral rules of obedience. But since the turn of the century, capitalism and the social sciences have framed good students in terms of their utility, their social efficiency and skills. I argue that the modern social control of emotions through pastoral power occurs through the melding of religious and scientific measures of virtue. The (masculinized) values of rationality are embedded within both science and religion.

PASTORAL POWER AND SOCIAL CONTROL OF EMOTIONS

PASTORAL POWER IS a form of governing populations by teaching individuals to police themselves. Emotions are a primary medium through which we learn to internalize ideologies as commonsense truths. For example, children are increasingly taught not to express their anger, not to question authority, and not to resist those who have power. These rules are taught through differing forms of emotional discipline (shame, humiliation, etc., depending on gendered, racialized norms, for instance); depending on their gendered, raced, or social class standing children learn different rules regarding what emotional expressions are acceptable.

The following two examples demonstrate the theses of this chapter: that emotions as a site of social control are mapped onto girls and boys in different ways (similarly, onto women schoolteachers and male administrators differently) and that pastoral power manifests through a combination of scientific and religious authority which governs emotional discourses. These examples precede the mental-hygiene movement by only a few years but reflect the nascent merging of scientific and moral discourses slated to control emotions.

A New Manual of Method provides an example of masculinized discourses and reveals pastoral power at work through the authority of *scientific* and *rational* discourses that predominantly shape "boys'" behavior.[12] First published in 1897 and in its seventh publication by 1907, this handbook for teachers was made available in New York, Bombay, and Calcutta. Chapter 2 is titled "Discipline" and addresses how particular emotions should be rewarded and punished in the classroom.

The author, A. H. Garlick, headmaster of a boy's school, defines discipline as a "force for moral training." In its very definition, discipline functions through emotional vicissitudes.

> 1. [Discipline] must be based on Natural Principles.—It must recognize the child's love of activity and curiosity. . . . It must recognize that character is a growth, and that discipline is the natural trainer and corrector of growth.
> 2. Its Aims must be Good. . . . Do the scholars . . . love and seek their work? Is the discipline sufficient to restrain all the unruly impulses of the children? Is it maintained by love or by fear? . . . Does it cultivate the amicable sentiments? Does it check and regulate moral precocity, which is always an expensive luxury? Is it consistent, and does it tend to develop a self-governed being? Is it in harmony with the child's nature. . . ? (1897/1907: 12)

Teachers are instructed how to discipline many emotional behaviors including "Anger, Obstinacy, Crying, Cruelty, Kindness, and Cowardice." Garlick's discussion of "anger" provides an interesting example of how emotions and power are intertwined. Reflecting the different dominant discourses of pathology and rationality, anger is characterized as being "aroused . . . by an injury, real or supposed" with the various specific causes all reducible to the "sense of injury."

"Its treatment is difficult. The angry child is both physically and mentally disturbed" (22). Anger is understood first as a physiological disruption — the "action of the heart" and "digestive and other functions naturally suffer"; but "[t]he child is equally disturbed mentally. . . . The child is in no fit state for argument or punishment. The first effort must be to soothe the child, and to restore him to something like a normal physical and mental condition" (ibid).

The commonsense view of anger as a "physiological" upset that disturbs one's mental capacity is legitimated through the authority of medical science combined with the hypervaluation of rationality (a synonym for masculinity).

The corollary treatment— that one must "cool off" before thinking clearly after an angry upset to the system— persists in teachers', parents', and therapists' instructional directives today, as I will discuss in the next two chapters. (While there are certainly cases in which one benefits from "cooling" off before reacting, feminist analyses that emerge in the early 1970s recognize anger as a critical form of knowledge that need not be "pathologized.")

The headmaster's suggested "treatment" of anger offers insight into the power relations between teacher and student, and reveals culturally specific values imposed on a young person. While we might agree that, across different cultures and times, people experience the increased heartbeat of anger similarly, what varies tremendously is how the culture treats the expression of anger. In this instance, Garlick recommends such things as "the voluntary self-humiliation of the wrongdoer":

> 2. Later on the teacher might point out the dreadful effects of anger. He might show how it exhausts the energy, gives pain and annoyance to others. . . .
> 4. He should seek to cultivate the reflective powers of the child, and this will give him a healthier view of the irritating causes. . . .
> 7. He should appeal to the child's will, and make him understand that he should be the master, not the slave of his passions. He might also gently remind him that public opinion considers anger to be short madness.
> 8. Perhaps the best method of all will be to cultivate the social feelings; to appeal to the higher side of the child's nature (22-3).

This explicit educational discourse on anger resonates with histories of moral education that identify the historical shift to "good temper," self-control, and self-policing as the keys to harmony and efficiency within societies increasingly plagued by social conflicts. Garlick's targeting of the child's emotions reflects an early strand of what is known as the mental-hygiene movement.

How do these teachings apply to girls? I would argue that such emotional self-control has been assumed, implicitly, as proper feminine behavior. The following example shows that girls are *additionally* taught an entirely other order of emotional rules, designed to force them to take responsibility for all of society's ills through their "natural" altruism and caring. Preventing boys from expressing anger is discursively framed as being for the boy's own benefit; for girls, emotional control is especially for the benefit of others.

The 1898 *Domestic Economy Reader* textbook opens:

> Most of you are familiar with the word domestic, because you have some pet at home that you are fond of, such as a playful kitten, a mischievous doggie, or a happy little canary that is often singing so cheerily when you return from school.

> Each of these is a domestic animal, because it lives in or about the house. Every girl will now be eager to tell what she knows about those two words on the title page. Domestic—belonging to the house or family. Economy — Right management . . . .
> It is because so many homes are badly managed that crime, poverty, and misery are so common. Every girl hopes one day to be a woman, when she will most likely have to undertake the management of a home of her own. (1898: 1–2)

Assigned to the "domestic" sphere, girls are educated (ironically, by female schoolteachers and mothers) to accept her confinement in the home and her exclusion from public forms of power. Women's "domestic" role is presented as if it is natural — "God-given," biological, and virtuous. Her very existence is defined as an altruistic act for the sake of the healthy family and for the nation state.

How is this ideology presented as if it is "natural" and outside history, not reflecting the particular interests of patriarchy or capitalism? In this example, women's role is first *naturalized* through common sense: "Most of you are familiar with the word domestic, because you have some pet at home that you are fond of, such as a playful kitten, a mischievous doggie, or a happy little canary that is often singing so cheerily when you return from school." A woman's domestic role is equated with that of a pet: She is a feature of the home whose primary role is to be "cheerful." "Domestic" is then defined as "belonging to the house," which reflects the ideology of women as property. But rather than refer to this role in terms of religious values, the definition shifts to a discourse of social sciences and efficiency: "Economy — Right management." As the "domestic scientists" who learn the "right skills," women's burden is nothing less than curing society of all its social ills. The text explicitly states that social ills are women's fault: "It is because so many homes are badly managed that crime, poverty, and misery are so common." This turn-of-the-century example reflects the scientized version of the ideal of the virtuous woman which shapes the role of the female common-school teacher.

The introduction of domestic science reflects the changing social climate at the turn of the century. Immigration, industrialization, and urbanization vastly increased social conflicts. The growth of the social sciences assisted in an ideological shift which shaped gender roles and education. This shift in social control is marked by increased emphasis on "utility" and social efficiency, a discourse that remains powerfully influential today.

What leads up to this turn-of-the-century form of pastoral power? I now examine the common-school movement, which precedes these explicit discourses on emotion. I analyze the different gendered narratives within common-school histories with respect to the social control of emotion.

COMMON-SCHOOL MOVEMENT AND PASTORAL CODES OF EMOTIONAL CONDUCT AND VIRTUE

ONE CAN ARGUE that, since feminists began rewriting educational histories, there are two predominant historical narratives about the common school movement of the mid-nineteenth century United States. Revisionist histories emphasize Protestant and/or capitalist influences on the shaping of schools. Feminist histories often focus on how similar forces shaped the "ideal of womanhood" and thus the predominantly female common-school teacher.

In revisionist accounts,[13] (usually male) historians emphasize religious and capitalist influences on the development of free, compulsory schooling in the United States. In these accounts, one finds little if any gendered analysis, nor does one find analyses of the "interiority" of schools. Feminist accounts, however, have been interested in the "everyday experiences of those who populate schools," an interest that "coincided with feminist attempts to make the 'private' public, to give voice to those who have been silenced, and to make visible that which has been excluded, marginalized, and forgotten in more 'mainstream' histories of education" (Rousmaniere et al. 1997: 275).

In the typical revisionist account, emotions are invisible because neither emotions nor women's and student's daily experiences have been foregrounded. Further, in Western cultures the absence rather than the presence of emotion signifies masculinity, the virtuous, and the good. Since the "ideal moral citizen" or student is understood to be both "rational" and "masculine," emotions generally fall through the cracks of history.

Pastoral Power and Invisible Masculine Emotions

AN EXAMPLE OF the masculinized erasure of emotions in history is found in Phillip Aries's book *Centuries of Childhood* (1962). This well-respected history (which strongly informs Foucault's *Discipline and Punish*) offers a detailed tracing of how the modern notion of the "family" came into Western culture, explored through the changing conceptions of "childhood" since the Middle Ages. Aries argues that the major historical shift that defines conceptions of childhood is a shift from "coddling" to "disciplining" the child. Although this is most significantly a shift in emotional attitudes towards children, emotion is not cited in the index, and few emotions are mentioned within the volume. Of the few emotions mentioned, "humiliation" crops up frequently as a method of disciplining within schools, yet Aries does not analyze how this emotional discourse shapes discipline. Finally, the title of the book evidences the complete erasure of women's and girls' experiences: The book should be

retitled *Centuries of Boyhood.* The children who are being disciplined through the centuries of schooling are boys, the only ones permitted an education. We learn nothing about girl-children's experience of childhood for the several centuries described — yet the text speaks of "childhood" as a generic term!

Like Aries, revisionist historians frequently assume a generic child and rarely if ever describe the education of emotions. Before exploring the explicit mapping of emotions onto the virtuous female teacher, it is helpful to examine a representative common-school history. The typical account favors analyses of the social forces and public figures representative of the historical events and tends to overlook the questions of the "interiority" of schoolrooms.[14] In what follows, we find a discourse of norms and conformity — pastoral power— which reflects the subterranean social control of emotions.

The common-school movement is characterized as an "ambitious and successful social movement" and sometimes as a "crusade." The primarily male leaders of the movement were compelled by a "calling": Like missionaries, these crusaders were for the most God-fearing Christians who wanted to achieve character for the young as much as to teach them basic skills. A common, primary text for teaching literacy was the Bible; Sunday schools and the common-schools were in many cases nearly indistinguishable.

The relation of schoolteacher to morality was an explicit focus articulated by the influential "father" of common-school crusades, Horace Mann. The teacher's role was to teach children not to transgress laws, thereby replacing the police. "[The concept of teacher as police] made schools the central institution for the control and maintenance of the social order. . . . It opened the door for the explosive political issue of whose morality would be taught in the public schools" (Spring 1986: 85). As state institutions for the governance of young citizens, schools provided an ideal site for deploying the shift from authoritarian control to internalized self-regulation as a means of social control.

White Anglo-Saxon Protestant men headed this movement. They established curricula and set pedagogical precedent, and publicly debated what values were to be taught. "Superintendents in the twentieth century have almost all been married white males, characteristically middle-aged, Protestant, upwardly mobile, from favored ethnic groups, native-born, and of rural origins" (Tyack and Hansot 1982: 169). Tyack and Hansot note that it is no coincidence that the typical superintendent fits this profile: Women and non-white persons have been systematically excluded from holding positions of power.[15]

Tyack and Hansot explain the "conformity" of these superintendents to dominant cultural values in fairly benign terms. "Most occupational groups," they explain, "have norms to which the worker is expected to conform. 'When the teacher has internalized the rules which bind him,' Waller observes, 'he has become truly a teacher. . . . A person is not free in any occupation *until he has made conformity a part of himself*" (173, emphasis added). They describe the shaping and administration of schools throughout this century as determined by a "fraternity bonded by common personal histories as much as by shared ideals of scientific management" (180). The shared and common values remained wholly unquestioned, in part because the superintendents grew up with values that matched those of their community and because they rarely moved out of the communities in which they were raised. These men had no reason to question the dominant values and "accepted role prescriptions not as restrictions but as normal expectations—in short they were 'free' through unconscious conformity" (178).

The compliance of the common-school teacher and superintendent exemplifies pastoral power:[16] the maintenance of the status quo through individual's self-governance, acceptance, and in this case perpetuation of the dominant cultural values. The overriding goals of education within the common-schools has been shown to be not pupil freedom but " 'establishing a stable, orderly classroom, in which academic standards received a prominent position' " (Zeigler quoted in Tyack and Hansot 1982: 176). Although these authors don't explictly mention it, this educational goal required that individuals internalize self-control of their emotional behavior.

Visible Traces of Emotion in Education: The Ideal and Virtuous Woman

A SECOND PRIMARY narrative of common-schools has developed over the last two decades with the rise of feminist scholarship. Historical studies of education which recognize the central role of the female schoolteacher often focus on the dominant "ideal of womanhood." This ideology is constructed through the combined discourses of religion, science, and rationality. Because women are expected to uphold the virtues of the nation state and its young, it is possible to "see" the social control of emotions at work in terms of employing women as the "caring police." In what follows, I examine histories of the ideal virtuous teacher to exemplify how the discourses of religion, medicine, and rationality shape women's relation to emotion.

Women have been employed en masse to carry out the teaching of moral virtues, not only in the United States but in many Western nations.[17] In the United States, after the American Revolution, women's "private" domestic role gained a new public status. According to the refrain of such educators as Benjamin Rush, women were seen as crucial to the development of republican citizens for the nation. Just as the mother was expected to set a good example for the child in terms of restraining anger, so was the teacher. As of the

1790s, "Parents as well as educational theorists increasingly insisted on teachers of good character, and this in turn was to include mastery of temper" (Stearns 1986: 102).

By 1870 in the United States, "women constituted 60 percent of the nation's teachers; by 1900, 70 percent; by 1910, 80 percent" (Grumet 1988: 43). To assist in the project of assimilation to Protestant and middle-class values, women's naturally virtuous character was considered well suited. In the words of Catherine Beecher (1835),

> For a nation to be virtuous and religious, the females of that nation must be deeply imbued with these principles: for just as the wives and mothers sink or rise in the scale of virtue, intelligence and piety, the husbands and the sons will rise or fall. These positions scarce any intelligent person will deny: so that it may be set down as one of the current truisms of society, that the formation of the moral and religious principles and habits is the most important part of education, even in reference to this life alone. (in Cross, 1965: 71)

Grumet quotes from Louisa May Alcott an explicit list of what women were to learn (quoted in Grumet 1988: 42):

> "What virtues do you wish more of?" asks Mr. L.
>
> I answer:
>
> Patience, Love, Silence,
> Obedience, Generosity, Perseverance,
> Industry, Respect, Self-Denial.
>
> "What vices less of?"
>
> Idleness, Wilfulness, Vanity,
> Impatience, Impudence, Pride,
> Selfishness, Activity, Love of cats.

The epitome of these virtues is referred to as the "cult of motherhood" or the "cult of domesticity."

> The ideal of republican motherhood had provided the first rationale appropriate to the perceived need of raising virtuous citizens in the new nation. A second impetus arose with the renewed religious fervor of the Second Great Awakening

> that gripped much of the country from the late 1790s to the 1850s. The ideal of the Christian wife, mother, and teacher gave repeated urgency to women's education . . . .Republican and Christian rationales made a formidable combination justifying the education of women. (Solomon 1985: 15–16)

Revealing the contradictions embedded in ideologies, despite women being "naturally" suited to inculcate moral virtues in the young, not all women "naturally" embody the proper values. As Gerda Lerner traces in the binary of the "Lady and the Mill-girl" (1979), the virtuous woman is an ideal based on the white, middle-class Protestant female. Those women who entered the teaching profession from poor and working-class families were trained to adopt the proper values through-teacher training schools.[18] The ideal of womanhood was transported into Native American and into the indigenous New Zealand cultures, for example, by forcing young women of the indigenous cultures to live with white, middle-class families as part of their educational experience. These young women were then expected to return to their own culture and "Americanize," or colonize, from within.[19]

Women's "natural" skills in teaching moral virtues reflect the increasing modes of pastoral power. Women are conscripted as the agents of this power: required to enforce patriarchal values and laws, to instill virtues which are gendered. Not only do women assist in strategies of individualization, urging children to "self-control," they also participate in their own subjugation by reinforcing the control of emotions and gendered rules of emotions. As Grumet argues regarding this contradiction, the feminization of teaching "has both promoted and sabotaged the interests of women in our culture" (1988: 32).

Women's religiously defined "virtue" and her scientifically defined "utility" are intertwined in educational history as women became essential to the labor force. By the turn of the century, as was apparent in the excerpt from the *Domestic Economy Reader*, women's evil lies in her lack of skills in "domestic economy" or "right management." However, this is simply a scientific twist on the long-standing religious demonization of women.

RELIGIOUS BACKDROP TO WOMEN'S RELATION TO EDUCATION AND EMOTIONS[20]

LONG BEFORE THE spread of Christianity, rooted in Greek philosophy, patriarchy associated women with evil. Battles between the sins of the flesh and the purities of the soul were fought on the bodies of women; women literally embody sin and temptation, justifying the ancient patriarchal positioning of women as inferior.[21] Within religious doctrines one finds the powerful association of women's emotions and sin.

In the late 1600s and early 1700s, Mary Astell published powerful defenses of women against the contradictory requirements set upon them by religious order. Against the views of her time, she argued for women's education and interrogated the institution of marriage. Why do women experience disadvantage? Not from natural or divine causes, but from social: Young women are "'restrain'd, frown'd upon, and beat, not for but from the Muses: Laughter and Ridicule, that never-failing Scare-crow, I set up to divert them from the Tree of Knowledge' " (Astell quoted in Riley 1988: 33).

In an uncanny analysis of what I call the politics of emotion, Astell identifies how the fear of public shame and ridicule deters women from "knowledge." She criticizes women's no-win situation: Women are systematically miseducated, and then penalized for their shortcomings. Women have been educated "'to disturb, not to regulate their Passions; to make them more timorous and dependent, and in a word, fit for nothing else but to act a Farce for the Diversion of their Governours" (ibid). Astell soundly indicts the contradictory social construction of emotions, in which patriarchal law constructs woman as irrational and then makes her a clown because of her emotionality.

By the time Rousseau published *Emile* (1762), the idea that men's and women's souls were equal had become a weak postulate as the association of women with nature became further entrenched. Madame de Stael, writing in 1800, expresses the impossible status of women: "'The rank which women hold in society is still, in many respects, indeterminate.... In the present state of things they are placed neither in the order of nature, nor in the order of society'" (quoted in Riley 1988: 39).

Madame de Stael further depicts the struggle between reason and affective expression faced by the creative woman who dared to express herself:

> By what means can a distinction be made twixt the talents and the mind? How can we set aside what we feel, when we trace what we think? How impose silence on those sentiments which live in us, without losing any of the ideas which those sentiments have inspired? What kinds of writings would result from these continual combats? Had we not better yield to all the faults which arise from the irregularities of nature? (quoted in Riley 1988: 40)

Foreshadowing the politics of emotion, de Stael recognizes that in fact sentiments and thought are inseparable, and that sentiments inspire the thoughts. The view of emotions as symptoms of the failings and moral evil of women remains a bedrock of Western Protestant cultures.[22] In part because of their association with women's imperfection in the eyes of God, emotions signify vice rather than virtue.[23]

RATIONALITY AND THE PEDAGOGY OF LOVE

WOMEN WERE CONSCRIPTED as schoolteachers to function as what I call the "caring police," a description of women's role in pastoral power. The "ideal of womanhood," "the cult of domesticity" centrally require women's proper emotional behavior. Women should be caring and loving, and not express anger.[24] This ideal manifests as well in the "pedagogy of love." By the nineteenth century both educational and familial values markedly shift from overt coercion and authoritarianism as a means of social control, to "participatory democracy" and a "pedagogy of love." Valerie Walkerdine addresses how the female schoolteacher was positioned to carry out the values of the state. The social sciences combined with middle-class, Protestant values that pathologized social conflict such as "crime, pauperism, deviance" (1985: 206). Women were expected to teach children to "self-regulate."[25] Teaching children to internalize self-control through a pedagogy of maternal love was strongly favored over overt coercion.

Women are assigned as "repositories" of irrationality: They must embody irrationality (e.g., as the nurturing caregiver, and the embodiment of passions) while simultaneously they are held responsible for "removing" irrationality from children in order to civilize them. Walkerdine argues that a central goal of education is "the transformation of conflict into rational argument by means of universalized capacities for language and reason" (205). She demonstrates that as "covert self-regulation" became favored over more "overt" coercion, "love became the basis of pedagogical techniques designed to avoid problems with overt surveillance" (206).

Women's exclusion from the public sphere can be traced back to the Greek polis. The exclusion of women from positions of power — political, legislative and judicial, for example — is explained as the "natural" result of their inferiority and lack of rationality. Women's limited domestic power is "naturalized" through their emotionality, body, sexuality, and reproductive capacity.

Political philosopher Carol Pateman traces the differently gendered definitions of justice, virtue, and divisions of public/private labor in liberal political theory.[26] The privatized sphere of women's "love" and sentiment is deemed as a *social* virtue. Women's virtue is thus fundamentally divided from the masculine public sphere of justice is seen as a *conventional* virtue. The domestic family where women are permitted to "govern" is classified as a social rather than conventional institution. Women's power is confined to the privacy of the home (where, incidentally, public laws do not govern, and rape and domestic violence are hidden from public intervention and justice).

Not only are women excluded from public life, they are seen as potentially subversive to conventional justice and rational order.

> [W]omen . . . are incapable of developing a sense of justice. . . . The family itself is a threat to civil life. Love and justice are antagonistic virtues; the demands of love and of family bonds are particularistic and so in direct conflict with justice which demands that private interest is subordinated to the public (universal) good. (Pateman 1990: 23)

The overlap of ideologies regarding a woman's place in the family and her place in the (semi-public) sphere of the schoolroom positions her as a central agent of pastoral power. "The common-school movement and the feminization of teaching colluded in support of a program of centralized education that exploited the status and integrity of the family to strip it of its authority and deliver children to the states" (Grumet 1988: 39).

However, women have had to learn to live with ideological contradictions. For although women are seen as necessary to the healthy development of children and students, they are also unfit for "higher education" and public power. With respect to emotions, patriarchal ideology frames women as "naturally" hysterical, a hysteria that proves women's inferiority as moral (and as rational) beings. "Women have a disorder at their very centers — in their morality — which can bring about the destruction of the state" (Pateman, 1990: 18).[27]

The contradictions faced by female schoolteachers are inextricably intertwined with the contradictions imposed on women in relation to rationality:

> women are seen as guardians of order and morality as well as inherently subversive. . . . Women impose order and foster morality; but they are in daily contact with dirt and with natural processes only partly under our control. . . . Hence they represent both order and disorder, both morality and boundless passion. (Pateman 1990: 25)

To support the dominant discourses of rationality and the exclusion of women from the public sphere, emotions have been consistently individualized and privatized. Emotions are assigned as women's dirty work, and then used against her as an accusation of her inferior irrationality.

Feminist analyses like Pateman's evidence that women's gendered and emotional behaviors are not "natural" or "universal." To the contrary, emotional rules, like gendered roles, are historically- and culturally specific and shift accordingly to political and economic needs and climate (Mead, 1935; Rosaldo,

1984).[28] Ideals regarding schoolteachers and their "marriage status" provides a telling example. During the nineteenth century female schoolteachers were not allowed to be married. This reflected the ideological belief that an unmarried female teacher was "asexual," and thus more virtuous. However, recent historians document that in the 1930s after women had gained the right to vote and made significant gains in the educational and public sphere, this requirement was reversed.[29] Unmarried schoolteachers came to be perceived as a threat to masculinity. In a sudden turnabout, schoolteachers were suddenly expected to be married to assuage the growing anxieties surrounding masculinity.

MEDICAL/SCIENTIFIC DISCOURSES OF EMOTION: *The Pathologizing of Women*

HOW DO WE BEGIN to explain the contradictions faced by female schoolteachers — that they are portrayed as naturally emotional, yet expected to control teach children emotional self-control; that they are fit to attend teacher-training or nursing school, but not fit for other forms of higher education?

Scientific and medical authority have provided the ongoing justification to naturalize and pathologize women's emotions, particularly through the growth of psychiatry.[30] An early version of eugenics, "hysteria" was diagnosed as a female disease whose symptoms included hyper-emotionality and absence of reason.[31] Scientists argue that hysteria was caused by education. The stress of using her "mind" caused her womb to tear free from its moorings and float about the body. Education thus rendered women useless for childbirth. The fear of "hysteria" thus justified excluding her from education and enforcing her place as wife and mother.

The scientific and medical discourses regarding women's emotionality effectively excluded women from education. By the early 1900s the growing medical profession capitalized on scientific authority to bar women from education and keep her confined to the domestic sphere. As "cranium" theories lost force, the authority of scientists such as Herbert Spencer were invoked to support women's exclusion from education. Spencer's work supported the idea of the body as a system with limited energy. Columbia University psychologist James McKeen Cattell writes in the *Popular Science Monthly*, (1909): "Girls are injured more than boys by school life: they take it more seriously, a and at certain times and at a certain age are far more subject to harm. It is probably not an exaggeration to say that to the average cost of each girl's education through high schools must be added one unborn child" (quoted in Rosenberg 1982: 89). Authorities agreed that the strain of educational endeavors rendered women unfit for childbearing. These arguments supported preventing women from higher education, and development of sex-differentiated curriculum, emphasizing domestic science rather than academic curriculum for girls.

The scientific and medical discourses found their way into education through the burgeoning of the social sciences. By the early twentieth century, social scientific management (still in combination with religious values) was seen as a primary solution to maintaining order within the fraught educational systems.

In short, within narratives of educational histories, emotions are largely "invisible" because the dominant historical methodologies do not foreground women's experience nor the "daily" material substance of emotional interactions between students, and between students and teacher, in the classroom. With the emergence of science as the new "god" at the turn of the century, the discourses of explicit obedience and the scientific discourses of utility and skills work in tandem. I turn now to examine the effect of the emergent discourses of social sciences on the social control of emotion.

THE SHIFT TO UTILITY-BASED MORALITY AND THE SOCIAL SCIENTIFIC DISCOURSE OF EMOTIONS

FOLLOWING THE TURN of the century, the social sciences become a dominant force in educational theories and practices and are systematically applied to maintain conformity. Though Protestant values remain embedded in cultural ideologies, educational curricula and debates are increasingly shaped by questions of scientific measurement. With the growth of the social sciences, new forms of social control are introduced.

Rapid increases in urbanization, industrialization, and immigration at the turn of the century forced educational institutions to adapt, almost overnight, to demands for centralized school systems.[32] The community-based schoolroom proved to be an unfeasible model for a rapidly expanding national population. The increased bureaucratization of schools was accompanied by centralized administration and the rapid growth of the social sciences as new tools for measuring efficiency and "virtue."

CAPITALIZING ON EMOTION: *Social Efficiency and "Human Resources," 1900 – 1920*

THE SOCIAL SCIENCES provided new tools for "blaming the individual," and functioned to proliferate pastoral power. The social sciences emphasize efficiency and utility: "school would be reduced to teaching mechanical skills and virtues associated with living in an industrial society. As morality became embedded in behaviors identified by supposedly value-neutral 'scientific' methods, it was distanced from the idea of moral development through critical and conscious thought" (Beane 1990: 28).

Emotions are increasingly recognized less as a symptom of *moral* degeneracy and more as the disruption of the organism's equilibrium. Emotion also signifies disruption of the equilibrium of the "social organization." Constructed as antithetical to reason and social efficiency, emotion is subdued by emphasis on the rational functioning of the organism as one part of a larger industrial organization of harmony.[33] Social harmony, like the organism, is increasingly conceived a well-oiled machine of functioning parts.

The following excerpt, from a 1912 New York City High Schools Teachers Association Bulletin, attempts to measure and rate efficiency of students, and describes the student literally as a version of what is now called "human resources." Students provide the "flesh-and-bone" material for capitalist production:

> B. Comparisons between schools and mercantile establishments:
> 1. The teacher obviously corresponds to planning department, superintendent, manager of a factory.
> 2. The elements in the enterprise (the workmen, the raw material, and the finished product) are combined in the pupil. The other elements (tools, etc.) are the text books, charts, and apparatus. . . .
> E. Difficulties in the way of making exact applications of scientific principles:
> 1. *So many different elements are combined in one (i.e., the pupil).*
> 2. *The raw material (pupil) is affected by so many outside conditions.*
> 3. *Poor raw material cannot be exchanged for good.*
> 4. Teacher never sees or deals with a finished product. (quoted in Callahan, 1962: 58, emphasis added)

Schools recognized that students provided the "raw material" for capitalist production. However, there was the problem of "poor raw material": schools needed to sort out the "poor" from the "profitable" raw material/student. How were schools to distinguish between the good and the bad student, without violating the rhetorical commitment to democracy and equal opportunity?[34]

The IQ test provided a solution: science could "measure meritocracy." Those who performed poorly were, through their own lack or fault, justifiably "tracked" into the less valued strata of society.

MEASURING MERITOCRACY

STANDARDIZED TESTING offers a key means of measuring the rational virtues and skill-based "capacities." In 1908 Alfred Binet's "intelligence scale" made its debut and was quickly adopted by Edward Thorndike of Columbia Teacher's College. Thorndike (1874–1949), profoundly influential in the testing movement, offered a view of intelligence as fixed and measurable. The IQ test provided a "neutral," scientific means for measuring the valuable student. "Coincidentally," the overemotional, criminally inclined, poor students would be weeded out through standardized testing. Through the "disinterested" gaze of science, social inequality is justified through scientifically measured meritocracy. "By invoking the highest ideals — talent, merit, achievement — the educational system sanctioned the privileges, indeed, the affluence, of an accredited individual in American society. Theoretically, neither birth nor prejudice nor favoritism restricted those privileges" (Bledstein 1978: 127).

Serving pastoral power, "failure" is blamed on the individual rather than on the social inequalities that set them up to fail or on the possible cultural bias of standardized tests.

> Meritocracy is a concept of society based on the idea that each individual's social and occupational position is determined by individual merit, not political or economic influence. Scientific management of human capital and scientific management of organizations are central ideas in the meritocratic concept. For the schools, meritocracy was both a social goal and a method of internal organization. (Spring 1975: 224)

Meritocracy enforces the internalization of discipline and desire for reward, thus incorporating democratically engineered individualism: Again, "equality was everyone's right to occupy one's natural place determined by disinterested science" (Haraway 1991: 56). Meritocracy places success and failure squarely on the individual, decontextualizing the student from any mediating factors of social or cultural context.

MENTAL-HYGIENE: The Social Scientific Portrait of Emotions

TWO MOVEMENTS IN education sought to control emotions in the early part of the century: character education, and the "mental-hygiene" movement. Simultaneous with the social scientific measures of the "good" student, a movement in "character education" enters American schools. The character education movement is usually dated 1920–40, but is rooted in the mid-Victorian values that establish higher education institutions prior to the turn of the century. Character education represented a break from classical humanism, directed instead towards shaping children's conduct through such agendas as Americanization and social efficiency (Beane 1990: 23). Through social efficiency, "morality became embedded in behaviors identified by supposedly value-neutral 'scientific' methods" (Beane 1990: 28). This notion of moral development was understood as distinct from morals developed through cognition: rather, the emphasis was on embodying the social values of efficiency and productivity through one's industrious nature and conduct. Virtues become embedded in efficient and industrious action which prepared young people for industrialized society.

However, character education didn't ensure conformity to cultural norms. The challenge of the emotional student was becoming apparent by the end of the 1920s, as reported in the Third Report by the Character Education Inquiry at Teacher's College, which found that "character education had little effect on some of the virtues cherished by its advocates. Among the findings were that moral lessons taught in school largely dissipated under the ambiguities and demands of real life situations, that in school life itself often contradicted the very moral lessons that were taught, and that didactic moral lessons ignored the need for experience in their application. . . . " (Beane 1990: 29)

The shift to an explicit discourse on emotions, framed largely in social scientific terms, invoked the concept of "mental-hygiene." In an essay titled "The Mental-Hygiene Movement, the Development of Personality and the School: The Medicalization of American Education," Sol Cohen contributes a missing focus of revisionist educational histories. His essay resonates with my research on how social sciences sought to control emotions. Cohen dates the mental-hygiene movement with roots in "turn of the century Progressive reform movements," officially recognized through the 1909 establishment of the National Committee for Mental-Hygiene (1983: 125). Cohen describes the movement as almost "evangelical," motivated by an optimism and unbridled faith in the new social scientific conception of the personality: "the mental-hygiene movement took on aspects of a quasi-religious phenomenon: the truths of psychiatry a surer foundation of the New Society than the truths from the Bible" (141).[35] The NCMH "considered mental illness [and poorly developed personalities of children] the most serious evil of the time (1983: 126). Echoing Lesko's (1996) analysis of how the adolescent in particular was targeted as a "primitive other", who threatened social equilibrium, Cohen notes that "delinquency, crime, and deviant behavior . . . could all be understood as symptoms of underlying personality maladjustment" (1983: 127). These symptoms, if corrected, would solve society's ills. The increasing anxiety about social conflict thus became fixated on adjusting youth through techniques of mental hygiene.

The mental hygiene movement framed emotions not as religious "sins" but as pathological "symptoms". To cure students, education emphasized not academic curricula but child-centered pedagogies aimed to reduce "stress" on the child. Like the eugenics movement of the previous century, the mental hygiene movement represented a "crusade" which Cohen characterizes as an "attempt by scientists, professionals, and experts to cope with social problems through a scientific control of behavior" (1983: 128). Unlike in the eugenicists' analysis, the "primary cause of social pathology was not innate feeble-mindedness" (ibid.) but personality problems. Mental hygienists (like today's contemporary advocates of "emotional intelligence" as I discuss in the next chapter) saw emotions and personality as "malleable". Emotions were thus a prime target for social control, the correction of which would solve social conflicts: "the problems facing the nation were those of the individual personality" (141).

However, despite the mental hygiene emphasis on individual pathologies as the root of social conflicts, mental hygiene also represnts a veiled response to quite real and fraught political issues. For instance, the conflicts which gave educators's anxiety had significantly to do with vast increases in immigrant populations, social conflicts which were reduced to individualized pathologies in mental hygiene discourse. Thus the mental hygiene movement represents a significant historical example of pastoral power.

Cohen obliquely recognizes that women were recruited to play a central role as mental hygienists, as well as being themselves objects of mental-hygiene's scrutiny. "Here was a form of social control without coercion of laws, rules, and legal prohibitions." (ibid.) This method coincides directly with analyses of the pedagogy of love and child-centered pedagogies which women were assigned to carry out.

THE MEDICALIZATION OF EMOTION AND FEMALE TEACHERS

WOMEN, WHO CONSTITUTED the majority of teachers, were now assigned a central role in developing not only "virtuous" citizens but in developing "mental hygiene." Here one finds a fascinating point of overlap between women's naturalized role as nurturer and the growth of mental hygiene after the turn of the century. The underlying ideologies of ideal womanhood, which are rooted in ideas of women's virtue and piety, by no means disappear with the growth of scientific discourses. The

> hygienists would call upon teachers to establish non-authoritarian classroom environments. . . . Harsh and authoritarian teachers forced children to hide their emotions, thus contributing to . . . personality maladjustment . . . the success or failure of mental-hygiene depended upon the teacher's own personality. *She was the one in continuous contact with the child*. . . . All attempts to make the school a therapeutic milieu and an institutions for children's personality development would fail if *the teacher herself was emotionally immature*. . . . (Cohen 1983: 131 emphasis added)

Thus the female schoolteacher's "mental hygiene" was also blamed as a cause of social problems. By the 1930s, the emotional student had become a central concern of educational administration.[36] In *The History of Manners*, Norbert Elias traces the sublimation of overt aggression into Enlightenment codes of civilization, and notes the 1930s as a new and firmly established historical moment of self-control. The industrial United States, at least rhetorically,[37] favored patient "toleration" of temper tantrums until the child learns self-control, rather than overt punishment.

> [A] certain relaxation is setting in. . . . The freedom and unconcern with which people say what has to be said without embarrassment, without the forced smile and laughter of a taboo infringement, has clearly increased in the postwar period. But this . . . is only possible because the level of habitual, technically, and institutionally consolidated self-control, the individual capacity to restrain one's urges and behavior in correspondence with the more advanced feelings for what is offensive, has been on the whole secured. ([1939] 1978: 140)

THE LABILE, OVEREMOTIONAL STUDENT: 1938

IN 1991, MANY years prior to my recent study of the mental-hygiene movement, I came upon a book which grabbed my attention and led me to identify the 1930s as a unique historical movement in emotion's explicit emergence within educational histories. I was captured by the description of the overemotional student as "labile," a term which turns out to have an interesting definition.

The text *Emotions and the Educative Process* was first published in 1938 and reprinted ten times before 1961. Collaboratively authored but essentially written by Daniel Prescott, the book represents a centerpiece of the mental-hygiene movement in part because it was sponsored by the American Council on Education. Prescott and his co-authors identified the overly emotional, "labile" student as a problem for educational curricula and pedagogies. "Labile" is defined by the Oxford English Dictionary in five central ways: (1) liable; prone to lapse: (2) liable to fall from innocence into error or sin: (3) slippery, unstable: (4) prone to undergo displacement. In its fifth definition, in reference to woodworking — as in a "labile construction material," it resonates with John Dewey's description of mutable subjectivity as "plasticity." These meanings contradictorily suggest both a passive material that can be shaped, and tendencies to "lapse or degenerate" as a result of physiological, social, or internal factors.

Prescott recognized that a central motive for "disciplining" emotion is to balance discrepancies between desires produced within capitalism, on the one hand, and the "reality" of unfulfilled needs that cause "frustration," maladjustment, and conflict on the other. Social scientists shared with psychoanalysts and educational administration a concern about how and where to channel the growing anxieties experienced by the modern and civilized subject. Influenced by Charles Darwin and John Dewey, educational psychologists analyzed the relation between industrialization and immigration, and the modern anxieties and stresses that threatened the smooth administration of large school populations. In a highly unique but short-lived period, educators explicitly addressed the "emotional student." This book articulates a rule of industrial capitalism, namely, that the school should not set up expectations that will not be fulfilled within the society.

> [T]he existence of conditions which drive large blocks of the population to hold attitudes too sharply antagonistic . . . can only cause conflict, lowered efficiency, and ultimate disintegration in a society. . . . Not only is affect important in connection with the formation of attitudes, but attitudes themselves are important sources of affect when the behavior they imply is obstructed or penalized. If certain factors in society such as the school, advertising, or the teachings of the church develop attitudes favorable to types of behavior made impossible by prevailing social conditions, then tension, disappointment, and feelings or frustration are inevitable. Either the attitudes must be replaced, or social changes must come about, or the individual must compartmentalize his thinking and submit to permanent dissociation due to the lack of harmony between his beliefs and his actions. (Prescott 1938: 43)

Although as Sol Cohen argues (1983) the mental-hygiene movement targets students' emotions as the cause of social ills, Prescott's text doesn't blame the labile student entirely for his overemotionality; in fact, he recognizes that social influences cause "overemotionality." However, social and economic revolution was not an option advocated by social scientists or school administrators. The next solution — "to replace attitudes" which are in conflict with existing social structures — reveals a rationalist emphasis. Attitudes, like beliefs, are much more easily explained within rationalist terms than emotions, and lend themselves more easily to measurement. The third effect of unchecked lability is that the individual will suffer "permanent dissociation due to lack of harmony between his beliefs and actions." This reflects the combination of "medicalized" discourse and Deweyan influence: the concept of "dissociation" and the ideal of an achieved "harmony" and equilibrium within the self. The educational aim was, in short, to "adjust" the child's personality and emotions to handle the stress of social conflicts.

In *Emotions and the Educative Process* Prescott expresses deep concern regarding the "startling" fact that "[a] significant proportion of the country's teachers are either mentally ill or suffer from serious mental and emotional maladjustments. . . . [This is to be taken as] an indication of genuinely *unhygienic* conditions in the profession" (1938: 252, emphasis added). In 1939 the *Harvard Educational Review* published a book review of Prescott's *Emotions and the Educative Process* and Mandel Sherman's *Mental Conflicts and Personality*; Sherman's text is a follow-up book to his text *Mental-Hygiene and Education* (1938). Representative of the movement, Prescott and Sherman both subscribe to increasingly "medicalized" discourse regarding emotions.

However, these scientific notions are not divorced from explicit analyses of morality and "criminal behavior." The reviewer of Prescott and Sherman writes "emotions may lower or raise the efficiency of the pupil. . . . Surveys in industry show that a large part of the failures of youth are caused by personality defects. The improvement of the 'Three R's' depends much upon healthy emotional conditions. . . . The criminals in our State prisons usually know right from wrong but are governed by undesirable attitudes" (Bosshart 1939: 453).

The social control of emotions is thus reflected in the *combination* of moral and scientific discourses that function to govern individuals and teach students to internalize blame. These modes of pastoral power become increasingly intertwined through emphatic rhetoric regarding democratic participation. By the 1930s and certainly during and following WWII, "democracy" becomes a rallying cry as a "solution" to social conflict. Fueled by American faith in scientific as well as religious authority, democratic rhetoric promises equality but therives on illusions.

In educational discourses, "democracy" was interpreted in at least two key ways. In 1932 George Counts advocates a fairly radical notion of "social reconstructionism," in which schools are envisioned as helping to move the larger society towards democracy. In a quite different emphasis, historian William Graebner characterizes the use of democratic process in schools as a version of "engineered consent," a modern articulation of pastoral power. Graebner is alarmed at the ways in which "democracy" is used to mask insidious "autocratic control" through educational emphasis on "group process." Skeptical of the emphasis on democratic participation, Graebner and others argue that through this rhetoric individuals are led to believe they are actively shaping their moral world, when in fact the illusory sense of "participation" simply leads people willingly to comply with economic, political, and national interests of the ruling class. I point out the concerns regarding democratic rhetoric because these continue to be invoked in contemporary curricula using emotional literacy, through such discourses as "creating a caring community" which emphasize democratic participation. Such discourses are frequently interwoven with models of what counts as natural, healthy and normalized child development.[38]

Mental hygiene, Cohen argues, "fades out by the Cold War period." He writes that the "NCMH is no more and the mental-hygiene movement qua movement is but a shadow of its former self" (1983: 143). However, I suggest that since Cohen's 1983 remarks we find a re-emergence of the mental-hygiene movement, revived in a "postmodern" version for the 1990s: "emotional intelligence." It is to this new mode of the social control of emotions that I now turn.

Pastoral power is by no means a force of the past; it is alive and well. The historical backdrop of this chapter sets the stage for a close analysis of emotional intelligence, a popularized paradigm rooted in contemporary discourses of science and skills, mobilized to regulate morality, emotions, and education. In the present generation's educational theories and practices, the gendered contradictions also continue to thrive. Though it is largely women who have developed contemporary curricula of emotional literacy, and women still constitute the majority of schoolteachers, the popular embrace of emotional intelligence functions largely as blueprint for male CEO success, and it is men who govern the public debates on emotional intelligence.

1 From "The Mental-Hygiene Movement, the Development of Personality and the School: The Medicalization of American Education," (1983: 141).

2 1997: 5.

3 "Babylon System," *Survival* (1979).

4 The work of Hayden White (1978) pioneers "histories of historiography," detailing for example how historical "facts" are themselves shaped by discourses, narrative, genre, trope, and metaphor. See also Barzun(1950); Stern ([1956] 1970); Finkelstein (1992); Gay (1974). I have found using the literature of Vietnam veteran Tim O'Brien (1990) useful in teaching students to interrogate what counts as "fact" vs. "fiction." See also the video on Tim O'Brien, *How to Tell a True War Story*; dir. Christopher Sykes, (1991).

5 We need histories of education that investigate how conformity is achieved through specific emotional terrains. The work of Norbert Elias ([1939] 1978) is one such example; also Bourdieu (1984). But most often, we find histories of ideas which trace, for example, changing philosophies of emotion rather than examining how emotions are embodied and enacted in material practices.

6 Rather than attempt to give an exhaustive analysis of the history of emotion in education, or of different philosophies of emotion that have influenced education, I focus on selective examples of how emotions are tied to social control. A key feature of the social control of emotions, is that we find differently gendered emotional rules or discourses. Similarly, the rules applied to people of different ethnic, cultural, and social class backgrounds vary. I cannot explore all of these dimensions here. I focus on how the social control of emotions is gendered, and try to understand how we can "see" emotions in educational history. I argue that we can "see" them most explicitly in terms of social control as well as in differently gendered rules.

7 Histories and philosophies of moral education offer one central to approach to a project such as the study of disciplined emotions. As I try to argue in this chapter, to focus on moral education as the site of emotion's education eclipses the myriad "inexplicit" ways in which emotions are educated. Nonetheless I am indebted to work in the philosophy and history of moral education. See for example in philosophy Noddings (1984); Feinberg (1975); in the area of histories of education see Beane (1990); Aries (1962), Cleverley and Phillips (1986); Spring (1986); Bledstein (1976).

8 A burgeoning area of study examines how race (intertwined with categories of social class, gender, and ethnicity and cultural differences) defines social hierarchies and educational structures. For analyses related to discourses of racial formation see for example Omi and Winant (1986); McCarthy (1990); McCarthy and Chichlow (1993); West (1992); Williams (1991); Goldman (1990).

9 The explicit aims of assimilation and Americanization are apparent in examining the education of Native Americans, African Americans, and immigrants. On U.S. issues of colonialism see Mohanty (1988). For histories regarding U.S. educational policies and the education of Native Americans see Churchill (1992, 1993); Guerrero (1996); Johnston (1993); Noriega (1992). For histories on the education of African Americans see DuBois ([1903] 1989); Aptheker (1973, 1974); Genovese (1968, 1972); Davis (1983); Lerner (1972).

10 Revisionist histories and sociologies explore the relationship of education as a social institution to ideologies and economic and political interests. See for example in educational histories: Tyack and Hansot (1982); Katz (1971); Katz et al. (1982). In sociology see Apple (1990); Dale (1989); Bernstein (1975, 1990); Popkewitz (1991).

11 Histories of gender and education have proliferated over the last two decades. For historical studies that combine with cultural and sociological studies, see for example Steedman (1985); Steedman et al. (1985); Walkerdine (1985). See the special issue on women's educational histories in *Harvard Educational Review*, (Winter 1997);

Solomon (1985); Gordon (1990); Aisenberg and Harrington (1988). For New Zealand histories see Brookes et al. (1992); Middleton and Jones (1992).

12 This excerpt on the internalized social control of emotions reflects a view of emotions that has roots in the mid 1800s.The "mental-hygiene movement" discussed in the final section of this chapter should, I believe, be traced not just to the early part of this century but to the mid 1800s. See for example Brigham (1833); Ray (1863); Sweetser ([1850] 1973).

13 I elect to focus on revisionist histories, as these exemplify pastoral power but do not analyze the more insidious forms of (emotional) internalized submission and resistances within the everyday lives of teachers and students, which are always marked by gender, race, and class. Some readers might inquire whether revisionist historical accounts are sufficiently representative. I can attest to reading widely in educational histories seeking analyses of emotions and interiority, and coming up empty-handed.

14 Again see Rousmaniere et al. (1997) for an exceptional collection of historical analyses of these subtler forms of interiority and moral regulation. See also Lawn et al (forthcoming).

15 As Tyack and Hansot note, "[p]robably none of these [typical characteristics of the superintendent] is surprising. Surely they are not accidental. If such characteristics as sex, age, and race did not count in a systematic way, one would have found a more random distribution. In most respects the superintendents matched leaders in comparable occupations. . . . Superintendents also tended to match the characteristics of the school board members that hired them — again not accidentally" (1982: 170).

16 What one discerns more explicitly in these historical accounts is how pastoral power governs relations between administrator and student: "Learning to adapt to the moral and educational demands of the community and to preserve the tenuous authority of the classroom . . . were important parts of the socialization of the teacher" (Tyack and Hansot 1982: 170) and consequently of the administrators who moved always from teaching to their supervisory roles.

17 The "cult of domesticity" and "virtuous ideal of womanhood" has a powerful influence in the United States: See Nicholson (1980); Solomon (1985). On Great Britain and New Zealand; see Middleton and Jones (1992); Jenkins and Matthews (1995); Fry (1985).

18 See especially Grumet (1988); MacKinnon (1990); Theobald (1990); Prentice and Theobald (1991); the 1997 *Harvard Educational Review* issue on women's educational history.

19 Linda Smith provides an invaluable analysis of indigenous and colonial histories of education in Aotearoa/New Zealand (1996); see also Graham Smith (1997); Jenkins and Matthews (1995); Simon (1993); Bird (1928); Pihama and Mara (1994).

20 Despite U.S. public schools being legislated as secular, ongoing heated debates regarding religious teaching in schools (e.g., evolution vs. creationism; what is allowed to be taught in sex education) continue. Religious values shape the moral teachings in schools not only for women, but for all students, explicitly as well as implicitly. In contemporary sex education, for example, topics such as abortion, teenage sexuality, and lesbian and gay lifestyle are most often excluded from the curricula. This omission is in no small way due to the powerful influence of religious values in the United States.

For example, I use the video *It's Elementary* (Chasnoff 1996) to offer inspiration for how lesbian and gay issues can be incorporated into elementary and middle school curricula — not as an explicit discourse about sexual practices or intimacy, but in terms of stereotypes, inclusive curricula, what counts as a "family," and lifestyle issues. However inspiring this tape may be — documenting children's genuine open-mindedness, and the courage of heterosexual and gay teachers in introducing such topics — many of my students refuse to even mention the word lesbian or gay in their elementary, middle, or high school classroom. While fears of parental upset or even losing their jobs may be real, it is likely that most of their fear is rooted in the unexamined moral authority that governs school curricula. I discuss this in greater depth in the final chapter of this book.

21 Religious doctrines worried whether the "soul" is common to both men and women. In Renaissance formulations, though woman is hopelessly "tainted" in this life she is permitted to aspire to moral perfection in the afterlife: "'woman is, therefore, the inferior of the male by nature, his equal by grace'" (MacLean, quoted in Riley 1988: 25).

22 A shocking example of religious control of women's emotional/sexual lives are "virginity tests" conducted on young teenage women in Turkey. Recently in the news because five young women attempted suicide to protest these laws, both the shame deployed within the culture to police women's virginity, and the women's anger at this enforced shame reflect the ways in which emotions can resist the policing of women's bodies and sexuality.

Another contemporary example of shifting discourses of emotion is reflected in The Promise Keepers, an international men's Christian movement claiming 1.1 million members. This movement represents an alarming appropriation of feminist discourses into an extremely conservative movement. The Promise Keepers garner public appeal in part through an appropriation of a discourse borrowed from the "men's movement," which seeks to "reclaim" men's vulnerability. The Promise Keepers also represent what might be seen as "twisted" appropriation of feminist calls for men's responsibility to their families.

A *Time* cover story (13 October, 1997)on the Promise Keepers opens with a seductive lead about men's "vulnerability," describing thousands of men in an auditorium weeping publicly to express their grief at their "failures" (e.g., infidelity) as fathers and husbands. The mission of the movement is a conservative return to family values, calling for women to return to their role as full-time wife and mother in the home as commanded by God. Alarmingly, *Time* quotes feminists from the National Organization of Women who are represented as "seduced" by the appeal of men "keeping promises" to their family.

23 Most contemporary analyses of shame and guilt reveal religion as a primary basis for women's moral failings. For cross-cultural ethnographies of shame see Lutz and Abu-Lughod (1990); on sociology and shame see Parker et al, Shame and the Modern Self (1996); in feminist philosophies see Card (1991); and on Victorian ideals, Poovey (1988, 1984). Shame and guilt continue to police women's sexuality and compulsory motherhood as demonstrated in the public embrace of religious-cum-political values espoused by influential new right politicians. See for example Newt Gingrich's *Contract with America* (1996); see also Brown (1995).

24 Kate Rousmaniere (1994, 1997) offers excellent analyses of the contradictions women faced in the actual classroom. She explores how women were contradictorily bound by the norm of being the "virtuous loving mother," but in fact had to resort to various forms of physical discipline to maintain authority and control. In her essay in Rousmaniere et al. (1997), she analyses oral histories with female teachers who continue to feel guilty, decades later, for physical discipline used even if only on one or two occasions during their careers.

25 Walkerdine writes: "the regulation of conflict (of crime, pauperism, and deviance as pathologized) is central to . . . sciences and technologies. . . . From the outset a regulation of conflict and rebellion was aimed at the poor, at a population newly contained in towns and cities. At first such regulation involved overt surveillance and attempt to inculcate 'good habits.' But . . . covert self-regulation became favored. That children who were so obviously watched and monitored might still rebel . . . remained a continuing problem. In transformations relating to pedagogy, love became the basis of techniques designed to avoid problems with overt surveillance. Now the aim was to produce citizens who would accept the moral order by choice and freewill rather

than either by coercion or though overt acceptance and covert resistance" (1985: 206).

26 In the work of John Rawls, for instance, "'justice is the first virtue of social institutions'" (quoted in Pateman 1989: 20). Yet in the analyses of Freud and Hegel, she writes, "it is love, not justice, that is the first virtue of the family. The family is a naturally social, not a conventionally social, institution, but justice is a public or conventional virtue. In the family, individuals appear as unique and unequal personalities and as members of a differentiated unity grounded in sentiment" (ibid.).

27 The previous examples of the Promise Keepers reflects not only the prevalence of religious discourses but also the discourses of rational political theory of containing women in the home.

28 Margaret Mead aptly recognized this in 1935: "'whatever the arrangements in regard to descent or ownership of property, and even if these formal outward arrangements are reflected in the temperamental relations between the sexes, the prestige values always attach to the activities of men" (quoted in Rosaldo 1984: 302) Feminist anthropologist Michelle Rosaldo echoes Mead's crucial observation: "... what is perhaps most striking and surprising is the fact that male, as opposed to female, activities are always recognized as predominantly important, and cultural systems give authority and value to the roles and activities of men" (1984: 19).

29 See Blount (1996).

30 Foucault's *Discipline and Punish* (1979) and *The History of Sexuality* (1978) offer important analyses of the growth of psychiatric discourses as they shape the subject. He does not, however, offer systematic studies of women or of emotions.

31 Feminist studies of science document the persistent effects of sexism and male-defined paradigms in the sciences. See for example Harding (1986); Keller (1984); Haraway (1989, 1991); Merchant (1980); Rose et al. (1984).

32 See Katz (1971); Katz et al. (1982); Cremin (1988).

33 See chapters in Haraway, Part One (1991).

34 After 1917, alongside the recognition that efficiency and testing were necessary to develop the nation state, the question was not whether to use these scientific means but how: "The larger problem involved the question of how to fit a program of schooling, established to meet certain predetermined national needs, into a society whose rhetoric emphasized democracy and self-determination" (Feinberg 1975: 69).

35 There is vast room for a full discussion of how Freud's work influenced American conceptions of the child, sexuality, and personality within such educational movements. The scope of my study does not allow for this here; but see Hale (1971).

36 Freud's *Civilization and Its Discontents* was published in 1930. Though during this period psychoanalysis had less influence in the United States during the 1930s than did the work of John Dewey, for example, it is interesting that psychoanalysis, social psychology, and moral education also shared concern about how the individual would channel social conflicts. Much more work remains to be done examining the influence of psychoanalysis on pedagogies and emotion. See Hale (1971); Britzman (1998).

37 See Rousmaniere (1994, 1997) for discussion of contradictions between nurturing schoolteacher and actual disciplinary practices.

38 For brilliant analyses of these intertwined discourses see the collection *Changing the Subject* eds. Henriques et al (1984).

CHAPTER THREE

CAPITALIZING ON EMOTIONAL "SKILLS"

"Emotional Intelligence" and Scientific Morality

The eugenics movement appealed to many in the early 1920s as an attempt at a scientific management and control [of social pathology which was seen to be caused by innate lack of intelligence]. . . .The mental hygiene movement stepped forward as a competing manifestation of the same impulse — the attempt by scientists, professionals, and experts to cope with social problems through a scientific control of behavior. The primary cause of social pathology was not innate feeble-mindedness. The cause lay in the personality.

—Sol Cohen[1]

Goleman's highly popularized conclusions as demonstrated in his book [Emotional Intelligence]. . . *"will chill any veteran scholar of psychotherapy and any neuroscientists who worries about how his research may come to be applied." While many researchers in this relatively new field are glad to see emotional issues finally taken seriously, they fear that a notion as handy as [emotional quotient] invites misuse.*

—(*Time*, 2 October, 1995: 62)

INTRODUCTION

EMOTIONAL INTELLIGENCE provides a contemporary site in which to explore discourses of social control and the "postindustrial" moral person. Within a history of pastoral power, the discourse of "emotional intelligence" is an almost predictable evolution: The most alien, unmanageable feature of human behavior—emotions, the most interior and private experience—has now been placed under the scientist's microscope and dissected for the benefit of mankind. Science, working hand in hand with postindustrial interests, has identified emotions as profitable to global capitalism.[2] Emotional intelligence allows a glimpse of power's arbitrary manifestations. Suddenly identified as profitable, emotions are associated with success and corporate power. Emotional intelligence, as packaged and popularized through Daniel Goleman's 1995 bestselling book, is in no way associated with weakness or femininity.

By *capitalizing on emotion* I refer to how scientific narratives are employed to shape the human resources necessary for capitalist expansion. Rooted in the scientific authority of cognitive science and behavioral psychology, emotional intelligence justifies a new conception of the moral person. Like earlier historical incarnations, the moral self is measured both though his capacity for skills and efficiency as well as his good character and rule-obedience. However, unlike earlier scientific conceptions, moral behavior is increasingly depicted as hard-wired within the brain. The good person is he — and I do mean "he" — who is taught the right skills to capitalize on the hard-wired virtues.

More so than the mental-hygiene movement of the early part of this century, emotional intelligence is a popularized phenomenon consumed by the public as a version of self-help and dinner-party conversations. Unlike previous modes of self-control, emotional intelligence invokes the growing authority of cognitive science. Popular as well as scholarly interests in emotions are increasingly influenced by cognitive science — and, the new developments in cognitive science may push us to rethink some of the long-standing binary oppositions of cognition and emotion. Emotional intelligence invites increased public debate about emotion, pulling it from its less visible absent-presence to the level of explicit discourse. In its popularity, emotional intelligence opens the potential for a discourse about the relationship of emotional labor to capitalism and the workplace.

However, like the mental-hygiene movement emotional intelligence also reflects historical roots in the most conservative versions of social control. After defining emotional intelligence and looking at its popular consumption, I briefly examine parallels between "emotional quotient" and the history of IQ testing. I examine the application of emotional intelligence as a mode of social control, and how this application is rooted in workplace management and behavioral psychology as a basis for increased social efficiency and cultural assimilation. I then examine how cognitive science shapes the new package of the moral person. Whatever its promises, cognitive science provides a "scientific" welding of the traditional "rules-based" morality, with the more modern "skills-based" morality which has potentially alarming implications for social control. This chapter provides an understanding of the discourses and global interests that motivate the integration of "emotional literacy" into school curricula, the subject of the next chapter.

The "postmodern," emotionally intelligent person reflects a paradigm of hard-wired morality combined with the neoliberal, autonomous individual "chooser".[3] Rather than exhaustively review the scientific research on the brain, I examine the deployment of authoritative discourses of cognitive and neurological science and behavioral psychology in relation to emotion. I investigate how and why these sciences maintain an interest in controlling emotional behaviors, particularly in relation to the increasingly globalized workplace and the profits to be gained by creating "smooth" and efficient worker relations, which have been found to depend significantly on what is called "emotional intelligence."

While it may be that new developments in cognitive science and neurobiology are shifting the binary relationship of emotion and reason, the relative paucity of definitive "scientific" understanding of emotions—which themselves continue to be extremely idiosyncratic and unpredictable despite the advances of "new brain science"— compels me to analyze the social uses and significance of these new narratives about emotion.

Why worry about any of this? Why not celebrate emotion's new popular status? I argue that, whether or not these new conceptions of the person/brain are accurate, or are based on replicable and adequate scientific evidence, a central worry is how science in its application utilizes these models for social control. Second, the contemporary discourses such as "emotional intelligence" erase gendered and cultural differences through the discourses of universal biological circuitry of emotions. In this erasure of differences, we find science by no means free from social agendas and ulterior motives. The ideal virtuous citizen is still he — and again, I mean "he"— who controls his emotions through rational choice and the ruling neo-cortex.

THE POPULAR CONSUMPTION OF EMOTION

THE PACKAGING OF emotional intelligence has popularized emotions in a way that few previous "scientific" theories can claim. Daniel Goleman, who holds a Ph.D. in psychology from Harvard, published his book titled *Emotional Intelligence* in 1995. Primarily a science writer for the *New York Times*, in 1992 Goleman authored a number of articles on emotions and school curriculum (drawing on the notion that had been coined in 1990 by psychologists Peter Salovey, from Yale, and John Mayer, from the University of New Hampshire). The popularity of the topic and best-selling status of Goleman's book spurred international coverage in *Time* magazine and on the *Oprah Winfrey Show*, received extensive coverage on National Public Radio in the United States, and was publicized through *Time* and *Oprah* in

New Zealand and Australia as well as through various male spokespersons and agencies who use Goleman's work to advocate self-help and organizational management strategies. A 1998 article in *Better Homes and Gardens* printed a version of emotional intelligence "instructions" for mothers to give to children.[4] During 1998, magazines such as the *Atlantic Monthly*, *Life*, and *Newsweek* featured discussions of cognitive science and emotion, often framed as debates between religious faith and science. Internet discussions, websites, publications, and commodification of emotional intelligence into educational and self-help circles have increased exponentially since the publication of *Emotional Intelligence*. In addition to these popularized representations of emotion, proliferating scholarly texts in neuro- and cognitive science signal the rapidly increasing interest in emotions: these include Antonio Damasio's *Descartes' Error: Emotion, Reason, and the Human Brain* (1994); debates within cognitive and neurological science, as represented in the MIT anthology *Mind and Morals: Essays on Ethics and Cognitive Science* (1996); and neurobiologist Joseph LeDoux's *The Emotional Brain: The Mysterious Underpinnings of Emotional Life* (1996).

What does this popularity reflect? In the particular case of emotional intelligence, it may reflect Goleman's access to mass media as a science writer for the *New York Times*; or, that his publisher helped him to do an excellent job of packaging; or, that the historical moment/market was ripe for this concept. It is certainly true that within the American cult of individualism and "narcissism," we are increasingly aware of or obsessed by "dysfunctionality." "We" are not doing okay; everyone is taking Prozac; and like other self-help books *Emotional Intelligence* offers a consumable package for the layperson.

Rather than the moral person being shaped either through (religious) moral obedience, or simply through skills of industry, the new moral person combines the two in a different package. The moral person is he who accepts his *neurobiologically determined* fate, alongside the disciplined (Aristotelian) *self-control* in order to express the right emotions at the right time, in the right way, through acquired *emotional skills*. The equation of emotional intelligence with self-control evidences the fact that the emotionally intelligent person is still the *man* of reason. Although at first glance one might think that this explicit "valuing" of emotion would place women — with her long-standing, stereotypical emotional sensitivity — at the head of the race, in fact *Emotional Intelligence* reads as a blueprint for male CEO success.

None of the representations of emotional intelligence analyse how people are taught different rules of conduct for emotional behavior acccording to their gendered, racialized, and social class status. Instead, we are all supposed to feel the same "empathy" and "optimism." Gender is powerfully ignored. Women have histroically been characterized as naturally caring and empathetic; yet in the new discourse of emotional intelligence there is no longer any mention of women's "natural" or historical relation to these emotions. There is certainly no discussion of the possibility that women might be of superior emotional intelligence!

I do not mean to argue that women are "naturally" more emotionally intelligent. The point is that what is valued and assigned as gendered characteristics changes in any culture according to the demands of economic need and social harmony. Anthropologist Margaret Mead noted this decades ago in 1935: "'whatever the arrangements in regard to descent or ownership of property, and even if these formal outward arrangements are reflected in the temperamental relations between the sexes, the prestige values always attach to the activities of men'" (quoted in Rosaldo 1984: 302). Feminist anthropologist Michelle Rosaldo echoes Mead's crucial observation: "... what is perhaps most striking and surprising is the fact that male, as opposed to female, activities are always recognized as predominantly important, and cultural systems give authority and value to the roles and activities of men" (19).

The popularity of emotional intelligence also demonstrates how information, particularly high-status "scientific" information, becomes a consumable commodity. The authority upon which the popular commodification rests is largely the "new science of the brain" advertised on the front cover of Goleman's book. "Self-help" is a profitable market in which one can sell information about "cognition and emotion." The playing field of science is not limited simply to how it is used by institutions or workplaces to control its subjects: Through mass culture, we have been created as consumers of science as well as the human resources subjected to science's applications.

DEFINING EMOTIONAL INTELLIGENCE

THE DEFINITION OF emotional intelligence focuses on self-control (delayed gratification), identifications of emotion in oneself and others, and managing other's emotions effectively. Emotional intelligence has been measured by a "marshmallow test," conducted at Stanford University: the researcher tells a four-year-old, "I'm leaving you in this room with a marshmallow while I go out. If you don't eat the marshmallow, when I return I will give you two marshmallows." Fourteen years later, the researchers found that those children who resisted the marshmallow became more "successful": more popular and confident, with SAT scores 210 points higher than their counterpart failures who were "more likely to be lonely, frustrated and buckle under stress." Psychologist Dr. Martin Seligman, author of *The Optimistic Child*, developed a related test to measure successful salesman: namely, those who don't blame themselves when doors are slammed in their face. Optimism and empathy are two specific emotions highly valued in this paradigm. Both Goleman and Seligman maintain that optimism, empathy, and the other skills of emotional intelligence can be taught and learned. A key selling point of emotional intelligence is that, unlike IQ, which supposedly is genetically given and unchangeable, we can improve our emotional intelligence.

Goleman defines emotional intelligence by drawing in part on the model of "personal intelligences" introduced by Howard Gardner. Five primary domains characterize emotional intelligence:

> 1. Knowing one's emotions. . . . People with greater certainty about their feelings are better pilots of their lives, having a surer sense of how they really feel about personal decisions from whom to marry to what job to take.
> 2. Managing emotions . . . the capacity to soothe oneself, to shake off rampant anxiety, gloom, or irritability.
> 3. Motivating oneself. . . . Emotional self-control — delaying gratification and stifling impulsiveness — underlies accomplishment of every sort.
> 4. Recognizing emotions in others. Empathy . . . the social cost of being emotionally tone-deaf, and the reasons empathy kindles altruism . . . This makes them better at callings such as the caring professions, teaching, sales, and management.
> 5. Handling relationships. The art of relationships is, in large part, skill in managing emotions in others. . . . These are the abilities that undergird popularity, leadership, and interpersonal effectiveness. (1995: 43–4)

In the most narrow and individualistic way, *Emotional Intelligence* is about social relations: Goleman recounts countless stories of interactions, detailing reasons why one experiences particular feelings in different contexts. However, analysis is entirely dehistoricized and does not discuss cultural differences or social hierarchies that account for the particularity of our emotional responses. Despite the apparent interest in social relations, what is reiterated is *individual choice*: the ability to autonomously choose how one acts and controls one's emotions. The emphasis is on how individuals can either manage and control undesirable emotions (e.g., anger and anxiety), or augment and acquire the desirable emotions (e.g., optimism and empathy). Both as a management strategy, and as a curriculum that can teach students to manage conflict and delay gratification, emotional intelligence casts the social self in entirely individualistic terms.

A built-in contradiction, which frames not only Western discourses of emotion but the debates over intelligence and virtue, becomes visible. In the new version of the skills- and rules-based disciplines, emotions are simultaneously explained as neurobiological processes largely beyond our individual control, which we are nonetheless expected to control and manage through our industry and education.

Who gets to decide what counts as the "appropriate" emotional response and who therefore counts as the good citizen? Even *Time* magazine signals these alarms, quoting various scientists' concerns about the uses of "EQ" as indicated in the opening quote of this chapter. *Time* comforts us that the skills of emotional literacy are in themselves "morally neutral," while the issue of morality is "another book." But this is a false distinction. There is nothing "neutral" about emotional literacy skills. The overlap of "neutral science" and its patently "biased" application is already evidenced in similar narratives of IQ and standardized testing. One must then ask: To what extent does "emotional intelligence" signal a direction parallel to standardized testing of IQ?

EQ AND IQ

ALFRED BINET DEVELOPED the intelligence test in 1905. In the preface to its Americanized version, the "Stanford-Binet" test was introduced with this vision of its application: "in the near future intelligence tests will bring tens of thousands of these high-grade defectives under the surveillance and protection of society. This will ultimately result in curtailing the reproduction of feeble-mindedness and in the elimination of an enormous amount of pauperism, and industrial inefficiency" (Terman quoted in Kamin 1995: 476). Thanks to the myth of science's "neutral" gaze, standardized tests appear to measure the individual's pre-existing deficits and degeneracy, hiding the fact that the IQ test itself produces a "degenerate" population and justifies social stratification necessary to capitalist production.[5] The association of IQ and eugenics is not a thing of the past: Recent debates regarding the "bell curve", and renewed interest in equating intelligence with biological heredity are evidence that science continues to be applied toward questionable ends.

"Emotional quotient" is billed as the "newest measure of intelligence and success."[6] The cover states in capital letters: "The groundbreaking book that redefines what it means to be smart." And the full title is *Emotional Intelligence: Why It Can Matter More Than IQ*. Closer examination reveals that emotional intelligence is a neoliberal variation of genetic discourses regarding intelligence.[7] Goleman claims that this new research challenges "those who subscribe to a narrow view of intelligence, [those who argue] that IQ is a genetic given that cannot be changed by life experience, and that our destiny in life is largely fixed by these aptitudes" (1995: xi). The reader may think that Goleman is challenging the ideology of innate intelligence recently reinvoked by such books as *The Bell Curve*. But he is not challenging genetic theories of innate intelligence quotient. Rather, his concern is that a bell curve "argument ignores the more challenging question: What can we change that will help our children fare better in life?" (ibid.) One can see the shift from the strictly genetic argument regarding intelligence, to the neoliberal and humanist discourse which instead emphasizes self-control and individual choice. Emotional intelligence packages marketable solutions for "success" and "self-improvement."

Goleman concludes that the difference between those with mediocre IQs who are successful and those with high IQs who fail "lies in the abilities called here emotional intelligence, which include self-control, zeal, and persistence, and the ability to motivate oneself. And these skills, as we shall see, can be taught to children, giving them a better chance to use whatever intellectual potential the genetic lottery may have given them" (1995: ix).

Emotional skills enable us to maximize the "intellectual potential" we have won in the "genetic lottery." Intellectual potential has been firmly rooted in genetic inheritance. One can recognize a familiar conservative discourse, in which the individual's only hope against biology's determinism is her own bootstraps. The socially constructed environment (e.g., the market) is instead a "natural" given. Goleman leaves intact the possibility of genetically-determined IQ and EQ and moves on to the ostensibly liberal question of how parents can help the quality of children's lives. The move away from the more conservative discourse of eugenics to "caring for our children" reflects liberalism's insidious modes of social control. It is a paternalistic discourse that combines surveillance with "caring protection."

Unlike an explicit eugenics theory, in the neoliberal version social class is erased and unmentioned. Instead, Goleman's text teems with descriptions of "society falling apart," and "good people" being hurt as a result of individuals' temperaments. However, as with the conservative view of IQ, which roots intelligence in biological heredity, the scientific discourses that authorize this new measurement of the emotional self are centrally founded on neurobiology and the potential for "hard-wired" morality.

The two primary scientific narratives mobilized to discipline the moral citizen for postindustrial capitalism are behavioral psychology and cognitive science. Within the history of the sciences, cognitive science represents a major paradigmatic break from behavioral psychology. Yet the two sciences share social and economic interests, and emotional intelligence reveals cognitive science's interest in emotions. I turn now to a brief overview of the historical emergence and application of these two discourses in relation to human resources.

FROM "HUMAN ENGINEERING" TO "CYBERNETIC SYSTEMS"

IN HER ESSAY "Sex, Mind and Profit" ([1979] 1991) Donna Haraway contrasts the work of two scientists to illustrate the shifting concerns of life sciences in relation to the body politic, specifically production and reproduction as central concerns of capitalist economy. Prior to the Second World War, Robert Yerkes developed "personality sciences" in psychobiology in the context of scientific management industry. Psychobiology was concerned with the "microcontrol of individual workers, establishment of co-operative hierarchies" (45) with particular focus on the "individual organism and hierarchies of intelligence and adaptivity . . . building an evolutionary picture of . . . instinct and rational control" applicable to "capitalist science" (46). Human engineering in the 1930s was interested in "personnel management . . . in order to produce harmony, team work, adjustment. . . . Co-operation most certainly included rational organization of hand and head, of subordination and dominance, of instinct and mind." Haraway notes that management's challenge to encourage "cooperation" was also a "biomedical problem, necessitating detailed physiological knowledge of the 'irrationalities' which could become pathological"(48). She concludes this part of her analysis noting, "Human engineering was a kind of medical encouragement of natural homeostatic mechanisms of intelligent integration" (ibid.).

Following the war, biology was "transformed from a science centered on the organism, understood in functionalist terms, to a science studying automated technological devices, understood in terms of cybernetic systems" (1991: 45), particularly through the work of biologist E. O. Wilson. In this shift from psychobiology to sociobiology, sociobiology is defined as a "communications science." Post Second World War control strategies required changed metaphors: "from organism to system, from eugenics to population management, from personnel management to organization structures." There is a distinct shift from focus on the individual in terms of human engineering to the interactions within groups and the kinds of information communication that occurs within social networks. Within the discussions of emotional intelligence, both of these strands are still present —

the former in terms of behavioral psychology, and the latter in terms of cognitive science.

CAPITALIZING ON EMOTION IN THE WORKPLACE

"EMOTIONAL MANAGEMENT" is not a concept new to workplace psychology, as Haraway's study indicates. Even earlier in this century, the demand for social efficiency spurred industrial psychologists to devise methods to involve workers strategically in workplace management through emotional investments. The social efficiency movement in the early decades of this century developed industrial psychologies to assure worker harmony and contentment. Under the guise of "democracy," these strategies emphasized the importance of interpersonal relations, a sense of agency, and emotional manipulation as means to assure worker contentment.

A fruitful direction for understanding the historical interest in "emotional management" is found in labor practices, developed since the first decades of this century. In a book titled *The Stirring of the Soul in the Workplace* (1996), Alan Briskin analyes the "management of emotion" in labor practices. At the same time Taylor was promoting efficiency as the aim of the workplace in the early years of this century, Australian Elton Mayo brought to the United States another approach to industrial labor. Mayo, who published the results of his experiments in 1933, believed in adjusting the "individual's mental outlook and emotional attitude to his or her surroundings." "Reenchantment" is a word used to describe the worker's requisite attitude towards the workplace. In Mayo's view, "external conditions such as pay incentives" were not the crucial key to worker unhappiness. Rather, "the worker's relations with each other and their supervisors must be studied and reformed so that the kinship patterns of their group could be brought back into equilibrium" (Briskin 1996: 168).[8]

In a classic example of how workers could be made to feel in control of their workplace, known as the Hawthorne experiment, two women "were allowed to suggest their preference for increased lighting. In reality, however, the replacement bulb was the same size as the one removed." The women, unaware that they had been deceived, "commented favorably on the 'change' " (171). By the middle of this century, industrial psychologists were favoring Mayo's approach over Taylor's (175). However, scientific management was by no means abandoned: The manipulation of human resources was simply combined with efficiency models.

At this same factory, an early example of an "employment-related counseling program" was instituted. "The counselors, primarily women, were available for workers to express their grievances" (176). There was a sharp demarcation between this unit and the actual workplace supervisors, with little overlap between the two spheres. "'On the contrary, workers, tenderness, feelings, relationship . . . [and] femininity would all be in one department: and management, toughness, intellect, distance. . . . and masculinity would all be in the other. The latter would, of course, dominate the former"(Hampden-Turner, 1970, quoted in Briskin 1996: 176). Today, in the United States, New Zealand, and Australia we find a contemporary version of these counseling programs called the Employment Assistance Program which provides therapy at cost to the company for employees "stressed" by company restructuring.

WORKPLACES AND OTHER PUBLIC SITES OF EMOTIONAL INTELLIGENCE

CONTEMPORARY EXAMPLES of the adaptation of behavioral psychology to the globalized workplace in terms of discourses of emotion are plentiful. In New Zealand, for example, a nation whose government and mass media presently consume at a rapid rate any imported ideologies that support privatization, most of the major press on EQ has been shown on TV or pasted on magazines. A New Zealand talk show *Good Morning* featured writer Harry Mills, Australian author of a book titled *The Mental Edge: Unlocking the Secrets of Inner Selling* (1996). Several weeks later, American entrepreneur Greg Jemsek gave a public talk titled "Emotional Intelligence." Jemsek lists himself as the "former National Program Director of the prestigious American Leadership Forum. He has a 22-year background as a corporate and community consultant, university lecturer, psychotherapist and storyteller." Jemsek charged the audience, about 35 people, $10 each to listen to him tell stories straight out of Goleman's book, and for an additional $95 many would join him for a full day.

Emotional intelligence capitalizes on informal networks between individuals, an example of what Haraway describes as the "zones of communication and exchange of information," a key focus of sociobiological study (Haraway 1991: 62). Domination and aggression are explicitly demonized in Goleman's depiction of the new collective information networks workplace; the new value lies in "trust networks." In a chapter titled "Managing with Heart," Goleman writes, "By the end of the century, a third of the American workforce will be knowledge workers, people whose productivity is marked by adding value to information — whether as market analysts, writers, or computer programmers" (1995: 159). The new emphasis uses the language of "collective" — collective emotional intelligence and collective teamwork. Studies of so-called "group intelligence" show, among other things, that "people who were too eager to take part were a drag on the group, lowering its overall performance; these eager beavers were too controlling or domineering. Such people seemed to lack a basic element of social intelligence" (160). Finally, "the single most important factor in maximizing the excellence of a group's product was the degree to which the members were able to create a state of internal harmony" (161). In a study of scientists at Bell Labs, a renowned think-tank, it was discovered that while simple problems were handled by the formal organizational networks, "unanticipated problems" were best handled through the informal networks. Informal networks consist of three types: communications webs, expertise networks, and "trust networks." Goleman explicitly points out transnational corporate desire to profit from "trust" networks. Trust networks in part function to inform top-level managers which team members are functioning as deadweight, or as heavyweights — which worker is not functioning smoothly with the team for maximum profit. Without "emotional intelligence", even an expert will not be trusted with coworkers' "secrets, doubts, and vulnerabilities." In other words, profit from human capital relies increasingly on an interpersonal dynamic that fuels *smooth and efficient production* within *virtual communities*. Isolation is no longer the name of the game. Those individuals most capable of creating friendly and trusting networks for information and gossip are the most valuable workers.

The increasingly overlapping ground of the private, internal space of emotions and the public workplace or school marks a radical shift in defining the public and private spheres in Western capitalist culture. No longer is the private space of the family the only site expected to deal with emotion and its training.

COGNITIVE SCIENCE AND THE NEW MORAL PERSON

LIKE MANY OTHER scholarly domains, cognitive science has frequently avoided accounting for affect and emotion when developing models of human intelligence and activity. Howard Gardner, whose models of "intelligence" have had a huge impact on education, offers one example of emotion's absence. In his account of cognitive science (1985) he devotes two paragraphs to the question of emotion as a feature of human mind and behavior.

These two paragraphs are subtitled "De-emphasis on Affect, Context, Culture, and History." Gardner writes,

> though mainstream cognitive scientists do not necessarily bear any animus against the affective realm, against the context that surrounds any action or thought, or against historical or cultural analyses, in practice they attempt to factor out these elements to the maximum extent possible. . . . This may be a question of practicality: if one were to take into account these individualizing and phenomenalistic elements, cognitive science might become impossible. . . . At least provisionally, most cognitive scientists attempt to so define and investigate problems that an adequate account can be given without resorting to these murky concepts. (1985: 41–2)

In the decade since this writing, as Goleman tells us, new research on the brain suggests that we may be challenged to rethink the relation of cognition and emotion. Further, both popular and scholarly explorations of emotion increasingly invoke the authority of cognitive science. In Goleman's popularized version, he cites new research on the brain as the foundation for far-reaching claims about how we can now understand emotion:

> The last decade . . . has also seen an unparalleled burst of scientific studies of emotion. Most dramatic are the glimpses of the brain at work, made possible by innovative methods such as new brain-imaging technologies. They have made visible for the first time in human history what has always been a source of deep mystery: exactly how this intricate mass of cells operates while we think and feel, imagine and dream. This flood of neurobiological data lets us understand more clearly than ever how the brain's center for emotion moves us to rage or tears, and how more ancient parts of the brain, which stir us to make war as well as love, are channeled for better or worse. This unprecedented clarity on the working of emotions and their failings brings into focus some fresh remedies for our collective emotional crisis. (xi)

What does the "new brain research" actually tell us? The latest neurobiological research on brain lobes reveals that the (emotional) amygdala frequently "hijacks" the (rational) neocortex — which explains behaviors ranging from murder to marital stress. A number of the studies referenced by Goleman are based on studies of stroke patients and faulty lobes, not "new findings," data that may be far from representative of the fully functioning brain.[9]

A major slippage occurs between what the new "brain-imaging technologies" make visible on the one hand, and what we may then conclude about emotions, human behavior and culture, on the another. Does it follow that images of the brain can explain the "more ancient parts of the brain" that move us to make love or war? This new technology may offer some understandings about rage, some kinds of anger, and fear, and how neural circuitry between the amygdala exchanges information with the neocortex. Only by a great stretch can we assume that understanding some of the basic neurobiology of rage and fear suggests "fresh remedies for our collective emotional crisis." Any solutions to our collective emotional crisis do not issue from new science of the brain, but from the application of these sciences and their translation into new moral values. Goleman's slippage reveals not only that he invokes both behavioral psychology and cognitive science to authorize emotional intelligence, but also reflects a historical split between the two sciences.

Cognitive science developed in the 1950s in part as a reaction to the oversimplifications of behavioral psychology. An interdisciplinary field, it is constituted by the studies of artificial intelligence, psychology, philosophy, linguistics, neuroscience, and anthropology. Inspired by Turing's proven theorem (1936) that a binary code apparently could enable a computerized machine to "think" like a brain, cognitive scientists began to doubt the model of a passive brain that simply responds to external environmental stimulus.

A primary goal of cognitive science is to discern some form of "hard-wired" rationality. Cognitive science tends to subscribe to a "representational" account of such complex human activities as language and problem-solving abilities. It draws on the philosophical traditions of Plato, Descartes, and Kant which suggest different versions of an a priori, hard-wired "rationality" that explains human ability for complex activities that cannot be explained through reductive nature or nurture accounts. At the present historical moment, cognitive science seeks to explain emotions and their relation to moral evaluation through a universal and hard-wired cognitive system.

RETHINKING THE COGNITION/EMOTION BINARY

LET US TAKE the most optimistic view of the "new brain research," and assume as some scholars suggest that the work in the area of cognitive neuroscience and artificial intelligence helps us rethink the long-standing binary opposition of cognition and emotion. Antonio Damasio's *Descartes' Error: Emotion, Reason, and the Human Brain* offers a widely-read and balanced scholarly account. He draws on neuroscience to outline emotion's role in rational decisions, arguing that the two are inseparable in significant ways previously not recognized by scientist and philosophers — in ways that surprised even his traditionally-scientific conceptions.

Damasio writes,

> The picture I am drawing for humans is that of an organism that comes to life designed with automatic survival mechanisms, and to which education and acculturation add a set of socially permissible and desirable decision-making strategies that, in turn, enhance survival, remarkably improve the quality of that survival, and serve as the basis for constructing a person. At birth, the human brain comes to a development endowed with drives and instincts that include not just a physiological kit to regulate metabolism but in addition basic devices to cope with social cognition and behavior. . . . The neurophysiological base of these added strategies is interwoven with that of the instinctual repertoire, and not only modifies its use but extends its reach. The neural mechanism supporting the suprainstinctual repertory may be similar in their overall formal design to those governing biological drives, and may be constrained by them. Yet they require the intervention of society to become whatever they become, and thus are related as much to a given culture as to general neurobiology. (Damasio 1994: 148)

What Freud called the superego, the moral part of the psychic processes, Damasio calls the *suprainstinctual*. The basic portrait is that we are neurologically programmed to compute social perception and dynamics. These "social-neural" mechanisms "support" the moral guide of the "suprainstinctual," but may be "constrained by biological drives." But Damasio concludes that all of these instinctual and neural wirings "require the intervention of society to become whatever they become, and thus are related as much to a given culture as to general neurobiology." The basic conception of human nature appears to be one that emphasizes the ways in which we are *neurologically* designed to allow us to *learn social rules and relationships*. In the words of Zoe Sofoulis, attempting to bridge the opposition between fears of essentialism and social constructionism, "We are predesigned to be cultural, but we still shape our own history."[10]

However, we are pushed again to rethink the implications of these new discourses by the potential marriage of cognitive science and moral psychology. A 1996 MIT edited volume titled *Mind and Morals* brings together work from cognitive science with work in moral philosophy, and represents the increasing interest in aligning ethical theory with scientific observations about how people make choices.[11] *Mind and Morals* sees itself contributing towards the possibility of "a fully satisfying union between cognitive science and ethical theory" (May et al. 1996: 14). According to the editors, the most conservative "radically naturalised ethics of this kind would hold that normative ethical questions were adequately and exhaustively answered by empirical knowledge of people's actual moral behavior and attitudes" (3).

In selections such as Paul Churchland's "The Neural Representation of the Social World," neuroscience and sociobiology (founded in part on studies of crabs, ants, and bees) suggest models for classifying how humans interact affectively in social relations. Churchland argues,

> Social and moral cognition, social and moral behavior, are no less activities of the brain than is any other kind of cognition or behavior. We need to confront this fact . . . if we are ever to understand our own moral natures. We need to confront it if we are ever to deal both effectively and humanely with our too-frequent social pathologies. (92)

The basis for his claims has to do with an artificial intelligence network called EMPATH, which "[succeeds] in modeling some elementary examples of social perception" (93). The task was to recognize emotions, "eight familiar emotional states," which it did with a "qualified yes". It had "high levels of accuracy on the four positive emotions (about 80 percent), but very poor levels on the negative emotions, with the sole exception of anger." Its weaknesses parallel similar weaknesses in studies of human recognition of emotions.

EMPATH, writes Churchland,

> has no grasp of any expressive sequences. . . . EMPATH cannot tap into the rich palette of information contained in how perceivable patterns unfold in *time*. . . . Lacking any grasp of temporal patterns carries a further price. EMPATH has no conception of what sorts of casual antecedents typically *produce* the principal emotions, and no conceptions of what *effects* those emotions have on the ongoing cognitive, social, and physical behavior of the people who have them .(95)

EMPATH's shortcomings are in fact analogous to the emotionally "unintelligent" person. On Churchland's account, the moral person is "one who has acquired a certain family of perceptual and behavioral skills" as opposed to "the more traditional accounts that picture the moral person as one who has agreed to follow a certain set of *rules* (for example, 'Always keep your promises') or alternatively, as one who has a certain set of overriding *desires* (to maximize the general happiness)" (1996: 106). This quote clearly exemplifies the shift from religious morals to hard-wired skills.

Churchland's cognitive science expresses an agenda of social control entirely compatible with those expressed in *Emotional Intelligence*: "If that person has no comprehension of what sorts of things genuinely serve lasting human happiness; no capacity for recognizing other people's emotions, aspirations, and current purposes; no ability to engage in smoothly cooperative undertakings . . . then that person is not a moral saint. He is a pathetic fool . . . and a serious menace to his society" (107).

The mode of governing the subject of pastoral power, the moral person as defined through a scientized version of moral rules, is explicitly articulated in cognitive science. The question becomes not "Why should I follow some set of rules?" says Churchland, but "Why should I acquire those skills?" His response to this last question is deeply disturbing, and begs the central question: Who gets to decide which rules/skills are important and valuable? Churchland sidesteps this crucial question entirely and merely states "'because they are easily the most important skills you will ever learn'" (107).

The virtuous person is conflated with he who acquires the right skills. In this discourse, we find that rules are "hard-wired" into the brain, and we are expected to develop the skills to utilize best these hard-wired rules. While the conception of a person as consisting of hard-wired knowledge and emotions is not new, the developments regarding hard-wired *morality* are a new development. Postindustrial morality is bolstered through advances in "brain science" that begin to refigure the hard-wired relations between cognition and emotion.

What remains within our control and tied to moral and religious notions of "character" is still our disciplined behavior and ability for self-control: in short, *emotional intelligence*. Behavioral psychology continues to capitalize on the exploitation of human resources. Emotional intelligence capitalizes on a repackaged version of industrial psychology and democratic participation, authorized by cognitive science.

•

THE FRAMING DISCOURSES OF EMOTIONAL INTELLIGENCE

AS I TURN to examine how emotional intelligence has influenced educational curricula programs, it is helpful to summarize the defining features of emotional intelligence. Emotional intelligence is characterized by three dominant discourses, which together situate educational curricula as an insurance of pastoral power, more likely to institute social control than a creative program of social inquiry or political analyses.

- Emotional intelligence is based on a *universalized portrait of human nature and emotions* which entirely neglects significant differences of culture or gender. The universalized portrait of emotions is "imposed" in terms of discourses of "skills" that are common to and can be learned by all, taught through behavioral modification. As noted by Linda Lantieri, co-director of the Resolving Conflict Creatively Program (an emotional literacy program), the "dominant culture would love to see emotional literacy programs replace diversity trainings."

- In addition to the absence of cultural analyses, all gendered associations with emotion have been entirely erased. Within the emotional intelligence literatures as well as within the existing curricula I have observed and examined, the question of gendered patterns of emotion are rarely if ever mentioned. Within the popular discourse, not a single woman or person of color has been quoted, interviewed, or allowed to occupy a position of authority within the public discussions of emotional intelligence. Every authority cited in the studies that found "emotional intelligence," and every spokesperson making public appearance, is a white man.
- The cognitive sciences of neurobiology and artificial intelligence conceptualize the person as an organism whose brain contains predesigned neural pathways to learn social behaviors. The emphasis is on how the autonomous organism acquires "skills." It is a shift in discourses, but not conception, from the autonomous moral chooser to the autonomous skill-acquiring organism. While these scientific literatures appear to carry a new emphasis on the biological capacity for learning modes of social interaction, the underlying model of self has not changed from scientific paradigms that emphasize individualist survival. The primary discourse is about mastery of emotions through biological potential for logical choice.

THE RISKS OF "EQ"

THE USE OF cognitive and behavioral scientific discourse to authorize emotional intelligence requires that we ask, What are the implications of these sciences for our conceptions of morality, moral education, citizen development, and globalized workplace? The risks associated with positing a measurable EQ are a concern I opened with, voiced even in *Time*. The risks of measuring EQ need to be examined in light of the effects of Edward Thorndike's reductive application of intelligence testing.[12] "According to Dr. Paul McHugh, director of psychiatry at the Johns Hopkins University School of Medicine, Goleman's highly popularized conclusions . . . 'will chill any veteran scholar of psychotherapy and any neuroscientist who worries about how his research may come to be applied.' While many researchers in this relatively new field are glad to see emotional issues finally taken seriously, they fear that a notion as handy as EQ invites misuse. Goleman admits the danger of suggesting that you can assign a numerical yardstick to a person's character as well as his intellect" (McHugh 1995: 62).

In his book, Goleman writes, "Unlike the familiar test for IQ there is, as yet, no single paper-and-pencil test that yields an 'emotional intelligence' score and there may never be one" (1995: 44). Disturbingly, however, he goes on to describe a version of testing already developed which measures "a person's actual ability at the task [such as empathy] — for example, by having them read a person's feeling from a video of their facial expressions." In fact this has been measured and studied at the University of California at Berkeley, among other places. Workplaces have already instituted tests such as those developed by Martin Seligman, administered to prospective employees to gauge their optimism and hence their potential profitability as marketing and salespersons. The final chapters of *Emotional Intelligence* explicitly make the link between emotional literacy in workplace management and in schools.

Emotional intelligence serves capitalism at several levels. If workers and schoolchildren are conversational in emotional literacy, the labor system profits. Simultaneously the "self-help" industry profits from information commodified and consumed by our own obsession with ourselves. The increasing authority of cognitive science fuels our popular and scholarly fascination with the self as a cybernetic system rather than simply a functionalist organism. Neurological science is systematically attempting to tame emotions, one of the most resistant sites of human and social life.

Does it make sense to speak of EQ as the taming of the alien, the colonization of emotion? We are in the midst of a shift from a climate of rationality to a climate of the cybernetic system which incorporates emotions. The older liberal conception of the free individual self who "chooses" to follow rules is replaced with the cybernetic self/system whose brain contains a "universally common" neural pathway that functions as the perceptual apparatus necessary to acquire (neoliberal) social skills and rules. Within these neural discourses about the social world, we find a combination of the rules-based morality rooted in traditional conceptions of the moral person, with the utility-based discourse of skills.

The compulsory educational curricula in emotional literacy, now taught in hundreds of public schools, are in large part behavioral modification programs that employ sociabiological discourses to authorize which emotional behaviors constitute the good citizen. Our futuristic visions may have invoked metaphors of machines and information coding processors, the ultimate in rationalistic dystopias. But the smooth operation of new systems of globalized networks may turn out to rely on a profitable emotional utopia, and on a hard-wired human consciousness defined by virtues of trust and empathy more than ever before.

---

1 1983: 128.

2 Neoliberalism characterizes the late-twentieth-century emphases on market-driven society within Western democracies. Historically this has involved systematic dismantling of the welfare state. Systems of "accountancy" and "self-governance" are two central ideological characteristics. For example, Alan Hunt emphasizes that in neo-liberalism there is often less concern with controlling the content of educational curriculum, for example, and more concern for an accounting of its outcomes. Other shifts indicate that rhetorical and resulting material allowances of fairness and egalitarianism are displaced by "freedom," which obviously works alongside the "choice" driven market model of progress (Apple 1993: 24). See also Giddens, *Beyond Left and Right* (1994).

3 For a valuable discussion on education in relation to this question see Marshall, "The Autonomous Chooser and Reforms in Education" (1996). See also Peters, *Poststructuralism, Politics and Education* (1996); and Peters and Marshall *Individualism and Community: Education and Social Policy in the Post-Modern Condition* (1996).

4 Meisner, "Emotional Intelligence," *Better Homes and Gardens* (May 1998).

5 A quote from John Dewey is worth noting here as it foresees the risks represented by new discourses of morality and emotions. "After ignoring impulses for a long time in behalf of sensations, modern psychology now tends to start out with an inventory and description of instinctive activities. This is an undoubted improvement. But when it tries to explain complicated events in personal and social life by direct reference to these native powers, the explanation becomes hazy and forced. It is like saying the flea and the elephant, the lichen and the redwood, the timid hare and the ravening wolf . . . are alike products of natural selection. There may be a sense in which the statement is true; but until we know the specific environing conditions under which selection took place we really know nothing. And so we need to know about the social conditions which have educated original activities into definite and significant dispositions before we can discuss the psychological element in society. This is the true meaning of social psychology." (Dewey [1922] 1983).

6 In a description which aptly describes how emotional intelligence serves capitalism through the quantification of knowledge, Foucault addresses power's relentless "interrogation" and "registration of truth" as "it institutionalizes, professionalizes, and rewards its pursuit. In the last analysis, we must produce truth as we must produce wealth" (1980: 93). In the case of EQ, we discover a new product or "form of wealth." EQ is susceptible to the same laws of truth as is intelligence.

7 For analyses of the social implications of genetic sciences, see for example Rose et al (1984); Gould (1981); Kamin (1995).

8 The emphasis on "kinship" as a model for the workplace resonates with Ann Ferguson's (1991) analysis of "sex/affective production" as the relatively unexamined site of the production and reproduction of people and relationships, whose production is simultaneous with material goods.

9 Goleman's sources include studies published by such scientists as Paul Ekman,

Joseph LeDoux, and Antonio Damasio.

10 Presentation at the University of Auckland, "What Scholer Would Endorse Me? Transference, Counter-Transference, and Post-Graduate Pedagogy," 23 October, 1997.

11 While moral psychologists like Piaget and Kohlberg have remained largely discounted by dominant psychology, interest has grown in the possibilities of connection between these disparate fields of psychology and philosophy. The editors of *Mind and Morals* (May et al. 1996) characterize this new interest as a version of moral naturalism. Holding forth crucial contesting views to this moral naturalism, essays by such feminist philosophers as Naomi Scheman and Helen Longino are included to pose very different views. The editors begin with G.E. Moore's critique of J.S. Mill's utilitarianism; Moore accused that to tell us what we "ought to do" could not be accomplished by "telling us what we do do" (2). They distinguish between moral realists and moral naturalists: the former, like Moore, have faith that we can ascertain some moral facts (stemming from logic and reason). Thus a moral realist has little interest in psychology, which has nothing to do with moral facts.

Moral naturalism is divided into two camps: normative ethical naturalists and metaethical naturalists. The former were the butt of Moore's accusation of the naturalistic fallacy: they rely on a "first order" sort of equation between what people are empirically seen to do, taking these observations as answers to our ethical questions. The new moral naturalists are of the second type, concerned with "what methods we should use to reach beliefs about what to do, value, or be, and tried to answer these questions using empirical knowledge of the ways which people actually reason morally" (3). See also Robin Fox, *The Search for Society: Quest for a Biosocial Science and Morality* (1989) NJ: Rutgers Univ. Press. Fox (author of *The Red Lamp of Incest*) who combines anthropology with evolutionary theory, and argues against what he considers the "irrational" opposition to claims for innate and essential human qualities. The dustjacket calls this book an "'equal time' response to Clifford Geertz's *Interpretation of Cultures.*"

12 See for example Wirth's *Education in the Technological Society: The Vocational-Liberal Studies Controversy in the Early Twentieth Century* ([1972] 1980).

CHAPTER FOUR

TAMING THE LABILE STUDENT

Emotional Literacy Curricula

The school must . . . establish a curriculum providing realistic experiences in which the pupil may have adventures producing the milder emotional reactions necessary to health and happiness; a curriculum in which the pupil may have stronger emotional experiences, not too long or disruptive, thus giving him the opportunity to analyze facts and use his reasoning ability toward that end that he may form generalizations and ideals which will lead him to the direction and control of these stronger emotions.

—Bosshart 1939[1]

ONE DAY IN OCTOBER 1995 will remain forever emblazoned in my memory: The day *Time* magazine hit the newsstand with a cover story on "emotional quotient." Alerted by my colleague, I rushed to the local store and there it was — "EQ" in huge red letters. What was being publicly announced in the mass media about emotions? My heart beating rapidly, I flipped open to the feature story to consume hungrily what felt like my first meal after a very long fast. As I read, I felt strong and contradictory emotions: a mixture of elation and alarm. Elation, because emotions, traditionally "silenced" though ever-present and expressed, had entered public and popular discourse. Alarm, because the emotions were addressed in complete absence of sociocultural and political analysis. The opening subtitle reads: "New brain research suggests that emotions, not IQ, may be the true measure of human intelligence." The sudden emergence of emotions into popular culture, I could see immediately, was sparked by "new science" and a "true" measure of "human intelligence." Knee-jerk fear? Eugenics in a new package.

Emotional intelligence emphasizes the ability to empathize and maintain optimism in the face of obstacles. Gender, race, and social class are discussed nowhere in the *Time* news feature. I have read and reread the article, and now the many popular and scholarly literatures sparked by Daniel Goleman's bestseller *Emotional Intelligence*, hoping to find some discussion of such questions as: Given the economic inequalities of our societies, who benefits from "delayed gratification?" Who can "afford" to maintain optimism in the face of lifelong poverty? Why is emotion suddenly valued as a universal ideal, entirely severed from its long association with women's assigned roles as the empathetic nurturers?

To its credit, the *Time* article does voice some alarm, as noted in the last chapter. "Goleman's highly popularized conclusions," says McHugh, "will chill any veteran scholar of psychotherapy and any neuroscientist who worries about how his research may come to be applied. While many researchers in this relatively new field are glad to see emotional issues finally taken seriously, they fear that a notion as handy as EQ invites misuse" (McHugh 1995: 62). To date, I have seen no tests developed in schools to measure EQ. In fact, Goleman himself rejects the term "EQ" and prefers "emotional intelligence" or "emotional literacy". However, corporations have developed tests to measure potential employees emotional intelligence. Further, the popular packaging of emotional intelligence is being translated into quick prescriptions. A 1998 *Better Homes and Gardens* feature titled "Emotional Intelligence" tells mothers how to teach their children. Instructions include:

> *How to accept criticism or a consequence:*
> . . . (2) Say "OK" (but not sarcastically) and nod your head to show you understand what the other person is saying (3) Don't argue; remember that the person who is giving criticism is only trying to help. (May 1998: 106)

Time concludes, however, by drawing a false distinction: They state that

> emotional skills, like intellectual ones, are morally neutral. . . . Given the passionate arguments that are raging over the state of moral instruction in the U.S., it is no wonder Goleman chose to focus more on neutral emotional skills than on the values that should govern their use. That's another book — and another debate. (1995: 47)

However, this false distinction between "neutral skills" and a "moral agenda" reflects only our culture's acceptance of science's language as "objective" and separable from moral or political agendas — a distinction that has been powerfully challenged for several decades. I will argue that emotional literacy skills are in no way neutral. Contemporary popular discourses in science, as discussed in the last chapter, increasingly encourage an understanding of human behavior as a combination of "hard-wired" impulses and an educable set of neutral skills for self-control. But this conception of the self reflects historically and culturally specific values which carry particular social and political agendas.

The popular representation of EQ provided me and my project with a new object of analysis and a new "legitimacy." In fact, I had seen the term "emotional literacy" in the *New York Times* three years earlier. (This had marked another memorable moment since I had, a year before the *New York Times* sighting, coined the term "emotional literacy" in my own project, but had been discouraged by a professor who suggested one should not put two "contradictory" terms together.) The need for analysis of how emotions infuse education and values was not only legitimized by its popularization but is now more pressing than ever. Daniel Goleman's popularization of emotional intelligence represents a gold mine after what had been far too many years of searching high and low for recognition of emotion as worthy of public attention. In Goleman's book I found descriptions of several curricula programs in emotional literacy. I set out to analyze all the materials I could find on these educational programs, and commenced a research project in which I interviewed curriculum developers in the United States, observed classrooms, and later interviewed the developers of similar programs in Australia.

Having now studied the educational theories and philosophies underlying emotional literacy and having seen the curriculum in action, I feel as torn as I did at the start. An explicit curricula in emotional literacy does seem an advance from the generally hidden curricula that guide emotional behaviors. Ideally, such explicit address of emotions would:

- invite collaborative, self-reflective analysis of emotions and critical analysis of cultural, gendered differences in emotions and how the rules of emotional conduct maintain social hierarchies.
- provide students with an opportunity to examine emotional experience within a context not usually provided in schools or elsewhere.
- allow teachers to explore their own emotional experience and develop conscientious "philosophies of emotion" to inform their pedagogies and interaction.
- allow young people to articulate and possibly develop an increased vocabulary, so that they can creatively examine their ethical relations with others and choose for themselves modes of integrating emotions in their lives.

However, to teach an emotional literacy curriculum runs real risks, both in theory and in practice. The risks include that such a curricula may:

- impose emotional rules or prescriptions, stemming either from particular values embedded in the curricula or the teacher's own arbitrary emotional values.

- in the absence of social, political, cultural, or historical analysis, reinforce a view of emotions as "natural," private," "individual," and "universal."
- reduce emotional literacy to yet another version of "blaming the victim" by advocating self-control as the end goal.
- uphold existing social hierarchies and capitalist interests in efficiency and social harmony, insofar as emotional literacy represents a prescription of imposed rules.

In sum, my greatest hope is that the explicit discourse of emotions leads us to develop, as a culture, a "meta-discourse" about the significance of different emotional expressions, silences, and rules in relation to the power relations that define cultural injustices. My greatest fear is that emotions are again reduced to an individualized phenomena, and that emotional literacy curricula function as a mode for continued social control and pastoral power through self-policing.

In this chapter, I define and describe emotional literacy curricula. I analyze the social, legislative climate that support the emergence of these curricula. I outline the historical roots of emotional literacy programs. I examine curricula programs and evaluate them in terms of the risk of individualizing on the one hand, and the promise of expanding our capacities to analyze the sociocultural context of emotions on the other.

Before proceeding, it is helpful to provide an example of what seems to me one best-case scenario of what can happen in the context of an emotional literacy program. In an interview I conducted with Resolving Conflict Creatively Program (RCCP) cofounder Linda Lantieri, she described to me a "teachable moment" in a classroom she was guest-facilitating. A "feelings barometer" had been put on the wall, ranging from rage to irritation. She posed a hypothetical situation to the students: "If you were to get off of a bus on your way home, and you were called a name, how would you feel?" The students grouped themselves along the feelings barometer according to their response. Lantieri then asked the young people, "What do you notice about who has gone to the different ends of the spectrum?" One white girl comments, "There are more African-American students under 'rage' and more white students under 'irritated.'" Another student asks, "Why would you feel rage? If someone calls me a name I don't let it bother me!" Lantieri asks, "What do you think accounts for that difference?" And one of the students who recognizes the rage she would feel in response to a verbal insult explains: "That happens to us almost everyday!" The class then had an opportunity to discuss the very different social situations faced by the different children, and how their emotional responses reflected different hierarchies and the effects of racism in their culture.

How often do such teachable moments occur? When and how can we be assured that teachers have the desire or skills to engage students in such discussions? These uncertainties seem built in to any educational project. In what follows, I hope to clarify some of the challenges and contradictions faced in evaluating emotional literacy curricula.

In my analysis and evaluation of the programs I have studied, I am guided by these questions:

1. Is there an opportunity to analyze how emotional expressions and rules vary according to cultural norms and context?
2. Are emotions portrayed as individual, natural, and/or as expressions to be controlled?
3. Who or what determines how and when to control and shape emotions—the teacher, the curricula, the student?

DEFINING EMOTIONAL LITERACY CURRICULA

ALTHOUGH THE TERMS "emotional literacy" and "emotional intelligence" have been adopted into numerous programs, particularly sparked by Goleman's popularized book, each program I have analyzed differs in significant ways. There is no one definition of emotional literacy. However, such curricula are likely to include:

- Teaching students to "identify" facial expressions as particular emotions, a kind of "mimicry" or "rehearsal." Part of the aim of this is to reduce "violence" that occurs because of "mis-recognition" of another's facial expressions: e.g., there are reports of gang violence sparked when one young person mistakes another's expression as "hostile." Based on a Darwinian model, this is troubling because it appears to reduce emotions to "universally" recognizable signifiers that mean the same things to all people at all times. It also risks reductiveness because this teaching is generally reduced to the "basic emotions,"[2] when in fact our emotional experience and expressions are much more complex. However, in one class I observed students performed an exercise for recognizing emotions that did emphasize the complexity of recognition. In this exercise, four students might be given a phrase such as, "Today is Monday!" The teacher directs each student to "say" the phrase in front of the class with a particular emotional inflection—e.g., disappointment, anger, shame, fear. The difficulty people had in "recognizing" the emotion was educational, and the aim of this lesson was "open-ended," a genuine inquiry into the complexity of how and when we recognize emotion through body language, inflection, intonation, etc.

- Developing more expansive vocabularies of emotions; in one instance I observed, students came up with an astoundingly long list of emotions brainstormed on the blackboard.[3] This "expansive" naming seems promising, and softens the impression of the above Darwinian model that suggests emotions have been reduced to "eight basic emotions."
- Increasing self-esteem: learning to identify the "positive and "negative" inner voices within us. This discourse tends to reduce emotions to individualized occurrences: Whether or not we "feel good about ourselves" is up to us, and situated within our own interiority rather than situated in relation to outside influences.
- Learning to verbally express "appreciations" of classmates by identifying their unique qualities. The emphasis here was not to appreciate someone's accomplishments, but their qualities.
- Learning to "control" emotions: to count to ten before expressing anger, or not to express it at all; to "use our words" and not physical violence or other forms of "acting out." The risk here is that there is little discussion of who, historically, has been taught not to express anger and who has been allowed to express anger. Neither is there discussion of the importance — both as emotional and physical defense — for some people in some situations to exercise anger.
- Learning conflict resolution skills: using interactive dialogue and expression of "When you did x, I felt y" to mediate conflict. This is taught usually by training "peer mediators" who help the two persons having a conflict to seek their own solution to conflict.
- Teaching tolerance, respect, and caring. These values need to be taught with respect to important cultural differences, rather than as "universal" values.

As I indicated, these represent aims of different programs; no one program does all of these, and different programs in theory and/or in practice offer greater and lesser opportunity for examining emotional skills in relation to cultural differences.

THE HISTORICAL EMERGENCE AND CONTEXT OF EMOTIONAL LITERACY

THE EXPLICIT DISCOURSE of emotional literacy has emerged over the past ten years within programs variously known for example as "conflict resolution, " "self-science," and "pro-social" development. Brought to public attention especially through several articles penned by Daniel Goleman, in 1992 and 1993, and then in 1995 by *Emotional Intelligence*, such programs are increasingly funded by private sources and implemented in public and private schools across the United States and in Australia. But the elements that make up these various programs are not new. Conflict resolution dates back to the 1920s industrial psychology;[4] discourses of racial tolerance and management date to the 1950s and 1960s;[5] and "affective" education developed in the 1960s and 1970s.[6] Each of these roots are visible within contemporary emotional literacy.

According to Tom Roderick, director of Educators for Social Responsibility (ESR), what *is* "new" in Goleman's vision is placing each of the above features under the "one umbrella" of "emotional intelligence." As he says, the concept of emotional intelligence gets away from isolating social development as simply a "violence prevention" program, and instead as part of a vision of "life skills" and teaching a worldview that includes "respect for people."[7]

Daniel Goleman's "umbrella concept" has offered new "authority" for many emotional literacy curricula programs. The book *Emotional Intelligence* refers to most of the programs I discuss here; Goleman's authority is quoted in the brochures and literatures of many programs, often commenting directly on their program. Goleman was the keynote speaker to the 1996 annual meeting of the Association of Supervisors of Curriculum Development, an eighty-thousand-member organization. Goleman spoke to an audience of six thousand, and five hundred then participated in a workshop run by Collaborative Association for Social and Emotional Learning (CASEL). CASEL is a newly established research and advocacy organization. It started at the Yale Child Study Center in New Haven and is now housed in the University of Chicago. The current budget is about $300,000, $200.000 of which has been given by the University.

An umbrella national organization developed during the mid-1980s, Educators for Social Responsibility (ESR), provides support through technical assistance, and curriculum development for many of the school programs. ESR works on an annual budget of over $2.5 million. They are funded primarily by private foundations and institutions. ESR has one thousand members, and twenty local chapters which function autonomously with respect to the needs of their regional community.

THE "CLIMATE": Modern Discourses of Crisis and Care

EMOTIONAL LITERACY CURRICULA might be interpreted as simply one of the latest "bandwagons" that reflect public, parental, and social concern about "youth in crisis." The history of education is replete with examples of curricula designed to respond to perceptions of youth in crisis.[8] "Caring for our children" is a rhetoric found within corporate,[9] legislative,[10] philanthropic, and media[11] discourses in our contemporary culture. While the concern and care for youth is real — in general, adult society really does want their children to grow up free from violence and harm — the discourse of care masks other rationales. For example, to teach young people to police themselves is more cost-efficient than outfitting an urban school with police and safety monitors.[12] In a *Washington Post* article "When Johnny Won't Learn," a social corrective program called "Pathways" is extolled as targeting middle school youth. The benefit of the program is centrally cited as economic: "'In education, we'll all end up paying for these kids. I think we get more for our money by taking on the problems before they get to high school'" (school principal quoted in James, 5 April 1998: 20). It is cost-effective to teach students to internalize appropriate control of their emotions by teaching them to take "responsibility" and learn "self-control." Thus the social, economic, and political forces that underlie these youth crises are masked, and the individuals are blamed for lack of self-control.

The social and economic environment that spurred federal funding for one of the programs I analyzed provides a compelling portrait of the extent of violence faced by young people. At the same time, the context evidences the degree to which such emotional literacy programs function to replace other forms of state-funded policing of schools.

> Officials are grappling with the increasing levels of urban crime and violence that are invading their schools. For the 1991–92 school year, the New York Board of Education reported 4,955 serious incidents in its schools, including homicide, robbery, sex offenses, and controlled substance and weapons possession. To increase the level of school security, the board has responded by installing metal detectors and X-ray machines and using student photo identification cards in high schools. The board has also funded conflict-resolution and mediation programs and increased the number of school safety officers in all schools. The board employs about three-thousand safety officers. *If considered a police department, it would rank as the ninth largest police department in the country. . . .* The budget for the Division of School Safety . . . totaled nearly $73 million in 1993. (April 1995 U.S. General Accounting Office Report on School Safety: 32, emphasis added)

This extract from the U.S. General Accounting Office Report employs the discourse of concern for the safety of young people. But of equal concern is the high cost of funding "the ninth largest police department in the country" to protect schools in only one public school system. Investing in programs that will function as a "self-policing" mechanism is clearly cost-effective if they work successfully.

Emotional literacy programs are largely framed as a "neutral set of skills," skills not necessarily value-laden or deriving from particular religious values or moral doctrines. But in American capitalist society, shaped by the values of the Protestant work ethic and social efficiency, a publicly and federally approved school curricula is inextricably linked with specific national and political interests. What may be sold to us in "commonsense terms" — of course, we "care" about the children — masks other political interests in social control and conformity. This is not a theory of "fascist" or even autocratic intentions, but an analysis of how the economy and existing social structure inevitably shape education. In the modern version of pastoral power, "skills" are emphasized, often in combination with particular cultural values such as respect, care, tolerance, democracy, "Just Say No," and sexual abstinence. Self-control and self-policing are hallmarks of the modern "virtuous" individual.[13]

To teach young people to be self-disciplined, self-motivated, and to get along benefits the workplace: Capitalism has an intrinsic interest in social efficiency. The popular appeal of "talking through our differences" infuses even corporate advertising on television. A recent advertising campaign for Telecom, the multinational corporation that owns the primary long-distance telephone service in New Zealand, ran a three-part ad series titled "Conversation Pieces." Each plays a popular song while depicting some form of interpersonal interaction (mother/infant, father/son, and boy/boy). The following ad represents an uncanny microcosm of "sociomoral" development and cooperation. Set to Cat Stevens's song "Where Do the Children Play" (an earnest song about children's innocence in the face of war), a six-year-old blond-haired boy enters a room where a dark-skinned boy of the same age sits on a couch. Subtitles state, "This is Ivan"; "This is Stephan." The music continues: "Bombs . . . fill the air, will we keep on fighting . . . but where do the children play?" The boys are looking at each other. "They have never met." The blond boy comes and sits on the other end of couch. Subtitles continue: "There is war and hatred between their countries"; "Watch."

The blond boy pulls out a toy airplane to play with, slowly begins to move closer to other boy. A brief time lapse is indicated through camera-melt, and we see them begin to play in earnest, chasing one another around the couch.

Subtitle: "What happened here?"

The last scene depicts the boys playing on the couch, smiling, touching each other.

"First"

"They talked."

"*Keep in touch. Telecom.*"

The Telecom advertisement suggests that the solution to cultural difference, to tensions between individuals created by national differences (differences that are themselves related to transnational corporate interests) is to "talk" (and to profit Telecom through large phone bills!). And indeed, if one motto had to be chosen to describe a skill common to each of the emotional literacy programs, it could easily be: "Use your words." The solution to violence, to cultural differences, and to improving self-esteem is to increase diplomatic and communicative skills so that we can play (work) harmoniously together. My point should come as no surprise: Goleman explicitly makes the case that emotional intelligence benefits the globalized workplace.[14] Emotional literacy programs directly benefit the globalized context of capitalism, and fit with organizational management and industrial psychology, which have been designed to serve capitalist needs for harmony.

As a "social program" in schools, emotional literacy is introduced to deal with such issues as violence, teen pregnancy, and drug use. In our society, these issues are strongly overdetermined by moral and religious values and norms. The anxieties surrounding the crises faced by youth is an example of an "affective epidemic." Describing the war on drugs as an affective epidemic, Lawrence Grossberg notes that "[i]n the name of protecting people from drugs, individual liberties can be sacrificed" (1992: 285). He details how the representation of these crises individualize social problems and neglect to analyze how the economy of "drug traffic" in fact serves capitalist interests. Nor is there analysis of how and why this "unacceptable" economy might even be said to be encouraged to exist within the dispensable communities of ghettoes.

We face the question: Which kinds of violence and crises become targets of moral discourse and behavioral modification? War, domestic violence and wife-battering, corporal punishment in schools, sexual abuse and rape are forms of violence regularly tolerated and even condoned, through silence and omission if not through explicit approval. Who gets punished, who is permitted "reprieve," and who gets publicly punished and humiliated must always be closely examined. The example of the four girls and female teacher murdered in 1998 by the two boys in Arkansas exemplifies these contradictions: The public concern and spectacle focuses on "How could these basically 'good,' if occasionally naughty, little boys commit such a horrendous crime?" There is no analysis in the media of this as a misogynist crime, as a children's version of the Montreal Massacre of female graduate students.[15]

Thus anxieties about the crises of youth cannot be understood as simply "caring about youth." The crises that schools address are intertwined with "moral panics" as well as with particular conceptions of young people as "out of control." Nancy Lesko's analysis evidences the diverse constructions of youth in our culture.

Teenagers, for example, are

> Simultaneously constructed in fictional and factual accounts as pets, wild animals, research objects, colonial subjects, criminals, and victims. Teachers draw upon professional accounts from medicine, psychology, sociology, and law, among others, to emphasize different natures of youth. Four professionalized definitions of youth can be distinguished. Conventional medical and social-science based views are one set of definitions that involve abstracted, universalized concepts of hormone-raging, identity seeking, and peer-conforming youth. A second category, youth as a major social problem, is composed of youth who fail to follow proper norms for development and are prone to violence, pregnancy, motherhood, school dropout, unemployment, and other deviances. In the therapeutic arenas, such as social work and mental health, youth are viewed as victims/patients: of sexual assault, of dysfunctional families, or of addictive patterns, such as alcoholism. A fourth discursive construction of youth is written in rights language, and opposes the child-as-property-of-parents view that contains youth within families. (1996: 453–4)

The constructions Lesko identifies are all present within the emotional literacy curricula in different forms, and these conceptions strongly pervade media and legislative representation of young people in crisis. All four conceptions involve a moral discourse in different guise. A site in which moral discourses are most obvious, whatever conception of youth is employed, is in issues surrounding sex education.[16]

Thus to situate emotional literacy programs within the climate of "caring for youth" and solutions to "youth in crisis" is to understand that any such program cannot possibly be a set of "neutral skills," as *Time* magazine states. Rather, these skills will always carry an agenda, determined by all of the above discourses and conflicting political, corporate, parental, administrative, and genuinely humane concerns.

LEGISLATIVE CONTEXT AND POLICY FRAMEWORKS ON YOUTH AND VIOLENCE

IN THE 1990s extensive federal funds were granted to promote social correction programs.[17] A General Accounting Office (GAO) report details the "variety of educational and non-educational approaches and programs" used to "address violence. Many school-based violence-prevention programs operate under the premise that violence is a learned behavior"(3). The argument of violence as a learned behavior recurs throughout these literatures, apparently as opposed to the idea of violence as an inherited or pathological symptom. The programs recognized by the GAO include:

- *Educational and curricula based:* These programs seek to teach students the skills to manage their behavior and resolve conflict nonviolently. Programs in this category focus on conflict resolution, gang aversion, social skills training, mentoring, and law-related education.
- *Environmental modification:* . . . home visitation . . . after-school recreational and academic activities . . . installing metal detectors and gates limiting access.
- *School organization and management:* These programs focus on establishing school discipline policies and procedures that pertain to student behavior, creating alternative schools, and developing operative relationships with police and other governmental agencies. Legal efforts to prohibit weapons in schools also fall into this category. (4)

The 1993 "Report on Violence in the Schools: How America's School Boards are Safeguarding Our Children" records "more than 750 different violence prevention programs." Of these, 66 percent "established alternative schools or programs for disruptive students" and 61 percent implemented "conflict-resolution and peer-mediation training," while only 10 percent developed "safe havens for students." Emotional literacy falls under the "educational and curricula based" programs.[18]

I now describe and analyze four different curricula programs that use some version of emotional literacy.

OVERVIEW OF EMOTIONAL LITERACY PROGRAMS

Teacher: R-e-s-p-e-c-t.
Children (in unison): I am in control of me.
— *New Haven social development program (1995)*[19]

THE FOUR PROGRAMS I have selected to analyze share discursive frameworks but also represent quite different conceptions of social problems and differently envisioned solutions. Every program I have studied and observed subscribes to some version of "I am in control of me." Every program seems to share the idea that schools must provide moral guidance where families are failing. Each program reflects strands of American discourses of a humanist model of cooperation and democracy, and the ideology of neoliberalism and self-control as the seat of virtue. However, beyond this there is great variation. I will contrast the programs through two generalized categories I call *individual developmental* models and *social inquiry/conflict-resolution* models.

I want to stress that my critical analysis is intended to examine the underlying assumptions of the programs. The people who have developed these programs and those who teach them are fully well-intentioned in their efforts to improve schools and their students' lives, and I have utmost respect for these intentions and accomplishments. Further, even in those instances where I offer critique of underlying assumptions, one could argue that the effect of the programs is in fact "good" and "useful." No doubt even those programs about which I had misgivings accomplish goals related to improving young people's lives. My critique is not of the people involved, but rather of how school practices are embedded in larger discourses that do warrant concern. More important, I think, than curricular intentions or my critique are students' experiences and perceptions of the different programs. Very little research is presently available that foregrounds young people's voices and evaluations.[20]

My analysis and evaluation stems from different sources: (1) In the case of the Resolving Conflict Creatively Program (RCCP) and Developmental Studies Center (DSC), I draw on interviews with curricula developers and observations of classrooms using the curriculum; in the case of DSC, observation not of classrooms but of videotapes produced by the DSC that document classroom interactions using the curriculum. (2) For each of the four programs I have examined, when available, scholarly literatures and research analyzing the curricular model; media representation of the programs; the "publicity" or other informational brochures produced by the curricula program (if available). In the United States, I observed four different programs in classrooms, and interviewed four different curricula developers. In Australia, I interviewed numerous people involved in different curriculum programs engaging emotions. In New Zealand, I studied the literatures employed in two very different curriculum approaches designed to decrease "bullying and teasing." The programs I have selected to discuss here are chosen to represent what I think are four representative programs that can said to involve emotional literacy in some form, though each uses different language to frame the education of emotions.[21]

Individual Developmental Models

The two programs under this heading exemplify, in the first case, conceptions of the self rooted in cognitive science and behavioral psychology as discussed at length in the previous chapter. In the second program I discuss, the conception of the self is rooted in developmental psychology and behavioral psychology, employing the discourses of "participatory democracy" and "caring community" and is thus related to the history of industrial psychology and organizational management. Both reflect significant overlap with the mental-hygiene movement conceptions of youth and emotions as discussed in chapter 2.

"Impulsive Individuals" and Skills-Based Morality

During 1995 when Goleman's book had placed emotion in the public eye, the U.S. National Public Radio program *All Things Considered* broadcast a fifteen-minute report on the success of the New Haven social development program, also referred to as an "emotional literacy program." The Yale–New Haven Social Competence Promotion Program, which calls itself "social development" training, is a program developed by Yale-trained psychologists, now housed at the University of Illinois, and currently offered to all eighteen thousand students in the New Haven public schools.[22] The motivating crisis in New Haven was that "fifty percent of the students were dropping out by the eight grade, one-quarter of the girls were having sex by the sixth grade, teen pregnancy was rampant" (10 December, 1995 broadcast NPR). The schools' children come significantly from low-income families. This program exemplifies an emphasis on "impulse-control," a highly individualized conception of reducing delinquent behavior through increased "social competency"[23] (Goleman 1995: 308). In a *New York Times* article (1993), Goleman states that the "program's effectiveness" is revealed in teachers' reports that those who had undergone the program were "markedly better at resolving classroom conflicts, controlling impulsiveness and being more liked by their fellow students." Goleman also reports that "among the New Haven statistics was a sharp decline in the rate of suspensions among students as their time in the program increased" (ibid.).

A review of the curriculum programs that were being used in New Haven in 1990 "to fight the wars on drugs, violence, and school truancy" had shown that most programs were ineffective, but that the successful programs had "common elements" (10 December, 1995 broadcast NPR). They invited Daniel Goleman to address the success of the Yale–New Haven Social Competence Promotion Program on the NPR radio broadcast.

> Goleman: [The programs that] work for pregnancy are very like the ones that work for violence and very like the ones that work for dropouts — they teach this core skill, set of skills, emotional and social skills. Things like knowing what you're feeling, managing your feelings, knowing what other people are feeling, empathy and taking another person's perspective, and being socially appropriate, knowing how to cooperate, knowing how to negotiate.
>
> Margot Adler(reporter): In fact, most of the kids who were getting into trouble had poor communication skills, poor problem-solving skills, and above all, had poor impulse control.
>
> Goleman: The trajectory of impulse . . . puts you in prison, essentially, in this culture, if you're a boy. If you're a girl — impulsive girls don't get violent, they get pregnant. (ibid.)

Their discussion reveals a distinct portrait of the conceptual model underlying some individualized social development programs. "Impulse control" portrays the individual as an organism ruled by impulses, or instincts. Rooted in developmental and cognitive psychologies, the discourse of impulses reflects the idea that one's emotions are hard-wired through evolutionary and neurophysiological features of the brain. However, we are expected — as part of the "normal" developmental process — to exert our individual control over these biological impulses. For those who don't seem to develop "normally" we can teach the skills of impulse control.

As Adler reiterates after Goleman, the program "doesn't teach values and attitudes, it imparts *skills*" (emphasis added). As discussed in the previous chapter, the individual as conceived here is born "naturally predesigned to acquire social skills." "Skills" fits both the scientific and neoliberal cultural portrait of the autonomous organism or individual chooser. In the contemporary market-driven climate of high unemployment, it is difficult to argue against the development of skills: Skills are what give you jobs. As *Time* magazine states, "IQ may get you hired but EQ gets you promoted."[24]

The universalized portrait of the individual as a bundle of impulses allows for an extraordinary decontextualization of actions, events, and choices. This decontextualization is especially marked when Goleman says "The trajectory of impulse . . . puts you in prison, essentially, in this culture, if you're a boy. If you're a girl — impulsive girls don't get violent, they get pregnant." "Impulse" is entirely decontextualized. What is an impulse? Where does it come from? Which boys are sent to prison for their "impulses"? There is an extraordinary lack of sociological analysis regarding who is sent to prison, and for what offenses. There is no discussion about why African-American and Hispanic boys are disproportionately labeled as delinquent.

Similarly, *why* do girls have unprotected sex — because they are "naturally" inclined to avoid contraception? We find no discussion of religious influences on education about contraception, or of federal and state mandates against the provision of contraceptive information for juveniles; there is no discussion of the cultural expectation that places responsibility for birth control on girls rather than on boys.

In the social competency program, "skills" or "lack of skills" are isolated within the *individual* whose aim should be virtuous industry and good habits: "Most of the kids who were getting into trouble had poor communication kills, poor problem-solving skills, and above all, had poor impulse-control." As with the mental-hygiene movement early in this century, individual children are blamed for "poor skills and impulse-control." The pervasiveness of the individualism is startling: Even communication, which, of all skills seems most obviously to occur in a social context, is portrayed as rooted solely in the individual. There is no discussion of the fact that rules of middle-class politeness may not serve the cultural context of inner-city children's material lives — not only that, to use middle-class skills of politeness in some contexts could conceivably put one at risk. Children develop survival skills that make sense within their social environment. This is not to say that violence is the only answer, but rather that the social development programs offer no analysis of how and why children have *intelligently* developed the particular social strategies they *do* have.

Caring Community Model: The Illusion of Democracy

A nonprofit organization called the Developmental Studies Center (DSC) formed in the 1980s, and their "Child Development Project" (CDP) curriculum has been adopted into dozens of schools in California, as well as in three other states. The Child Development Project includes "four major elements: cooperative learning, developmental discipline, the use of literature, and other means to highlight prosocial values and promote empathy and interpersonal understanding, and helping and other prosocial activity" (Solomon et al., 1992: 385). This program emphasizes creating a "caring community" in a classroom. The need to "create a caring community" is seen as a solution to the fact that "social changes have reduced the availability of other traditional sources of moral guidance" (Solomon et al. in Oser et al. 1992: 383). Schools are called upon to "explicitly," rather than "implicitly," "enhance children's moral development" (ibid.).[25] "[S]tudents will be learning about important values, such as fairness, respect, helpfulness, and responsibility. They'll be learning how to work together, to accept each other's differences, to play by the rules — *rules that they often have helped shape*" (DSC Brochure, 1 emphasis added). My inquiry here is: When and how are students invited to "help to shape the rules?" Representative of many educational programs, upon close examination it appears that the rules are developed by adults, and "taught" through a pedagogy of "caring" and illusory democracy.

Goleman is quoted in the DSC publicity brochure: "Some programs in emotional and social skills take no curriculum or class time as a separate subject at all, *but instead infiltrate their lessons into the very fabric of social life . . . essentially, as an invisible emotional and social competence course* (II, emphasis added). Goleman inadvertently confirms precisely what I see as the risks of such a program: Emotional and social values are taught "invisibly," the very definition of pastoral power and "engineered consent."[26]

While the CDP emphasizes students "participation" in "creating the caring community," the teacher "plays the critical role in creating a classroom that students experience as a caring community" (Solomon et al. 1992: 384). The teacher is explicitly named as the authority, not the child. The discourse of "community" thus masks the predetermined authority of the teacher or school — what some call the "illusion of democracy." I would argue that in shaping "community rules," it is entirely conceivable that young people *could* actively engage in developing rules specific to their own community needs. In one conflict resolution program that I analyze later on (RCCP), the students are explicitly told that they "were as much the bosses as anyone." The CDP model, in contrast, appears to operate as a version of subtle consent to predetermined values of "democracy." Perhaps the difference is only rhetorical. Yet one can see explicit overlap between the CDP program with the emotional management techniques used in the workplace, as discussed in the previous chapter.

> The teacher creates a climate of mutual concern and respect by showing concern for all students and by being sincerely interested in their ideas, experiences, and products. . . . Students are given the chance to see for themselves the importance of the things they are asked to do and, in many cases, are allowed to decide for themselves when or in what way they will do them. *They come to see themselves as doing these activities for their own intrinsic reasons rather than as a*

> *response to external coercion.* . . . It then becomes less necessary to entice students with the prospect of rewards or to threaten them with the fear of penalties or punishment. (1992: 384, emphasis added)

A model of what has been called "illusory democracy" in terms of a version of child-centered pedagogy is reflected in their claim: "To be prosocial, people must *understand* other people's motives, intentions, and needs; they must *want* to take appropriate actions to safeguard or improve the well-being of others; they must have the *abilities* needed to take the necessary actions; and they must then actually *perform* them in the appropriate situations" (383). How does a curriculum create this kind of internal change and adherence to norms? What methods are required to achieve the forcible directive that people "*must* understand," "*must* want" to do or feel any particular thing? Who decides what counts as "appropriate actions . . . to improve the well-being of others"?

"Prosocial development" is a modern version of educational philosophies rooted in the behavioral psychology of Edward Thorndike and B. F. Skinner, and the developmental psychology models of Piaget and Kohlberg.[27] The conception of the person is based on a universal and naturalized conception of children's development. "The teacher helps this process by creating and maintaining a setting in which children can progress, with guidance, towards increasing levels of autonomy, responsibility, and interpersonal concern" (1992: 384).

Like workplace management strategies, the caring-community model aims to teach students that they are "freely" choosing to carry out norms without imposed coercion, through a rhetoric of democracy. The rhetoric of students' "democratic participation" in establishing the norms of the classroom community offers an especially slippery model for analysis. The term "community" is used unproblematically with broad assumptions of universal values. While watching several videotapes of classroom interactions and discussions (videos prepared by the DSC as part of its teacher training), I had the strong impression that this program potentially allowed for each classroom to develop its own model of community. None of what I saw recorded on video suggested an imposition of particular values. However, as I read more closely and interviewed program developers, it was made clear that *variation* was not necessarily encouraged: The CDP program does espouse particular foundational norms for the caring community. In response to my query about this, I was told that, in fact, one finds across cultures (such as the United States and Japan) and across socioeconomic contexts (e.g., inner-city schools and private schools of wealthy areas), "very little variation" in basic values such as respect and tolerance, etc. This troubling assumption forces me to question the theoretical and ethnocentric framework underlying such a curricula.

This model does not appear to engage students in direct analysis of interethnic conflict; in analysis of broader social context; or in a genuine choice regarding their own set of guiding principles and solutions to conflict. Yet my misgivings arose only after close investigation: In fact, the appearance and rhetoric of the program are very seductive. The videotaped interactions that I watched were extremely touching: Young people negotiated their conflicts and learned to "share," which powerfully testifies to a certain "success" of such a curriculum.[28]

Social Inquiry /Conflict Resolution Models

I now analyze the Resolving Conflict Creatively Program (RCCP) and a program initiated in Australia that can be called "Taking Responsibility." The former is, clearly, a "conflict resolution" program, and the latter, while not explicitly referencing these literatures in the description I examined, also can be grouped under the umbrella of "conflict resolution."

Conflict resolution is defined significantly in terms of cooperative learning. Cooperative learning emphasizes several key features, including "positive interdependence." According to Morton Deutsch, who has been writing about conflict resolution for almost fifty years, "Students must perceive that it is to their advantage if other students learn well and that it is to their disadvantage if others do poorly" (Deutsch 1993: 510). Other features of cooperative learning include "face-to-face interaction, individual accountability, interpersonal and small group skills, and learning to process and analyze the dynamics of their learning groups" (ibid.). In describing the role of emotions in conflict resolution training, Deutsch addresses emotions in the following terms: Students should become

> aware of the causes and consequences of violence and of the alternatives to violence, even when you are very angry. Become realistically aware of . . . how many young people die from violence, the role of weapons in leading to violence, how frequently homicides are precipitated by arguments, and how alcohol and drugs contribute to violence. Become aware of what makes you very angry: Learn the healthy and unhealthy ways you have of expressing anger (1993: 512).

According to Deutsch and Coleman's recent study (1998), very little research has been done on the use of conflict resolution introduced to address interethnic conflicts. However, two key aspects of conflict resolution speak directly to my inquiries regarding analysis of cultural context. First, conflict resolution centrally recognizes that individuals are not isolated beings but rather live in interdependent ways. Second, it fosters *cooperative learning*, learning to understand oneself in relation to others. These seem valuable emphases for inquiry into cultural and political contexts and differences. However, the discourse on emotions invoked in the above quote poses a model of "healthy" vs. "unhealthy" emotions. Thus we still face the question: Who decides what counts as healthy? Further, there is still the risk that what is called for in relation to emotions is primarily self-control. However, in the examples I describe below, students seem to be engaged in a genuine search for their own "creative" resolutions to conflict.

Resolving Conflict Creatively Program

The Resolving Conflict Creatively Program represents one of the most widely adopted, and in many circles well-thought-of, curricula program using emotional literacy across the United States.[29] My observations and research indicate that this program offers promising potential as a curricula that allows students to think creatively and to consider the broadest possible social context and interpretations of emotions. Nonetheless, through no inherent internal flaw to the curriculum, RCCP or any other conflict resolution-type program still risks being "co-opted" or practiced without addressing cultural norms and contexts.

RCCP was founded in 1985, sponsored by the Board of Education in New York City and by the New York chapter of Educators for Social Responsibility. The program began based in three Brooklyn schools, and now has been adopted in nine states for a total of 360 schools serving at least 150,000 students. The RCCP National Center was opened after the shooting of a principal killed when attempting to intervene in a student conflict in 1992. I had the opportunity to observe the curriculum being taught in the school in which RCCP was first introduced; RCCP had been part of the school community for five years.

Approaching the front entrance to the school is a large, colorful, and collectively painted mural that honors the memory of Principal Daly. The mural depicts the principal as a spirit who is present, within a multicultural environment of different children united by their commitment to nonviolence. Inside the school, all of the corridors showcased hand-painted butcher paper drawings and mottoes about respect and nonviolence; art exhibits related to peace and conflict resolution; and in one corridor, stories written by several classes about the best world for girls and women, as it was Women's History

Month. The work produced by students which hung on the walls was moving, creative, and inspiring, and though the theme was "nonviolence," the students' expressions reflected quite diverse interpretations of their vision of an ideal world.[30]

Based on what they call the "Peaceable Schools Model," RCCP emphasizes "preventing violence and creating caring and peaceable communities of learning . . . making a significant contribution to the social and emotional development of young people, showing them that they have many choices other than passivity and aggression for dealing with conflict" (RCCP statement).

The largest such curriculum program in the U.S., RCCP operated with a $2 million budget in 1992–93 in New York City and is now used in over 360 schools nationwide in eleven school districts. RCCP co-founder and director Linda Lantieri has recently coauthored a book with Janet Patti titled *Waging Peace in Our Schools* (1996). Although the RCCP curricula used the language of emotional intelligence in their own right prior to Goleman's popularity, *Waging Peace in Our Schools* is introduced within the context of Goleman's work.

The RCCP curriculum, like the other programs I observed, is classified as a "skills-based program," and the "development and promotion of social responsibility is an expected outcome. We hope to inspire everyone to play an activist role in shaping our society's future" (*Educational Leadership*, September 1996: 29). However, it is the emphasis on "responsibility" rather than "development" or "social competence" that distinguishes conflict resolution from more individualized programs.

RCCP emphasizes empowering young people to develop creative solutions to a range of social problems. RCCP is one of the few programs I observed which consistently reiterates cultural diversity and "interrupting bias." RCCP describes its goals to include:

- reducing violence and increase intercultural understanding;
- transforming the culture of participating schools so they model values and principles of creative, nonviolent conflict resolution and respect for diversity. (Handout A)

"Emotional literacy" is understood as one aspect of a broader project: teaching young people how to identify creative, alternative responses to violence. RCCP does not prescribe an exhaustive list of "correct" or "possible" solutions to conflict. As the name suggests, there is a genuine emphasis on resolving conflicts "creatively"— students are expected to think through these solutions as best meets the needs of particular situations. "Emotional literacy" is one of the lesson plans or tools taught as part of this larger process.

The "Peaceable Schools Model" that underlies RCCP is introduced to all members of the school's community, through a K–12 curriculum, professional development for teachers, student-led mediation, administrative training, and parent education. The curriculum

> focuses on teaching . . . active listening, empathy and perspective taking, cooperation, negotiation, the expression of feelings in appropriate ways, and assertiveness (as opposed to aggressiveness or passivity). Classroom lessons include role-playing, interviewing, group discussion, brainstorming, and 'teachable' moments that arise from classroom situations or world events. We also help students appreciate cultural diversity and show them ways of countering bias" (Lantieri with Patti 1996: 30).

Here my analysis becomes more difficult. Like other programs, RCCP's use of emotional literacy uses such language as "teaching . . . expression of feelings in appropriate ways." Who gets to decide what counts as appropriate? Like other "skills-oriented" programs teaching emotional literacy, RCCP teaches students to identify a range of emotions; to recognize emotions expressed by others, especially through their facial expressions, tone of voice, and body language; to "control impulsive reactions," and instead consider alternative, nonviolent response options when faced with conflict.

In the earlier sections of this chapter, I discussed an example described by Linda Lantieri in which she, as the teacher, had used a "teachable" moment of emotions to analyze racial conflict and difference. I have no way to estimate how often such productive analyses occur in RCCP lessons. In my own observations of RCCP in the classroom, I had three strong impressions. First, that the emphasis on conflict resolution is a framework that potentially—but not assuredly — invites analysis of emotions within cultural contexts. Second, I observed students engaging in sophisticated analyses of emotions. Yet, third, I was aware that the sophistication of the emotional literacy lesson I witnessed was in no small part due to the skill of the particular teacher I was observing. I observed that even highly skilled teachers easily slip into arbitrary assertions of their own emotional rules and values. In the course of a forty-minute lesson, this exceptionally skilled teacher also evidenced at one point what I felt to be an arbitrary assertion of an "emotional rule" which gave me pause. I imagined myself in her shoes: I, too, as any teacher, would be inclined at certain junctures to state my own idiosyncratic values regarding appropriate emotional conduct.

In this class exercise each student was asked to mark on a scale on the board how they felt at the moment, from –5 to +5. One girl walks up and puts her marker at -3. The class expresses surprise at her level of "not feeling good." The teacher points out, "We may not *see* how someone is feeling," meaning feelings are not always visible through body language or facial expression. The next girl ranks herself at –5 (and indeed in my estimation "looked" very sad). The teacher responds to this, "What do we need to know, class?" Before any student had opportunity to respond, and without asking the girl herself what she needed or wanted, the teacher answered her own question: "We want to give her space rather than tease her." It seemed to me that "what the class needed to know" was what the young girl herself wanted in response to her distress. The teacher's quick conclusion about how to react to the unhappy student is a fairly minor example of setting an arbitrary norm, which might have adverse effect on the girl. But one can easily imagine other examples of arbitrary impositions of the educator's authority with much harsher effects on students.

Again, we need research evaluating students' perspectives regarding their experience of different programs. My next comments should not be taken as a point of comparison to other programs discussed in this chapter, because it was only in RCCP that I had a chance to hear directly from students about their perceptions of the program. I observed and participated in a meeting between eight children from third to sixth grade who had been trained as peer mediators, and adults including the curricula developer, the RCCP "guidance counselor" (a trained employee funded by RCCP to work with the school community), and other adult visitors. These students were remarkably articulate about their interpretation of the RCCP principles. Each student had developed relatively varied interpretations of the RCCP philosophy and had very different stories to tell of their experiences. They expressed sophisticated understandings of the wider social context of violence that faced their communities. With respect to RCCP, they reported extremely positively on their perceptions of the changes the practices and skills had made not only in school interactions but in some instances at home and on the street.

Also striking were the questions they posed to the founders of RCCP who were present that day. One student asked: "Who is the boss of RCCP?" The child then turned to the white man in the group of visiting adults. "He's the boss?" the child demanded. Linda Lantieri replied, "You're the boss as much as anybody," elaborating that there are people helping but nobody being ordered around. After a bit more discussion, the student who had the asked original question "Who's the boss?" rephrased his question another way: "Who wrote the book?" They accurately perceived the book as issuing from a source of authority which was quite different than their authority as peer mediators.

The young children's "savvy" was clearly revealed in this discussion. The adults stated that, in this meeting, the young people were invited to ask questions of the adults. One young person said, "I want the adults to tell us how RCCP has changed *your* lives." Their insightful demand for accountability stood out as a unique questioning of authority. The students were well aware that, on some level, this was a curriculum designed by others and imposed on them; that in the end, someone had power over them to evaluate their performance, as later another young person asked, "Do you get fired in RCCP?" Provided space to interrogate the structure of the program they were involved in, this event was a striking contrast from a program emphasizing a hidden curriculum of "democratic" values.

Australian Programs: Social Context Frameworks

Another program that recognizes emotional expressions and literacy as part of a nexus of social relations is demonstrated in a report by Alice Morgan called "Taking Responsibility: Working with Teasing and Bullying in Schools" (1995).[31] Morgan's work with young girls represents an exceptionally creative approach to "social responsibility." In Australia and in New Zealand, discourses revolve primarily around the phenomenon of "bullying and teasing" rather than school violence.

While not yet a systematized curriculum program, Morgan's description of her work represents an increasing discourse within Australian curriculum programs: "taking responsibility." Frustrated with the psychological, individualistic model reflected in existing frameworks developed to address bullying and teasing, Morgan turned to Alan Jenkins's *Invitations to Responsibility* (1990). Jenkins has developed programs and written about men taking responsibility. Morgan reports that her work is inspired by Alan Jenkins's book; and by a recent film, titled *The Color of Fear* (Stir Fry Productions, 1994), on racism and emotion.

Of seeing this film, Morgan writes "The abusive use of power by the dominant group, and their inability to see the consequences of their actions, reminded me very much of the perpetrators of bullying and teasing"(1995: 19). She decides to work with groups of "perpetrators" in the schools. Her sessions are conversations with the girls about their behavior. Impressive throughout Morgan's description are her questions which genuinely ask for the girls' ideas and reflections rather than imposing a moral code. The discourse of "responsibility" she uses is based on the assumption that "only the abusive person can change his/her beliefs and behaviors" (20) (which might be read as another version of "I am in control of me)."

As a Junior School Counselor Morgan held ongoing group meetings with girls 8–10 years old who were "perpetrators" of teasing. At the first sessions, the group brainstormed definitions of teasing. The girls began to discuss their own behavior. Through the course of these meetings, Morgan replies to their discussion and disclosures by posing such questions as: "How does it affect you to talk about your teasing like this" (20)? "How do you think teachers could be involved in this project, talking about teasing" (22)? "I asked them if [teacher] 'policing' was a good or bad thing. They thought it was bad for many reasons" (21). Morgan says there were times she asked herself, "Am I putting words in their mouths?" In response to her self-reflection, she would sometimes say, for example, "When you said 'courage' before, is that because I said it or because you really thought it? Is there a word that would suit you better? How would I know if you answered a question and it wasn't what you really thought" (27)?

Morgan's approach represents the potential of social inquiry: Rather than imposing or teaching a program either "insidiously" or from the top down it is indeed possible to engage the students themselves in an analysis of the dynamics of the teacher-student relation; the significance and interpretation of words and meanings; and the relevance of the approaches to the students' own perceptions.

CONCLUSION

THESE CURRICULA represent a Pandora's box. First, they reflect the tension with which I opened: Any one of these skills may be taught in a way that either invites analysis of social and cultural context, or instead closes down discussion and teaches a skill in purely individualistic terms. The majority, if not all, of the classroom instances I observed engaged discussion of emotions without attention to political and cultural differences or analyses. Very few of the readings or literature in this area analyze social conflict in terms of social injustice and how emotional rules are embedded in power relations.

Second, any one of these skills can function both as a creative expansion and opportunity for growth, and/or as a way to "blame the individual" for lacking appropriate skills. This follows from the earlier statements: Because I find so few examples of emotions analyzed within their wider cultural context, I must conclude that students by and large are learning to perceive "pragmatic" and "utilitarian," if not downright prescriptive, rules regarding emotional behavior.

Third, how are we to ensure the quality with which any such curriculum is taught? Teachers' relationship to the material varies tremendously; teachers are often given very little, if any, training or follow-up; not to mention, teachers already have their own ways of "educating emotions," and, teachers' own sense of expertise may be offended by imposing on them a new curriculum. In short, a great deal of "harm" and imposition can conceivably occur in the course of an apparently benign or well-meaning emotional literacy lesson.

Fourth, although I would argue that every curriculum developer or institute is entirely well-meaning, and every program has some "good" that comes out of it, how such programs are in fact institutionalized, and for what ends, is a real and crucial question. For example, a program that wants to develop students' capacity for critical inquiry may in fact be used by a school to enforce forms of self-control that are simply a version of behavioral modification and enforced peer policing.

Despite these risks, I still celebrate the emergence of explicit curricula in emotional literacy. I believe we owe it to students and to teachers to be explicit about what values we are teaching and to create opportunities for collective self-reflection and evaluation of emotional rules and conduct which are inevitably a part of school curricula.

I am grateful to Myra Hird and Jane Abraham for their comments on this chapter.

1 Bosshart, *Harvard Educational Review*, (1939: 455).
2 Goleman lists eight "basic emotions": anger, sadness, fear, enjoyment, love, surprise, disgust, shame (1995: 289–90).
3 The list brainstormed by these 10- to 12-year-old children included: "lonely, sad, the best, down, disappointed, glad, mad, happy, excited, angry, discouraged, terrible, scared, petrified, frightened, nervous, hungry, despair, hopeless,upset, unhappy, lovely, friendly, shy."
4 See my discussion in previous chapter.
5 See for example, "The Mediation of Interethnic Conflict in Schools," by Peter Coleman and Morton Deutsch (1998).
6 See Beane (1990) for a synopsis of "affective education."
7 From a conversation, February 1998. See also Roderick (1987–88).
8 Lesko (1996) offers an invaluable analysis of conceptions of adolescence, and how discourses of psychology have created the "adolescent-as-primitive." She utilizes postcolonial discourses and arguments against linear time/models of progress and development to chart the shifting discursive social control of adolescence. It would be valuable to do a full reading of her approach in relation to the conceptions of youth within emotional literacy curricula.
9 In the United States, the corporate sense of crises and care is prevalent, as exemplified by these titles from two corporate philanthropic foundations that fund emotional literacy programs: "Losing American Youth to Violence" (Mott Foundation,

1994); the Prudential Granting agency opens its annual report: "Prudential cares about the vitality of our communities. We demonstrate this concern by supporting innovative nonprofit organizations that help improve the quality of life—especially for our children" Annual Report (1995: 4).

10 "Promising Initiatives for Addressing School Violence" (General Accounting Office 1995).

11 Newspaper features headline stories such as: "Schools Try Conflict Resolution to Help Students Stay Focused on Facts, Not Fights" (*Christian Science Monitor*, 21 October 1996).

12 As Jane Abraham pointed out to me, the "cost efficiency" rationale is sometimes an argument pragmatically used to acquire funding. Yet to invoke "cost efficiency" for utilitarian reasons doesn't mean that this invocation doesn't reflect the "real" material interests of a capitalist society. In other words, "caring for children" needs to be analyzed in greater depth.

13 See Peters and Marshall (1996) for valuable analyses of neoliberalism and education. See also Apple (1993).

14 See chapter 10, "Managing with Heart" (Goleman 1995). "The cost effectiveness of emotional intelligence is a relatively new idea for business, one some managers may find hard to accept" (149). Goleman details how overemotional employees disrupt working groups; how getting into a "flow state" while working or being an empathetically "attuned" workers benefit the company and public service sector; and how "[l]eadership is not domination, but the art of persuading people to work towards a common goal" (ibid.).

15 The Montreal Massacre refers to an incident which occurred in Canada (1989) in which a man took open fire and murdered fourteen female graduate students at Montreal's École Polytechnique.

16 Two excellent examples of analyses of gender and sexuality in sex education include Michelle Fine (1993) and Cris Mayo (1998).

17 Congressional "concern for student safety and school security" resulted, after extensive hearings, in the passing of "two bills explicitly targeting schools violence." One is the "Safe Schools Act of 1994, which authorizes the secretary of education to make grants to local school districts with high rates of youth violence" (U.S. General Accounting Office Report on School Safety 1995: 3). A total of $20 million was granted to this program in 1994. A second bill in 1994 is the "Safe and Drug-Free Schools and Communities Act" similar to the above bill but additionally targeted to "deter the use of illegal drugs and alcohol." These funds could be used for "violence prevention and education programs . . . [involving as well] parents and coordination with community groups and agencies." In 1995, $482 million was appropriated to fund such programs. A third act was passed by Congress in 1994, the "Family and Community Endeavor Schools Act and the Community Schools Youth Services and Supervision Grant Program," the former receiving $11 million and the latter $26 million (GAO 1995).

18 However, there appears to be no simple correlation between a particular type of emotional literacy program adopted and particular school problems. One might expect that conflict resolution programs would be adopted into schools facing the more severe forms of violence, while "social development" models would serve the middle-class privileged and private school settings. In schools impacted by high rates of violence, one finds the Resolving Conflict Creatively Program. But one school suffering similar issues has adopted a quite different program, titled "Project Charlie," a social development program targeting poor youth in New Haven, which does not emphasize conflict resolution. In one wealthy private school, a program has been developed and used for over twenty years called "Self-Science." Like RCCP, "Self-Science" uses the basic emotional literacy model and uses the language of conflict resolution, but the issues faced at this school are not

violence and teen pregnancy but developing self-esteem and group- and self-awareness. In other regional contexts, an overriding discourse is to boost self-esteem: "Running on Esteem Power," reads a *Santa Cruz Sentinel* article reporting on the California Task Force to Promote Self-Esteem and Personal and Social Responsibility. Similarly in Chicago: "Chicago School Program Boosts Self-Esteem" (1990).

19 National Public Radio *All Things Considered* (10 December 1995)

20 In Goleman's appendix he summarizes several programs and indicates which have been evaluated and whether this includes student evaluation. More generally, here I reiterate my appreciate of the work of such sociologists as Michelle Fine and Lois Weis and many others who make considered attempt in their work to "foreground" youth voices. I am involved in a three-year research program based in New Zealand, developed in collaboration with principal investigator Dr. Linda Smith, to examine what young people say about their schooling experience. This project culminates in a series of "Public Tribunals" which will allow young people to "testify" about their concerns regarding schooling.

21 I am not addressing two programs which I observed in the United States. The two I observed which are not discussed are the "Self-Science Program", and the "I Can Problem-Solve." I would classify both of these under the individual/developmental umbrella.

22 Goleman, "Managing Your Feelings 101," *New York Times*, 7 November 1993, Section 4a: I.

23 For further description and analyses of this program, see also Elias and Weissberg (1990); Caplan et al. (1992).

24 This educational debate is exemplified in the opposing philosophies of U.S. turn-of-the-century educators Booker T. Washington and W. E. B. Du Bois. Washington argues for industrial education while Du Bois argues for a liberal arts education. Industrialism represented an accomodationist stance, a willingness to accept status as a second-class citizen, a desire for the immediate reward of jobs and proving that newly freed slaves could contribute to the American economy. While arguing for liberal arts education was an argument for the healing of wounds, Du Bois also advocated the ability for black and white men to work together to create a better civilization. See Du Bois (1903) and Washington (1901); also Aptheker (1973, 1974); Giddings (1984).

25 This model has ancient roots: Aristotle's autocratic vision of education as an institution designed to ensure that citizens develop the "right" values in service of the state is but one example.

26 "Engineered consent" is a term used by such historians as Graebner (1987), traced back to the work of Walter Lippmann ([1922] 1977) and used as well by Herman and Chomsky (1994) and Neil Postman (1988) to describe the functioning of the state through mass media and education.

27 These conceptual underpinnings are reflected explicitly in the scholarly discussions published by Solomon et al. The DSC "prosocial development" includes "four domains: cognitive characteristics; affective, motivational, and attitudinal characteristics; behavioral competencies; and action tendencies" (1992: 383). This program thus envisions shaping of the self through cognitive, affective, and behavioral modification. "[T]eachers foster children's prosocial development by creating classroom and school environments that meet the children's *basic psychological needs*" (1992: 385, emphasis added). Such "basic psychological needs" are not delineated or discussed in terms of cross-cultural variation.

28 One can perhaps empathize with how hard I have struggled in my attempts to analyze these programs: The realm of emotions and interpersonal negotiation are complex and not simple to evaluate. Again, I stress that my critique is of the underlying discourses and not the people who are working to improve young people's

lives. My research could not fully investigate student's perceptions of the curricula, a perspective that should be foregrounded.

29 Evaluative studies of RCCP do show positive evaluations by teachers and administrators; and, a remarkable drop in violent incidents within schools environments. For example, during one year, five schools using RCCP were evaluated, and student mediators intervened in a total of 107 incidents in which arguments were prevented from escalating into fights (*New York Times*, 3 March 1992).

30 I describe these corridors because, in the course of my research, I observed numerous schools, and this particular school was, frankly, astounding in the sense of "ethos" and community participation. I believe that what I saw reflects the unique history of this particular public school, having adopted RCCP in a very consistent manner throughout the community of teachers, students, and parents over the last five years. Any "social program" might have such an effect; research shows that program effectiveness depends on being adopted throughout the community, from the principal to the parents, teachers to students. This begs the question of whether certain programs — e.g., those which invite the participant to creatively shape their own community — have greater likelihood of shaping the community ethos. Again, further research needs to be done in this area.

31 My data for this program is the essay I discuss here. Several of the people working in the area of emotional literacy in Australia spoke highly of Morgan's work, and of the work of Alan Jenkins.

CHAPTER FIVE

A FEMINIST POLITICS OF EMOTION

. . . the politic of consciousness-raising has earned a bad name precisely because it is a profoundly effective practice.

—Magda Lewis[1]

A few women's studies programs seem to be serious academic programs, interested in ideas, evidence, debate, and an open search for truth. But most aren't. Most are part therapy group and part training ground for feminist cadres to fight the patriarchy.

—*U.S. News and World Report* June 13, 1998

Dogmatic Marxists have regarded consciousness as a mere reflection of material conditions and therefore uninteresting as an object for study in and of itself. Even Marxists of a more humane cast of mind have not paid sufficient attention to the ways in which the social and economic tensions they study are played out in the lives of concrete individuals.

—Sandra Bartky[2]

HOW DO WE BEGIN to account for emotions as a site of political resistance? Thus far in this book I have examined emotions primarily as a site of social control. The practices of consciousness-raising and feminist pedagogy, which emerge as part of the second wave of feminism in the United States during the early 1970s, represent a historical turning point in the history of emotions and education. Radical feminists developed the first collectively articulated, politicized analysis of emotions as the basis for challenging gendered oppression.

My purpose is not to advocate feminist pedagogy and consciousness-raising as, necessarily, the ultimate liberatory pedagogies. However, in addition to representing a historical shift, I fear these significant feminist contributions are under threat of erasure. By and large, contemporary educational theories tend to distance themselves, ignore, or denigrate these radical feminist practices. In contrast to some authors, I perceive that critical pedagogy and Paolo Freire's work are more frequently referenced in contemporary feminist educational theory than are practices of consciousness-raising and feminist pedagogy. Are feminists contributing to their own erasure? The erasure of feminist theories and practices in such areas as critical theory and cultural studies is consistent and alarming. Again, while consciousness-raising and feminist pedagogies may have distinct shortcomings, they represent a radical turning point in the theorization of emotions as a site of political resistance and the transformation of gendered consciousness.

In this chapter I begin with an introduction to the risks of invoking a feminist politics of emotion. I then summarize how radical feminists emphasize emotions as a site of political resistance and transformation of gendered oppressions. I analyze how feminist pedagogies incorporate the politics of difference into their work. I then turn to explore the forms of erasure, dismissal, and reappropriation of consciousness-raising and feminist pedagogies. This denigration is rooted in the deep-seated bias against feminisms and emotions within higher education and scholarly work. Contrary to accusations, these invocations of "feelings" are not "acritical." I argue that the deceptive opposition between a pedagogy that either *invites expression of feelings* or *engages in intellectual rigor* signals not a shortcoming within consciousness-raising practices. Rather, this indicates how deeply the oppositions between feeling and intellect are built into Western paradigms and language that shape educational work and scholarship. Finally, I examine contemporary feminist educational theories and the absence of sustained analyses of emotions. I conclude by suggesting how contemporary feminist philosophies and theories might cross-fertilize with feminist poststructural educational theory to develop pedagogies that recognize feminist politics of emotion.

THE RISKY INVOCATION OF EMOTIONS

IN HIGHER EDUCATION and scholarship, to address emotions is risky business — especially for feminists and others already marginalized within the hierarchy of the academy. The privileging of reason and truth prevails and is manifest in differential funding status and reputations. In this hierarchy, emotions are culturally associated with femininity, "soft" scholarship, pollution of truth, and bias. Within the hallowed halls, and within a climate that rapidly eliminates arts and humanities while science funding increases, feminist scholars in particular risk being denied tenure, at worst, as well as earning the reputation as one of the "touchy-feelie" types.

A recent op-ed exemplifies a conservative reactionary attack on a curriculum project which will soon be introduced at the University of Massachusetts. Journalist John Leo of the *U.S. News & World Report* condemned this feminist program in a column written on June 13, 1998.[3] According to Leo, "Vision 2000" would require that "every academic department . . . hold an annual seminar on gender issues, and gender studies would be introduced into all pertinent programs of institutional research."[4] He voices his alarm, which summarizes a mixture of misconception, truths, and attacks on feminist pedagogies:

> The apparently innocent term "women-friendly" pedagogies might be enough to revamp the campuses all by itself. At colleges and law schools around the country, some feminists have argued that abstract argument, debating, logic, grading . . . are all male techniques that many women resent. In this view, "female knowledge" depends heavily on personal experience, feelings and cooperation, rather than competition or striving for excellence. . . .
>
> A few women's studies programs seem to be serious academic programs, interested in ideas, evidence, debate, and an open search for truth. But most aren't. Most are part therapy group and part training ground for feminist cadres to fight the patriarchy.

This kind of conservative attack on feminist work (however one evaluates the curriculum program of Vision 2000) powerfully infuses the climate of education and scholarship surrounding feminisms and pedagogies. Not long ago a male, tenured colleague interested in philosophy of education and emotion defended himself to me stating, "I'm not saying we should hold hands in the classroom and sway." In another recent conversation with colleagues who teach women's studies, they expressed their sense of a binary trap: They see the women's studies classroom *either* as a needed "therapy" session for blossoming feminists who have nowhere else to vent their feelings, *or* as a place for critical and intellectually rigorous study of the text. Feeling pressed by this either/or, both women noted that they feel more comfortable with the project of intellectual rigor.

I suggest that we are trapped by this deceptive sense of either/or. A pedagogy that recognizes emotions as central to the domains of cognition and morality need not preclude intellectual rigor or critical inquiry. The radical feminist practices of consciousness-raising and feminist pedagogy have been misconstrued as the uncritical sharing of "feelings," class time spent as "navel-gazing group therapy" in which students sit around and share their feelings to try to feel good about themselves, or gripe about their victimization. At the same time, Joan Scott's admonition regarding the invocation of experience poses a genuine challenge in classroom pedagogies. Scott writes:

> When the evidence offered is the evidence of "experience," the claim for referentiality is further buttressed — what could be truer, after all, than a subject's own account of what he or she has lived through? It is precisely this kind of appeal to experience as uncontestable evidence and as an originary point of explanation . . . that weakens the critical thrust of histories of difference. (Scott 1991: 777)

Granted, to develop pedagogies that effectively invite emotions into discussion as well as develop critical inquiry is not an easy task. Educators who invite students' experiences into classroom discussion face challenges: How do we challenge one another's claims to experience? In the era of identity politics, how can we respect differences as well as develop collective and self-reflective skills of critical inquiry regarding the nature of our experiences and claims to truth? Does the invocation of experience and feelings necessarily lead to essentialist claims? In the last section of this chapter, I examine these challenges.

A second, often-expressed concern is that consciousness-raising doesn't lead to political change or action. It is crucial to recognize that consciousness-raising was originally conceived as the basis for political action. If it does not lead to "action" in its subsequent adopted practices, this does not necessarily represent an endemic failing in the theory of consciousness-raising. Second, I would challenge educators to outline a pedagogy that *does* lead to *certain* transformation or action. Elizabeth Ellsworth's essay on developing an antiracist agenda raises this thorny question. Elsewhere, I explore the limits of institutionalized education as a site of political action.[5]

I examine these accusations in greater depth in a subsequent section of this chapter, but I want to signal my argument that these criticisms of feminist pedagogy and consciousness-raising often represent a form of misogynist backlash and meta-level fears of emotion bred within higher education. To evidence what I see as the possibly unfounded "bad reputation" of feminist contributions, I ask that we consider: Why is it that Paolo Freire's work is never accused of "embracing feelings uncritically?" To the contrary, Freire's methods of conscientizaçion are widely embraced as liberatory and sound, and much more frequently heroized than is consciousness-raising. Is this because Freire's methods are in fact more effective, by some measure? Is it because Freire's focus is not feelings and emotions as a central site of lived experience, and therefore he does not get accused of being "touchy-feelie"? Is it because Freire isn't a feminist, and doesn't analyze gender, and therefore does not get marginalized through stereotypical association with "soft" feminist scholarship? I believe it would be instructive to do an exhaustive research project comparing the use of Freire's methods and feminist methods to (a) document if Freire's methods are more effective than consciousness-raising in creating liberatory transformation (of course, how does one measure the "effectiveness"?); (b) identify instances in which feminist methods are used but not called "feminist"; (c) estimate the conceptual and strategic overlap in the two pedagogies; and (d) to see if one is more effective with some students than another. However, as this is beyond the scope of my work here, in this chapter I enumerate examples of the erasure and denigration of feminist strategies which, I argue, do not reflect an inherent problem with consciousness-raising and feminist pedagogy but rather reflect the powerful biases against feminism and invocation of "feeling."

DEFINITION OF FEMINIST POLITICS OF EMOTION

SANDRA BARTKY OPENS her invaluable study of "Phenomenology of Feminist Consciousness" (first published in 1976, in the midst of the second wave of feminism) by noting that

> Dogmatic Marxists have regarded consciousness as a mere reflection of material conditions and therefore uninteresting as an object for study in and of itself. Even Marxists of a more humane cast of mind have not paid sufficient attention to the ways in which the social and economic tensions they study are played out in the lives of concrete individuals. There is an anguished consciousness, an inner uncertainty and confusion which characterizes human subjectivity in periods of social change — and I shall contend that feminist consciousness, in large measure, is an anguished consciousness — of whose existence Marxist scholars seem largely unaware. (1990: 14)

The theme of "anguished consciousness" as indicative of the difficult paths to "freedom" is emphasized as well in the work of educational philosopher Maxine Greene. In an uncanny overlap, in nearly the same year as Bartky's writing Greene writes "anguish is the way freedom reveals itself" (1973: 279).

I argue that feminist theories and practices "step up" to this difficult question of how material and economic oppression reveal themselves in our daily lives and consciousness. What I call the 'feminist politics of emotion' is a theory and practice that invites women to articulate and publicly name their emotions, and to critically and collectively analyze these emotions not as "natural," "private" occurrences but rather as reflecting learned hierarchies and gendered roles. The feminist practices of consciousness-raising and feminist pedagogy powerfully reclaim emotions out of the (patriarchally enforced) private sphere and put emotions on the political and public map. Feminist politics of emotions recognize emotions not only as a site of social control, but of political resistance.

A BRIEF HISTORY OF CONSCIOUSNESS-RAISING

NUMEROUS POLITICAL movements have used consciousness-raising and a politicized discourse of emotions. During the U.S. civil rights movement of the 1960s the concept of "Black Pride" characterized a catalyzing emotion within the civil rights discourse. More recently, the lesbian and gay movement invokes similar discourses of pride. For the second wave of feminism that followed on the heels of the civil rights movement, consciousness-raising arguably represented the central strategy. In an often-quoted statement, Catherine MacKinnon writes in 1983: "'Feminist method is consciousness-raising'" (quoted in Lewis 1992: 177). In what follows I emphasize aspects of this history which evidence consciousness-raising and feminist pedagogy as a revolutionary shift in the articulation of politically transformative emotions.

In the late 1960s and early 1970s in the United States, women who had been involved with the civil rights and New Left movements began a grassroots movement of their own. Frequently, women were denied leadership positions within the civil rights and New Left movements and instead assigned to make coffee and mimeograph fliers while men planned strategies and headed the public debates. Many women were frustrated with the lack of gender analysis or concern with sexism. With the exception of the work of such thinkers as Engels, Marxism tended to privilege the politics of class oppression and generally failed to account for women's childbearing and housework in its analysis of how capitalism creates surplus profit through the exploitation of labor.[6] The left movements generally reinscribed traditional patriarchal distinctions of public and private, and perpetuated a definition of the "political" as the economic, public, and legislative realms occupied by men.

Radical feminism's challenge to the gendered spheres of "public vs. private" has forever changed Western thought, culture, and legislative, judicial, and political paradigms. The material changes that have occurred as a result of women's organized anger channeled into collective political action are innumerable: movements against violence against women — Take Back the Night marches; the demand for state and federal funding for battered women's shelters; major legislative gains such as *Roe* v. *Wade* (the right to legal abortion); legislation against domestic violence; and contemporary issues surrounding sexual harassment to name but a few.

The radical feminist slogan "the personal is political" symbolized the revolutionary reconceptualization of what counts as personal (women's lives, feelings, experience, and labor) and what counts as political (e.g., men's experience and rationality as the governing structure of political and public spaces). The emphasis on women's experiences, including her feelings, as *political* and not merely personal, was a key feature of the radical feminist agenda.

Consciousness-raising emphasized women's emotions as expressions to be publicly shared and critically analyzed. Through this process women's experience was removed from its privatized and isolated experience — from "I must be crazy! I'm the only one who's angry (at being confined to the home, being paid less than men, being battered and having no police assistance to intervene)." Instead, through collective expression of this anger, for example, women realized that they weren't alone. The shared experience of anger was one identifiable sign of women's collective dissatisfaction with being treated as second-class citizens. Thus the expression of feelings was political both in naming emotions and in making them public. But equally important, these emotional expressions catalyzed demands for justice and change.

The appropriation and legitimization of consciousness-raising by left theorists is demonstrated in a 1981 essay published in *Socialist Review*, by Peter Lyman, titled "The Politics of Anger: On Silence, Ressentiment, and Political Speech."[7] Lyman's text evidences an appropriation of consciousness-raising as a "leftist" strategy for giving new language to anger, once felt as a personal pathological symptom, but redefined as political:

> Consciousness-raising is also a collective activity, not only because speaking is a social activity, but because anger becomes a political resource only when it is collective. Consciousness-raising begins with the claiming of public space and political language for what were private feelings and personal sorrows. . . . Public space is necessary to consciousness-raising in order that the process of becoming angry can be recovered by the collectivity as part of its own past. . . . The psychological symptom is transformed into a political issue in that it reflects a collective experience. (1981: 69)

In an excerpt from her essays written between 1966 and 1978, Adrienne Rich (1979) describes the importance of public naming, and of recognizing how emotions are politically constructed:

> I was looking desperately for clues, because if there were no clues then I thought I might be insane. I wrote in a notebook about this time: "Paralyzed by the sense that there exists a mesh of relationships — e.g., between my anger at the children, my sensual life, pacifism, sex (I mean sex in its broadest significance, not merely sexual desire) — an interconnectedness which, if I could see it, make it valid, would give me back myself, make it possible to function lucidly and passionately. Yet I grope in and out among these dark webs." I think I began at this point *to feel that politics was not something "out there" but something "in here"* and of the essence of my condition. (quoted in MacKinnon 1989: 88, emphasis added)

Kathie Sarachild, a central activist and leader of consciousness-raising, confirms the importance of public naming as necessary to the transformation of consciousness. "'People who are without names, who do not know themselves, who have no culture, experience a kind of paralysis of consciousness. The first step is to connect and learn to trust one another'" (Sarachild quoted in MacKinnon 1989: 87). The importance of naming the obstacles to freedom and recognizing how one might picture the world otherwise is a recurring theme not only in feminist activism but across liberatory movements and educational theories dedicated to transformation of consciousness.[8]

Consciousness-raising provided a language of emotions to the women's movement, just as feminist pedagogy in turn seeks to provide a recognition of emotions for women's education. In both cases, women's experience and emotions are recognized as central to critical inquiry and political transformation.

WOMEN'S EXPERIENCE AND EMOTIONS AS A POLITICAL SUBJECT OF FEMINIST PEDAGOGY

CONSCIOUSNESS-RAISING methods were adapted into many educational contexts, most commonly into women's studies.[9] Women's studies burgeoned in colleges and universities during the 1970s and 1980s largely as result of the women's liberation movement.[10] Many women's studies educators drew on consciousness-raising as a central method of feminist pedagogies.

Feminist pedagogies cannot be characterized as a singular approach: "feminist pedagogy has no clear and readily agreed upon connotations amongst feminist educators . . . and is not a unitary or static discourse" (Kenway and Modra 1992: 159). These authors comment further that "a diversity of voices and practices make up the project of feminist pedagogy . . .

and it exists in a wide variety of educational settings and modes" (161). It is beyond the scope of my argument to summarize the different strands of feminist pedagogy and many debates which inform these educational approaches. I focus here on the recognition of women's emotions within feminist pedagogies, which represents a major shift in Western educational theories and practices. Those utilizing feminist pedagogies recognized the process of women's naming their experience and emotions as a starting point for political transformation and challenge to gendered oppression. They also recognized that emotions inform the cognitive process and "rational" production of knowledge.

Feminist writings on education and pedagogy proliferated in the 1980s addressed in journals ranging from the *Journal of Education* to *Feminist Teacher*, and anthologized into two landmark collections, *Learning Our Way* (1983) and *Gendered Subjects* (1985). These writings reflect ongoing deliberation regarding:

- women's liberation and education's role in radical change;
- the centrality of women's experience and emotions as a source of knowledge;
- the need to develop new methods of feminist scholarship that do not replicate patriarchal binaries;
- the importance of issues of pedagogy and process as part of transforming the academy as well as women's lives.

Women's studies sought to develop practices that would "not only raise consciousness about the existence and reproduction of male domination systems but also to create women and men who are agents of social change" (Ferguson 1982: 28). Rather than simply add women into the existing curricula, many feminists intended to make radical interventions into the existing male-defined systems of knowledge production.

How were feminists to create pedagogies that would continue to transform social consciousness even within male-dominated institutions built for capitalist gain? Ferguson articulates this challenge in the opening of her essay: "College teachers who were members of the New Left in the 1960s and who went on to become members of the Women's Movement have been struggling for a number of years to incorporate our radical critique of capitalist and patriarchal structures into our teaching practices" (26).

Radical educators recognized that political change required critique of the very institutions in which educators and students found themselves. Consciousness-raising provided an entrée into understanding oppressive systems not merely as distant reality but as part of the fabric of education and the university as an institution. As a practice that emphasized experience as well as theory, consciousness-raising offered a technique that made the personal political, and challenged the "academic distancing games" (27). Ferguson argues that consciousness-raising is one of the only ways to "get students in touch with repressed feelings of alienation, fear, anger, and despair that lie at the roots of the domination structures of racism, sexism, classism, and heterosexism" (28). To the extent that education is dedicated to social transformation, the recognition of these feelings provided a necessary starting point for taking action. Quoting Lusted, Patti Lather defines pedagogy as "that which addresses 'the transformation of consciousness that takes place at the intersection of three agencies — the teacher, the learner, and the knowledge they produce together'" (Lather 1992: 121). Feminist pedagogy recognized that the transformation of consciousness requires attention to this intersection of emotional experiences, theories, and analyses of social institutions.

Possibly the earliest publication defining feminist pedagogy is Berenice Fisher's "What Is Feminist Pedagogy?"(1981) published in an issue of *Radical Teacher* devoted to feminist pedagogies. Fisher highlights the "insistence that an awareness of feelings was integral to consciousness-raising" (21). Experience, she points out, is important not only to feminist pedagogies but that "educational reform traditions," articulated by "Rousseau and Dewey to Horton and Freire" also emphasized the value of "experience because [Horton and Freire] see adults as confronting social conflicts and contradictions which press them towards action, and which raise questions to their consciousness which true education can help to answer" (ibid.). But Fisher points out that in these patriarchal philosophies, "'having an experience' is taken for granted" (ibid.). Feminist pedagogies, unlike critical pedagogies for example, recognize that for women "experience" is not a category that can be taken for granted, as their experience has been systematically discounted and dismissed. Further, for women to explore emotions contains a central contradiction: "Ironically, it is our oppression itself which provides us with . . . the highly developed capacity for feeling. . . . This capacity for feeling has been a mixed blessing — the grounds for excluding us from public life and pressing us into service as nurturers" (ibid.).

INTEGRITY OF PROCESS IN EDUCATION

MANY FEMINIST educators recognized that the emphasis on women's experience and feelings needed to be addressed not merely as a subject of knowledge, but as part of the very process of educational exchange and community. Thus one finds women's studies conscious of their own methods and process, as a means of challenging the competitive patriarchal atmosphere of higher education. Feminist pedagogy is often associated with an emphasis on trust, collaborative learning, and collective process and facilitation as bases for feminist educational work.

In 1981 Nancy Schniedewind elaborated what are now familiar components of feminist pedagogies in "Feminist Values: Guidelines for Teaching Methodology in Women's Studies." "Feminist pedagogy demands the integration of egalitarian content and process" (25). In her essay she discusses "five process goals," which she heads as:

- Development of an Atmosphere of Mutual Respect, Trust, and Community in the Classroom
- Shared Leadership
- Cooperative Structures
- Integration of Cognitive and Affective Learning
- Action

In some contrast to this portrait of feminist pedagogy, Charlotte Bunch emphasizes critical inquiry and analysis, and addresses women's experiences and feelings only minimally in her influential 1979 essay "Not by Degrees: Feminist Theory and Education." Her opening sentence reads, "[t]he development of feminist theory and a rigorous analysis of society are more important for us today than ever before. Feminists need to understand the forces working against us, as well as to analyze our experiences as a movement, if we are to survive the anti-woman backlash and survive" (1983: 248). She details the "functions of feminist theory," and while stressing that theory is never "totally 'objective'" (249), she offers a four part model for feminist theory whose features are: "describing what exists . . . Changing people's perceptions of the world through new descriptions of reality is usually a prerequisite for altering that reality" (251). Second, she say that "[a]nalyzing why that reality exists involves determining its origins and the reasons for its perpetuation" (ibid.). (It is valuable to note that this echoes a basic tenet of the aims of consciousness-raising: Women's experiences were scrutinized and analyzed in terms of the question "Who or what has an interest in maintaining our oppression as women?") Third, Bunch emphasizes:"Vision: Determining what should exist require establishing principles and setting goals" (252). Fourth, she lists "Strategy: Hypothesizing how to change what is to what should be moves directly into questions of changing reality" (253).

Feminist pedagogies contributed radical directions that still inform educational theory and practice, however infrequently these historical roots are acknowledged.[11] Consciousness-raising and feminist pedagogies viewed emotions not as "raw, unmediated data" but as a starting point for critical inquiry. To conclude with an emphasis on this critical view of emotions present in early feminist pedagogy writings, Joan Cocks's essay "Suspicious Pleasure: On Teaching Feminist Theory" (1985) offers a fair assessment of how feminist educational theories and practices reconceptualized the binary either/or of "emotion" vs. "intellectual rigor."

In her essay, Cocks confesses her pleasure in theory, and examines student resistances to "theory," as if theory were inherently patriarchal and oppressive. Empathizing with her students she notes,

> a reason divorced from desire, anger, and everything that is generally moving about the human world is bound to be derided by women, who have spent much of their time attending to emotional life.
>
> Against both the dominant culture and its feminist critics, however, it must be argued that reason and emotion are not antagonistic opposites. Because emotions are felt does not mean there is no reason in them. . . . If emotional experience has such an intimate connection to thought, there is no more subtle kind of conversation than that which analyses a particular social context, set of characters and events, in order to determine what passions were felt in a given situation and what passions were warranted or at least reasonable to feel under the circumstances. (1985: 180)

Nearly a decade later, feminist pedagogies continue to bridge the tensions between emotions and theory through the discourse of consciousness-raising. In an essay called "Diversity and Representation" (1993) Jill Dolan writes:

> The necessary expressions of rage that accompany any sojourn into difference push at the limits of academic discourse. Classrooms suddenly house consciousness-raising meetings and people who might never interact by choice find themselves sharing intimacies by chance through registration. How can feminist teachers create an atmosphere that allows the discourse of experience —which created rage — to circulate meaningfully in the discourse of academia? . . . .
>
> We moved back and forth dialectically between experience, the storm for which rage provides the eye, and theory, which too often, in feminist, academic, and popular media discourse, is used to mask, aestheticize, and contain rage. I submit, from my own position as a feminist performance theorist, that theory can offer a framework to push forward the articulation of rage. Conversely, I sub-

> mit that the excess of rage is utterly necessary to theorize diversity and feminism and representation, and that the ideological apparatus of representation might be subverted if marginalized groups harness and theorize the power of rage. (1993: 21–23)

Dolan recognizes the necessary interconnection of rage and theory within consciousness-raising focused on issues of diversity.

The centrality of the politics of difference to feminist pedagogies were addressed early on. For example, by the 1980s issues surrounding the politics of difference — issues of racism and homophobia — challenged feminist pedagogies to consider the limits of feminist conceptions: Whose political agenda was reflected in these writings and visions of political agenda? Who would and would not feel "safe" in the women's studies classroom? Who felt "invited" into the "dialogue?" These and other tensions of the politics of difference are by no means unique to feminist pedagogies, nor have these tensions been resolved by any in the fields of feminist theory, postcolonial theory, or cultural studies.

THE POLITICS OF EXPERIENCE AND DIFFERENCE

BOTH RADICAL FEMINISM and feminist pedagogies have been embraced and articulated primarily by white women. It is important to note the ways in which feminist pedagogies have been challenged to recognize the centrality of politics of difference to feminist educational projects. Alternative models of liberatory education and scholarship for women have been articulated in the influential work of such theorists as Patricia Hill Collins and bell hooks. Collins's subtitle to *Black Feminist Thought* is "Knowledge, Consciousness, and the Politics of Empowerment." She does not situate her work in relation to consciousness-raising or feminist pedagogy. Like hooks, her approach resonates more strongly with a Freirean perspective. However, both writers address the centrality of women's experiences, and emotions, in their theories.

A political movement must, of necessity, claim shared experience as the basis of a political platform. In the case of women's liberation, a shared platform of women's "oppression" and an agenda of liberation is necessary in order to make such a demand as: "All women deserve the right to control their reproductive freedom and choice." Claims to a shared agenda necessarily face the contradictory need for recognition of women's differences. Early articulations of feminist pedagogy include numerous essays addressing questions of cultural and racial difference in the classroom. Less frequently are issues of homophobia addressed in the early 1980s.

To utilize the category "women's experience" erases significant differences.[12] Historically, the women's movement reflected an ethnocentric definition of "women's experience." Debates around the politics of difference began in the 1980s, often traced to a debate between Mary Daly and Audre Lorde and the publication of *This Bridge Called My Back* (1981). Women of color and lesbian women articulated their anger and frustration with their erasure and exclusion. This history has a long legacy; the first wave of feminism and struggles for suffrage are histories fraught with white women's racism and refusal to ally themselves with black women.[13] During the second wave of feminism, the politics of difference also manifest in the exclusion of public recognition of lesbians who worked in the women's liberation movement; those who came out were often shunned and excluded from recognition and forced to silence their sexuality.[14]

The politics of difference and experience pose challenges not only to feminist pedagogy but to all feminist theories and practices. These debates continue to define the work of feminist politics and theories. The dilemmas were recognized early on by feminist educators:

- If we need to claim women's "universal oppression," for example, as a basis for a political platform, how do we do this strategically without erasing differences?
- Within classrooms, how do we invite student expressions of unique experiences, but also create a space to critically challenge students' articulation of their experiences?[15]
- "Trust" and a safe space may not be an ideal goal, or a possible one, given the significant differences within a classroom and given the power and authority differential between educator and student. Is "community" then possible within the constraints of a classroom?[16]

By the 1980s, these questions were increasingly debated and complicated by many feminist theorists, by the burgeoning publications by women of color, and by articulations of multicultural and postcolonial feminisms.[17] Developing not only a politics of difference but directly questioning some of the key assumptions of feminist pedagogies, bell hooks offers a refreshing challenge to the question of "safe space" and "trust" as educational aims. *In Talking Back: Thinking Feminist/Thinking Black* (1989), hooks addresses the dynamics and politics of education at length. She draws on both Freirean vocabulary as well as models of feminist pedagogy; one chapter is called "Toward a Revolutionary Feminist Pedagogy"; another, "On Being Black at

Yale: Education as the Practice of Freedom." Regarding "safety" hooks writes, "Unlike the stereotypical feminist model that suggests women best come to voice in an atmosphere of safety (one in which we are all going to be kind and nurturing), I encourage students to work at coming to voice in an atmosphere where they may be afraid or see themselves at risk" (53).

TENSIONS OF THEORY AND EXPERIENCE

FEMINIST PEDAGOGIES recognized tensions between theory and experience in their first articulations in the 1970s and 1980s. Contemporary discussions of consciousness-raising, feminist pedagogy, and education continue to reflect the tensions surrounding experience and politics of difference. In short, these challenges are neither unique to "feminist pedagogies" not have they gone away despite many years of feminist theorizing.[18]

The risks of an "untheorized consciousness-raising format" comes about for two key reasons previously mentioned: the difficulty of challenging another person's claim to "experience," and the related issues of identity politics. Diana Fuss addresses this insightfully in the last chapter of *Essentially Speaking* (1989): "Nowhere are the related issues of essence, identity, and experience so highly charged and so deeply politicized as they are in the classroom. Personal consciousness, individual oppressions, lived experience — in short, identity politics — operate in the classroom both to authorize and de-authorize speech" (113). If Fuss is right, that "nowhere are these issues more charged," we indeed face a challenging order, and feminist pedagogies deserve some credit for engaging the charged issues of experience rather than being dismissed as "touchy-feelie." Yet despite her recognition of the centrality of this issue, Fuss speaks of women's studies relation to experience in a tone that might be interpreted as maligning. "The category of female experience holds a particularly sacrosanct position in Women's Studies programs, programs which often draw on the very notion of a hitherto repressed and devalued female experience to form the basis of a new feminist epistemology. Virtually all of the essays in one of the few volumes devoted entirely to questions of feminist pedagogy, *Gendered Subjects: The Dynamics of Feminist Teaching*, uphold experience as the essential difference of the Women's Studies classroom" (114). The first sentence does not have the tone of a compliment; and, the next sentence offers her criticism: She decries the invocation of "female experience" which assumes a unified, knowable, stable, universal entity(114).[19]

We face again the questions: Is feminist pedagogy inherently confounded by the tensions embedded in "experience?" Or does it become the lightning rod because it dares to engage experience?

Moving on to a concrete example of how experience challenges pedagogy, Fuss articulates a challenge that no educator I know has solved to this day: the issue of the "authority of experience." Her discussion indicates two distinct problems: first, the issue of the "privileged standpoint."[20] "Does experience of oppression confer special jurisdiction over the right to speak about that oppression?" (113) Fuss examines the dynamics in which speaking of experience tends to "freeze" the discussion, because we dare not "question" the authority of one another's experience. She writes, "While I remain convinced that appeals to the authority of experience rarely advance discussion and frequently provoke confusion (I am always struck by the way in which introductions of experiential truths into classroom debates dead-end the discussion), I also remain wary of any attempts to prohibit the introduction of personal histories into such discussion on the grounds that they have yet to be adequately 'theorized'" (117).

The second problem is the question of an exclusionary position. Fuss explores the ways in which the authority of experience creates "insider" and "outsider" groups, can lead to a ranking of oppressions, and functions to exclude in a potentially unproductive manner. She quotes Edward Said to make the point that it is "dangerous and misleading to base an identity politics on . . . 'exclusions that stipulate, for instance, only women can understand feminine experience, only Jews can understand Jewish suffering, only formerly colonial subjects can understand colonial experience'" (115). Yet, a decade later, educators and feminist theorists have not resolved this tension surrounding the "authority of experience."

The most promising approach (indicated in Fuss's discussion and articulated in the writings of many educators and theorists)[21] is the need to *historicize* experience.[22] Joan Scott (1991) persuasively argues that a simplistic invocation of experience as uncontestable evidence denies us the possibility of developing histories of difference. But I believe we *can* develop strategies that don't assume experience as authoritative or inherently "real" or "true"; we can introduce analytical approaches that frame emotional experience as a "window" into ideology. I am arguing that CR and feminist pedagogies were among the first to approach this through an analysis of gendered oppression and resistance as embedded in emotions. This approach "permits the introduction of narratives of lived experience into the classroom while at the same time challenging us to examine collectively the central role social and historical practices play in shaping and producing these narratives" (Fuss 1989: 118).[23]

The entrenched binaries of experience and emotion vs. intellectual rigor and theory persist in articulations surrounding feminist pedagogy. Yet the problems associated with theorizing experience are not problems created by feminist pedagogies. Rather, to theorize experience, to "validate" women's discounted experiences and still develop critical analytical skills, is simply an extraordinarily challenging task. The "bad reputation" of consciousness-raising and feminist pedagogy, I argue, reflects the entrenched misogyny of the academy, deceptive binaries between theory and experience that continue to force feminist teachers to feel they must choose to be either a "nurturing mother" or "castrating theory-bitch."[24] The riskiest business — politically, theoretically, and practically — is to theorize and integrate both experience and theory.[25]

I conclude this summary of consciousness-raising and feminist pedagogies by reiterating that we need to right the historical record, and acknowledge that the feminist politics of emotion paved the way for radically reconceptualizing emotions in education and scholarship. Contemporary discussions of feminist poststructuralism and theories of subjectivity more often than not fail to acknowledge the historical roots of consciousness-raising and feminist pedagogies. Feminists of the 1970s and 1980s deserve credit for catalyzing a radical paradigm shift that put emotions on the political and public map as a key to social resistance.

THE ERASURE OF FEMINIST HISTORIES AND CONTRIBUTIONS

I NOW WISH TO investigate some of the reasons for and manifestations of the erasure of these feminist histories. What accounts for the "bad reputation" of consciousness-raising and feminist pedagogy? I have selected examples of criticisms of feminist pedagogy and consciousness-raising articulated by authors whose work I respect and appreciate.

The first manifestation is the criticism that consciousness-raising unproblematically embraces and celebrates women's emotions without inviting critical reflection and inquiry. A valuable issue of the journal *Women and Performance: A Journal of Feminist Theory* (1993) dedicated to "Feminist Pedagogy and Performance" reflects the currency of consciousness-raising and feminist pedagogy and confronts the challenges associated with consciousness-raising. In a particularly astute and insightful essay titled "Trinh Minh-ha's 'Difference' as a Pedagogical Metaphor," Stacy Wolf uses Trinh's essay to develop a poststructuralist conception of pedagogy. Wolf's introductory discussion lays out the promises and risks of feminist pedagogy:

"Although most women's studies professors would probably agree on the importance of providing a safe space for feminist students, I would suggest that women' studies professors are increasingly insisting on intellectual vigilance" (1993: 31). This persistent binary opposition is deeply disturbing — why are "safe space" and "intellectual vigilance" portrayed as incompatible? Yet Wolf's comments reflect real tensions, which I hear repeatedly within women's studies: "Many professors have expressed a deep suspicion of an untheorized consciousness-raising format, a rejection of identity politics, and a desire for women's studies to maintain both institutional acceptance and its decidedly alternative intellectual and political agenda" (ibid.).

In a related critique, Moira Gatens charges that the "practice of consciousness-raising . . . functioned to entrench in feminist theory the split between ideology and truth, between illusory or imaginary conditions of existence and the true or real conditions of existence" (1996: 126). In Gatens's evaluation, consciousness-raising appears to embrace women's experiences (e.g., their collective expressions of anger at women's oppression) as raw, unmediated data immune to critical inquiry regarding how ideologies shape our feelings. As I have argued throughout this chapter, I am wary of the reasons that CR is accused of being naively uncritical.

The second erasure/reappropriation is visible in the tendency amongst both critical and feminist theories of education to privilege Freire's work over consciousness-raising and feminist pedagogy.[26] In their essay titled "Feminist Pedagogy and Emancipatory Possibilities," (1992) Kenway and Modra argue

> that there is an urgent need for far more rigorous theorizing of consciousness-raising by Women's Studies practitioners than we see at present. . . . Women's Studies practitioners certainly seem to be recognizing consciousness-raising as fundamental to the need for "naming" of oppression, which Freire and other liberatory theorists rightly valorize. However, naming is not nearly enough, and for Freire it was only the beginning of his process of "conscientizaçao." . . . Consciousness-raising, though many would claim that it has been powerful and of lasting value to them, can be engaged in a way that is not articulated with action. Awareness that "the personal is political" . . . does not automatically produce appropriate programs for action. In other words, consciousness-raising can so easily become the reflection without action which Freire calls wishful thinking. On the other hand, critical consciousness facilitates analysis of the context of problem situations for the purpose of enabling people together to transform their reality, rather than merely understand it or adapt to it with less discomfort. (156)

Nearly all descriptions of consciousness-raising and feminist pedagogies express explicit commitments to action and radical social transformation, as I evidenced in the previous sections of this chapter. It thus concerns me that these feminist practices are seen as less effective than Freire's work. I am left to wonder if in part the difference is largely one "shored up" through the (masculine) qualifier of "critical" consciousness:[27] The word "critical" is critical, creating the necessary "distance" between "naive" emotions and "critical" thought, thus maintaining the boundary between the less useful and more useful gendered delineations of emotion vs. reason.

I further suggest that another key difference between Freire's work and feminist work is that, in fact, feminist practice of CR functions as a genuinely "grassroots" movement: It has no "heroized" leaders; it is used in myriad and countless contexts and educational forms and political movements. No one person claims credit for this practice, and this reflects the fundamental political "integrity" and impetus behind CR. However, in the academic world driven by competition, in which masculine discourses and values dominate, theorization is a profitable enterprise. Freire, for example, offered us a body of work (inarguably valuable), which can be credited and marketed. He also fits the cultural symbolic niche as a masculine, revolutionary "hero." (1996)[28]

One final concern about the erasure of potential overlap between critical and feminist pedagogies: Kenway and Modra comment that "feminist pedagogy has been deeply influenced by Freirean thought" (1992: 161). Yet, why is this exchange not mutual — i.e., why is it that Freirean thought does not recognize and explore how feminist pedagogies might influence the critical pedagogy perspectives?[29]

The third erasure occurs as feminist poststructural theorists of education increasingly distance themselves from feminist pedagogy and consciousness-raising. As I address further below, even within feminist critiques of the limits of "critical pedagogy," it is rare to find feminist pedagogy and consciousness-raising invoked as an important theoretical analysis or historical development.[30]

Finally, the fourth erasure that adds insult to injury is that feminist strategies such as consciousness-raising are reappropriated within critical theories of education but are not credited as having been developed within radical feminist politics. Here examples abound, and to some extent it is difficult to demonstrate reappropriation because reappropriation occurs in the form of drawing on feminist practices, for example, without crediting them — so one must read between the lines. Perhaps more to the point is the erasure and ignorance of feminist contributions altogether within contemporary critical theories of education. I offer one random example.

In their insightful introduction to the collection *Critical Literacy: Politics,*

Praxis, and the Postmodern, editors Colin Lankshear and Peter McLaren provide a valuable overview of the contemporary intersection of political praxis and the postmodern, as related to literacy education and goals of emancipation. It is striking that in this fifty-six-page introduction, feminist theory, feminist pedagogy, and consciousness-raising are not once referenced. One could say their focus is not on feminist theory or feminist education. Yet as I have argued elsewhere, feminist theories and practices (even as articulated in essays within their own volume) have significantly shaped critical and postmodern theory.[31]

I offer a few quotes from their introduction. In each case, what seems glaringly absent is a reference to how feminist theories have contributed to these analyses of oppression, and how emotions function as key site of the ideological control they seek to challenge.

The first example evidences the privileging of Freire's work and the lack of recognition of feminist consciousness-raising:

> Many common and powerful ideologies can be understood as elements of naive consciousness. . . . These include diverse forms of blame-the-victim reasoning in which agents who should be assuming responsibility for their part in the problem and/or for addressing it effectively are enabled to escape, and those who suffer the consequences of the problem either see the situation as being of their own making or inadequacy, or else assume that their condition is inevitable and must simply be endured or adapted to. (1993: 28)

One of the most common experiences of this dynamic in "real life" is in gendered relations, or colonial relations: for example, the battering husband who refuses to take responsibility and the woman who blames herself. One example of relevant feminist work overlooked is that of political philosopher Sandra Bartky, which addresses the phenomenon of "psychological domination." Bartky's work first appeared in the 1970s and was published in 1990 in a collection of her essays titled *Femininity and Domination.* Her studies offer a critique of the limits of ideology as an explanation of our embedded situation in contradictory culture and consciousness. However, the absence of critical theory's recognition of feminist challenges and contributions leads one to believe either that feminists have had no impact, or that these two parallel intellectual and political movements are not mutually informing.

The editors of *Critical Literacy* define "praxis" as concerned to "make explicit the genuine self-conceptions implicit in ideological views, and to indicate how contradictions and inadequacies contained in exiting 'knowledge' and self-understanding can be overcome" (1993: 41). Again, Bartky's analysis of psychological domination, rooted in existentialism and phenomenology, emphasizes how oppression occurs precisely through such contradictions, which are embedded in our emotions. Representative of much critical theory, this lack of attention to emotions as a site of ideological control reflects a vastly undertheorized dimension of power and subjectivity.

A subset of this phenomenon is that the work of Freire is frequently invoked as offering a "better" approach than consciousness-raising because it is more "critical." Does Freire's theory and practice in fact offer a more critical approach to emotions and education, or is this turning to Freire symptomatic of the tendency to embrace the master's tools? By this I refer to the fact that, in contemporary feminist theorizations of pedagogy, (which rarely address emotion systematically), the primary theoretical frameworks are drawn from neo-Marxist, psychoanalytic, and poststructural theory. While these approaches are useful in theorizing subjectivity writ large, I have yet to find such an approach that analyzes the historical specificity of emotions in educational contexts. In sum, "feminist" contributions to theorizing emotion are erased, denigrated, or reappropriated under other names.

All this said, I am not advocating consciousness-raising and feminist pedagogy, so much as attempting to correct the historical record. Secondly, I pose the question: Are the "problems" associated with feminist pedagogy endemic to feminist pedagogy, or are they problems rooted in the deceptive binaries of Western language — emotion vs. reason, etc. In this sense, I am challenging the unsubstantiated myth that Freire's work is "more systematically critical" while feminist consciousness-raising embraces emotions unproblematically.

EVASIONS OF THE MURKY TERRAIN

I TURN FINALLY to examine two central moves I have identified in feminist theorizations of emotion and education. The first, rooted in Marxism, charges that to invoke or address emotions is to "psychologize" power and structural relations. The second is the tendency to evade systematic analyses of emotions, and instead invoke concepts such as "desire" or the "unconscious" as umbrellas under which the socially, culturally, and historically specific aspects of emotions are evaded.

This first argument is rooted in Marxist critiques of consciousness-raising as a bourgeois form of "navel-gazing."[32] On this view, the "real" work of revolution and material change is to take political action. Sitting around discussing "feelings" in consciousness-raising groups does not qualify as "political" action. What is the logic of this Marxist critique? Marxists recognize that ideology shapes our material world, and that radical change comes through changing material conditions. If women's material oppression occurs significantly through her internalization of her inferiority and consequent submission to her oppression, then an analysis of her emotions and consciousness would seem to provide a key starting point for changing material conditions.

At stake is how one defines "materialism" and "everyday life," vs. "idealism."[33] Analyses of ideology by Louis Althusser (1971)[34] move us to analyze how "ideological state apparatuses" are internalized through processes of interpellation — how we "identify" with symbolic, ideological representations of cultural constructions of values determined by capitalist interest, for example. However, in the end Marxism fails to systematically analyze emotions in relation to ideology.[35] Bartky's analysis of psychological oppression challenges the Marxist explanation of ideology. Like Marxists, she recognizes that contradictions are central to hegemony; however, analyzing the particular gendered form of these internalized contradictions, she argues: "It is itself psychologically oppressive both to believe and at the same time not believe that one is inferior — in other words, to believe a contradiction" (1990: 30). She analyses specifically how women are enculturated to internalize a sense of shame and lack of self-worth as an oppressive effect of ideological contradictions. In short, many Marxist explanations of ideology have not systematically excavated the gendered dimensions of consciousness, nor emotions as a site of hegemony.

In her insightful and invaluable essay "On Race and Voice in the 90s" (1989–90) Chandra Talpade Mohanty articulates a compelling case against the invocation of emotion within academic contexts. Mohanty's analysis reflects the type of language and discourses common to critical, Marxist, and postmodern social theory. She articulates what I recognize as the importance of our "interior" or "psychological" experience — but shifts to a less "problematic" Marxist discourse.

In her sketch of an ideal educational environment, a "public culture of dissent," she refers to affective structures but doesn't name them. Mohanty describes her ideal as follows:

> a public culture of dissent entails creating spaces for epistemological standpoints that are grounded in the interests of people and that recognize the *materiality of conflict, of privilege, and of domination*. Thus creating such cultures is fundamentally about making the axes of power transparent in the context of academic, disciplinary, and institutional structures *as well as in the interpersonal relationships* (rather than individual relations) in the academy. It is about taking the *politics of everyday life* seriously as teachers, students, administrators, and mem-

> bers of hegemonic academic cultures. Culture itself is thus redefined to incorporate individual and *collective memories, dreams, and history* that are contested and transformed through the political praxis of day-to-day living. (61, emphasis added)

She intimates the emotional, or psychic, dimensions of human existence — "collective memories, dreams" — but these remain undefined and unelaborated. I appreciate her emphasis on the political and historical context and her resistance to individualizing practices. Yet, representative of many radical social theories, Mohanty's analysis falls into a familiar refrain of contemporary academic discourse: a gesture towards the murky terrain of the interior, but an aversion to actually tread there.

The object of Mohanty's critique is a practice that proliferated in institutions during the 1980s: "Racism Awareness Trainings" (RAT). The invocation of this particular discourse of emotions results, she argues, in an erasure of important differences of power relations within a racist society.[36] To teach that "racism hurts us all" does not adequately address power inequities. RAT ends up privatizing the political. Reminiscent of early concerns regarding the ways that consciousness-raising was appropriated and used, not towards political action but for liberalizing and/or therapeutic goals, Mohanty points out what I would characterize as the ongoing risks involved in attempting to institutionalize any "politics of emotion." As I discussed in the chapter on emotional literacy, the tendency for emotions to be depoliticized within bureaucratic and institutional settings is a serious shortcoming. While I agree that this is a risk, particularly when we look at the case of commodified workshops on "diversity training" designed to make institutional relations function more efficiently and profitably, I am not convinced that all invocations of emotion necessarily psychologize power relations.

The second move is to shunt the difficult question of histories of particular emotions into the catch-all categories of "desire" and "the unconscious." This is a move frequently reflected in contemporary feminist poststructuralist analyses of education, some of which address pedagogy and which for the most part leave emotion tangentially addressed if at all. An example is provided by Ellsworth's 1989 essay, "Why Doesn't This Feel Empowering? Working Through the Repressive Myths of Critical Pedagogy." Ellsworth's essay offers a relatively rare, in-depth self-reflective engagement of the politics of pedagogy in terms of how one connects the classroom to the "real" world. In a sense extending critiques of critical pedagogy that had been developed in such articles as Fisher's and Maher's (though, again, we find no reference to the pioneering work of feminist pedagogies), Ellsworth's analysis develops a critique of rationality and critical pedagogies. She also offers an invaluable analysis of how pedagogies come up against the walls of racism, for example. Avoiding altogether the term feminist pedagogy, Ellsworth's discourse takes up the sexier vantage point of feminist poststructuralism. Poststructuralism does not run the risk of being called "touchy-feelie." Yet Ellsworth takes on the very "real" experience of difference, experience, and even emotions encountered in a classroom. In passing, she highlights emotions as genuine challenges to the pedagogy and social action she sees as the goals of education. Yet she doesn't sustain her analysis at the level of a politics of emotion, but invokes the notion of the "unconscious" and "desire" as umbrella terms to refer to this slippery domain.

Ellsworth writes, "As long as the literature on critical pedagogy fails to come to grips with issues of trust, risk, and the operations of fear and desire around such issues of identity and politics on the classroom, these rationalistic tools will continue to fail to loosen deep-seated, self-interested investments in unjust relations of, for example, gender, ethnicity, and sexual orientation" (1992: 105). She refers to Mohanty in this paragraph, noting that "[a]gainst such ignoring Mohanty argues that to desire to ignore is not cognitive, but performative" (ibid.).

In what follows, rather than pursue the particularities of "trust, risk, and the operations of fear" and "guilt" and "resentment"(107), Ellsworth addresses these issues in terms of the Lacanian language of how the "subjects are split between the conscious and the unconscious" (108).[37] Thus where Mohanty evades "emotion" in preference for Marxist notions of "everyday experience," Ellsworth shifts from emotions to a discourse of "the unconscious" and "desire."

Kathleen Woodward notes this phenomenon as common to academic discourses. Calling for histories of emotion, Woodward writes:

> Imagine histories of pity, resignation, sincerity, jealousy, tenderness, horror, and tranquillity; of grief, abjection, disgust, boredom, fear, resentment, ecstasy, pride, bitterness, gratitude, and irritation. . . . Such histories would offer us breathing room from the now banal rhetoric of poststructuralism and Lacanian analysis as it is summed up in the word "desire." In its ubiquity and virtual solitude, in the deployment of the discourse of desire everywhere, desire has assumed the status of a master category. . . . But it is also a curiously empty category. (1990–91: 3–4)

In the same way that "desire is a curiously empty category," so are the concepts of "consciousness" and "everyday life" broad umbrella terms that do not get us closer to histories of emotion and power.

PROMISING DIRECTIONS

THE CRITICISMS I have offered throughout this chapter are not meant to undermine the value of the feminist theories surrounding education. Neither do I exempt myself: Within the scholarly context in which I work, I am more likely to reference feminist poststructural theory than to situate myself in relation to feminist pedagogies and consciousness-raising.

I suggest that the continued development of radical and feminist pedagogies requires engaged conversations between the theories and practices of consciousness-raising and feminist pedagogies, feminist poststructural theories of education, and feminist philosophies of emotion. Elaborated conversations between the feminist theories of emotion discussed in chapter 1, and the educational practices and histories I have examined in subsequent chapters, would provide promising overlap across disciplinary boundaries.

For example, Bartky's analysis of psychological oppression might be explored more extensively in relation to different educational contexts. How might we develop pedagogies that address psychological oppression in all of its hegemonic complexities? Likewise, Susan Campbell's work on the collaborative construction of emotions may offer a key dimension to feminist poststructuralist theories of education. The work of Gilles Deleuze opens promising directions for theories of affect and the body, increasingly employed by feminist and other writers.[38] These directions conceptualize promising alternative to the reductive risks of emotional literacy curricula, for example.

Central to developing pedagogies that account for the intersections of power, emotions, and difference are the works of post-colonial, African-American, and Chicana scholars. The theoretical innovations contributed by Gloria Anzaldúa, Maria Lugones, Trinh Minh-ha, and Gayatri Spivak offer important directions that could be read alongside a feminist politics of emotion and extended further into educational theories and practices. Examples of interdisciplinary studies that address issues of representation, performance, emotions, and difference are found in two special issues of *Discourse: Journal of Theoretical Studies in Media and Culture*, one focused on emotions and one on pedagogy; and in the 1993 issue of *Women and Performance: A Journal of Feminist Theory* with a special focus on "Feminist Pedagogy and Performance." Both post-colonial and cultural studies/media perspectives foreground directions away from a reductive or dehistoricized invocation of "experience."

Conversations amongst what are at present disparate, yet intersecting, areas of feminist theory would vastly broaden educational theory and help to further the work begun by early radical feminists. In the chapters that follow, I elaborate the potential of interdisciplinary and feminist theories to develop pedagogies that recognize emotions as a site of political resistance.

1 Magda Lewis (1992: 177).
2 Bartky (1990: 14).
3 I am grateful to Kathryn Pauly Morgan for drawing this article to my attention.
4 It would be worthwhile to locate the documents and programs of Vision 2000 to evaluate the scope and intentions.
5 See chapter 6, "License to Feel: Teaching in the Context of War(s)."
6 Rubin's landmark essay "The Traffic in Women" (1975) offers an outstanding detailing of the beginning of socialist feminist theorizing of the sex/gender system. See also Haraway (1990); Young (1990); Acker (1994).
7 One might argue that in 1981 Lyman didn't have access to feminist writings on consciousness-raising. However, I rather think that this quote represents an example of the erasure of feminist uses of CR. Radical feminists writing on CR did exist by 1981 (see footnote 9). He opens his essay with a quote from Adrienne Rich, whose work represented at the time, as still today, a founding lesbian-feminist contribution to scholarship. However, aside from within a footnote to Rich's quote, he does not mention feminism or feminist pedagogy, even as he analyzes the importance of CR and the politics of anger. Rather, he proceeds to reference a series of white male theorists and philosophers from Wittgenstein and Nietzsche to Barthes and Marx and Freud!
8 Throughout her work, Maxine Greene emphasizes the importance of naming the obstacles to freedom; see especially (1988).
9 The diverse invocations of the term "consciousness-raising" is reflected in a simple search through the ERIC database. A search yields 132 records, and CR is used to describe projects that include: bilingual education, rural women's education in Nebraska, developing feminist ethics within educational technology, leading men's CR groups, and teaching lesbian literature. These publications date from the 1970s to the present, and the term appears even more widely used in contemporary discourse than in the 1970s.
10 For discussion of the development of women's studies, see for example Hull et al. (1983). She notes that in 1974 one source "lists a total of 4,658 women's sudies courses taught by 2,964 teachers" (1983: xxvi).
11 In a book that foregrounds students' experiences in gender reform environments, Kenway and Willis (1997) offer a powerful testament to the need for a "feminist pedagogy of the emotions: "the emotional dimensions of gender reform are under-examined and under-theorized and the practice of gender reform suffers as a result. Our evidence points to the need for a feminist 'pedagogy of the emotions' which would help those involved to understand why they feel the way they do, what it means for the ways they act, what to do about it" (132).
12 The second wave of feminism — like many other political movements — is frequently characterized as reflecting an agenda articulated largely by white, middle-class women. As a result, the agendas of being "freed" from the role of housewife, for example, did not reflect the demands shared necessarily by other women who have long been working outside of the home. However complicated the actual politics of the movement, it is equally important to recognize that many working-class and lesbian women were centrally involved in the women's liberation movement. For further discussion see Echols (1989); Hull et al. (1982) Snitow et al. (1993); Vance (1984).
13 See Davis (1983); Giddings (1984); Lerner (1972).
14 On the histories of sexual politics, see for example Snitow et al. (1983).
15 For an excellent discussion of the use of CR in teaching feminist studies, see Estelle Freedman's "Small-Group Pedagogy: Consciousness Raising in Conservative Times" (1994). The edited collection *Gendered Subjects* (1985) offers

complexified analyses of feminist pedagogies and contrasting views of their goals and aims. To their credit, those writing about feminist pedagogy have not adopted a unified, monolithic view that, for example, "trust" can be an assumed goal or feature of classroom community. Neither, upon examination, can these articulations be classified as advocating a touchy-feelie paradigm. For example, Joan Cocks's essay is precisely about the pleasure of feminist theory and the problematic phenomenon that women's studies students tend to spurn theory as "inherently male," which she finds inaccurate and disturbing.

16 On debates regarding safe space, empowerment, and dialogue see hooks (1989, 1984); Luke and Gore (1992); Burbules and Rice (1992) and response by Leach (1992).

17 For early discussions on the politics of difference, see for example Moraga and Anzaldúa (1981); Hull et al. (1982); Smith (1983); Echols (1989); hooks (1981).

18 Feminist theorists, who work primarily in what might be termed "high theory" discourses yet emphasize the importance of women's experience. I am thinking, for example, of insightful work by deLauretis (1987, 1990).

19 In fact, I would defend the collection against the accusation of assuming an unproblematic notion of experience, as many of the essays problematize experience through the politics of difference. Some essays define "theory," some explore the contradictions of "authority" and feminism; seven essays address, in their title, issues of "difference" in the women's studies classroom. Lesbianism, sexuality, on the other hand, appears in only one title.

20 I am grateful to Kathryn Pauly Morgan for her comments on this. For further discussion of feminist standpoint theory, see for example Harding and Hintikka (1983); Alcoff and Potter (1993).

21 In the 1990s one finds an increased emphasis on "politicized narrative theory." One might date this for example to Barbara Christian's catalyzing essay "The Race for Theory"(1988) in which she criticizes the academic definitions of what counts as theory, and explores alternative modes of theorizing articulated by women of color. See also Lugones; Trinh (1989); Anzaldúa (1987); Gluck and Patai (1991).

22 One of the best readings I know of to assign, particularly to white students reluctant to take responsibility for their "positionality," is Minnie Bruce Pratt's essay (1984) "Identity: Blood/Skin/Heart," the account of "coming to consciousness" through a critical historical analysis of her own experience growing up in the South.

23 Her remarks, along with Gayatri Spivak's advocation of "strategic essentialism" (the occasional, political necessity of claiming an "essential" identity even if one wishes, in the long run, to problematize the idea of a singular, essential identity) are referred to by several authors in the 1993 feminist pedagogy issue of *Women and Performance: A Journal of Feminist Theory*.

24 I do not have time to explore the extent to which these accusations are situated in relation to social class divisions. For example, part of the reason for accusing feminist pedagogies of being "touchy-feelie" is that often such methods as CR are used in community-college women's studies classrooms. In research universities, the admonitions against "touchy-feelie "work are stronger, and hence there appears to be an issue of social class discrimination overlaid on these questions.

25 For discussions that address these tensions in feminist education, see for example the collections in feminist philosophy of education: Diller et al. (1996); Grumet (1988); Stone (1994).

26 I explore this question in an essay "Posing Feminist Questions to Freire" (1998).

27 For valuable analyses of critical theory and critical pedagogy, which nonetheless reflect what I see as an erasure of foundational feminist histories, see for example Apple (1990); Lankshear and McLaren (1993); Giroux (1991).

28 In chapter 2, "What Are the Fears and Risks of Transformation?" Freire and Shor

(1987) discuss as a model for transformative work, how "revolutionary heroes" such as Fidel Castro were "afraid" when they took risks, but didn't discuss their fears. For a valuable discussion of distinctions between Freire's work and CR, see Peter Roberts, 'Rethinking Conscientisation' (1996).

29 Kenway and Modra do state that as feminists they "accept responsibility for going a lot further than he" (1992: 161). One assumes that their progress beyond the limits of Freire's work is not, however, due to their use of feminist pedagogies or consciousness-raising but other aspects of feminist theory.

30 See also my discussion in chapter 1. Reading the valuable work of such authors as Elizabeth Ellsworth and Patti Lather, consciousness-raising and feminist pedagogy do not figure as a significant theoretical discourse for theorizing education. While this may simply not be the central point of their analyses, it is striking that these radical feminist developments in education appear invisible as one of the starting points for feminist educational theories. It is important for me to include myself to some extent in this "camp." In the chapters that follow, neither do I find myself centrally invoking CR and feminist pedagogy!

31 See Boler, forthcoming in Peters (1999).

32 See MacKinnon for further discussion of the Marxist critique of feminist practices (1989: 50).

33 For a useful characterization of how Marxism, psychoanalysis, and cultural anthropology offer different paradigms for cultural studies see Hall in Dirks et al. (1994).

34 See also Appel (1996).

35 I refer readers to my discussions in chapter 1, regarding the work of such theorists as Raymond Williams, who offers analysis of structures of feeling (1977).

36 On 1950s histories in social theory, which similarly "privatize" race, see Henriques (1984). See also Omi and Winant(1986); McCarthy(1990) on discourses of race and racial formation.

37 In fact, a close analysis of what the "unconscious" and "desire" mean from a Lacanian perspective in terms of everyday pedagogical dynamics represents an underdeveloped terrain of politics of emotion. However, frequently the language is adopted without full explication. This vagueness is widely reflected within critical and poststructuralist pedagogical discourses.

38 See the work of Braidotti (1994); Massumi (1996); Gatens (1996b).

CHAPTER SIX

LICENSE TO FEEL

Teaching in the Context of War(s)

ON TUESDAY, January 29, 1991, at 6:45 A.M. I read the *Sentinel* headline and front-page story: Saddam Hussein threatens to attach nuclear warheads to his Scuds. In dawn's vulnerable moment, having read the news before establishing my usual media-guard censors, I am ravaged by this information and unable to focus appropriately on my role as composition and rhetoric instructor, on my agenda of thesis statements and this week's readings by Jewelle Gomez, Paula Gunn Allen, and Adrienne Rich. I enter the classroom at 8 A.M. feeling a sense of responsibility to my role in this community — or perhaps desiring a community that does not exist. I invite a discussion of the impact of the war and ask specifically how we are sustaining ourselves, where we are getting support. One after another the students tell me they have not read a paper or watched television in days or a week; they have chosen to "block it out," they say. In response to an in-class writing prompt, one student writes: "Since I'm not keeping up with the news, it's kinda nice to come in and know I'm not the only one ignoring the news because it bothers them too much. . . . When the war is over (hopefully very soon) I'm not sure it would have touched my life at all (except emotionally). I'm gonna forget about the war once it's over."

The examples of how this war has "emotionally touched" the students' lives perhaps won't be forgotten. One woman has a boyfriend in Saudi Arabia; laughing, she had told us that when they finally spoke on the phone the first time since war broke out, he told her he was "safe" in a surveillance tower — and then he told her the tower was one of Iraq's main targets. Another woman tells us that most of her friends are over there. And one young man fears the draft, as he believes his only other option would be deportation, given his immigrant status as a Korean. Yet today, not one out of sixteen speaks to the question of support or self-sustaining strategies. Their numbness reflects a profound isolation, not the least of which is our isolation from one another in this room. I am aware of a sense of hypocrisy should I remain silent about the question of the emotional impact of the Persian Gulf War on our lives. In a course dedicated to the "empowerment" of young writers, how can I not raise the haunting question about our distinctive emotional experiences at this historical moment? How can I not ask about the profound numbness, due to our veritable powerlessness, that seems to have rendered us both speechless, and further isolated from one another?

"There is a danger run by all powerless people: that we forget we are lying, or that lying becomes a weapon we carry into our relationships with people who do not have power over us" (Rich 1979: 189). Rich here speaks of women's skills of lying to men as a form of survival. We carry this weapon not only into our relationships with others but into our relationship with ourselves. This dynamic — lying in Rich's words, and numbness in mine — creates the modes of isolation I have described as crises. However, we might escape the implicit "realism" underlying these conceptions of falsehood/truth and argue that teaching is performance and that the dramatic element of teaching means a certain kind of pretense always takes place. In such a script, it appears I participate in an institutional acceptance of the war through the pretense that composition and rhetoric makes sense given a threat of nuclear disaster. What in turn does the performative element mean for students, or what might Rich's "lying" mean for them? How do the eruptions of isolation make sense either within a paradigm of performance, or in a paradigm of naive hope for community erupting through distorted representations? How do we make sense of a "real" war as it disrupts our "peace"? Or do we not make sense of it as "real," since to us it is in fact representation?

Our common experience as spectators of George Bush's war in the Persian Gulf prompted me to attempt to recognize our classroom as a community. And I know I am not alone in this attempt: Many instructors and professors I speak with use the language of "community ethos" to describe the climate they attempt to create in classrooms. At the time, another colleague told me she had asked of her class: We are a community; we are going through this together, so let's be here for each other.

The hyperdistinction of the "global" and "local" is one of the deceptive oppositions I encountered in this educational setting. If globalization refers to the web of economic, ideological, and political modes of domination and exchange whose effects include a flattening of cultures in the process of commodification and labor devaluation for the profit of few, then the common denominator of the local impact of globalization — although markedly varied—impacts communities and lives in "First" and "Third" World countries severely enough to warrant grasping this shared psychic imperialism. To privilege a discourse that builds on the distinction of global and local — economic/political versus individual/community — tends to assume that globalization doesn't require the ideological inscription of docile bodies and psyches.

To understand the effects of globalization, we must necessarily understand what gets referred to as a subset of the local: namely, the material effects of economic exploitation and ideology on the felt and thought processes of individuals and communities. No form of imperialism or colonialism has been possible without this localized engineering. As theorists producing discourses on such wrenching matters as transnational corporations and imperialist economic policies, we need attend to our own practices within equally imperialist-implicated institutions.[1]

Three features of modern life recognizably made community virtually impossible: identity politics, power relations, and fear. In this chapter, I concentrate on the latter two obstacles. All three obstacles share significant common denominators. Each is defined by negation — identification in terms of what it is not — and by predominant cultural silences. Each of these obstacles is significantly situated in a vector of the local and the global. The "local" that concerns this essay is the private, internal terrain generally segregated from the scope of education: In the instance of a war, this private domain is the site of anxieties, powerlessness, fear, and numbness, which defy language and are denied language within the educational institution. The global I examine includes the effects of media representations of the Persian Gulf War, which created our "community" or common perceptions of that war,[2] in terms of the effect of "repetitive trauma."

The identity politics of that particular classroom, in brief, were communicated primarily through the placement of our bodies rather than through language and posed a significant obstacle to any utopic notion of community.[3] We were in fact a very strange community if we were one at all. The six Anglo students — four women and one man — sat together, the two African-American women sit together, the two Chinese women sit together, the Filipinos and Chicana sat together, and the Chinese and Korean men sat together. The extreme variation of our cultural values with respect to emotional expression made for further silences.[4] The students had in common their age — all about eighteen years old; generally speaking, the social class of students at the University of California, Santa Cruz, is upper middle class; and the Filipina, Chicana, Korean, and Chinese students had in common that English was not their first language. Whatever commonalities, perhaps especially in war, the boundaries between us were not crossed, and we were shrouded in silence.

The second feature that prevents community and emotional literacies is, quite simply, the power relations that define the educator's relationship to students as an authority figure. To preserve authority, educators maintain immeasurable isolation and distance from students; for example, I generally do not reveal my social class background of growing up poor. Reciprocally, since I do have power over them, why should they make themselves emotionally vulnerable to me particularly in the public forum of the classroom?[5] In this chapter I analyze how educator/student relationships are defined by modes of pastoral power that preclude the possibility of community (Foucault [1982]

1984). Pastoral power functions as a contradictory catch-22 in which the educator, as the modern "pastor," by definition promises salvation. However, in the case of a crisis such as the Persian Gulf War, the educator cannot possibly deliver salvation. The modern educator is simultaneously positioned as globally impotent and as locally holding authoritative power. As a result, (student) resistance to this pastor is entrenched in such a way that community in relation to an outside crisis is virtually impossible. The overall effect is to isolate all involved.

The third feature that prevents community disturbs me the most. It is closely bound up with identities and with power relations but is rarely spoken of in these hallowed halls: In short, fear in its myriad forms. From the moment in 1982 when I commenced research on emotions' roles in subjectivities and knowledge production — the mutually defining relation of emotions and power — it has been patently obvious that what defines the discourses of emotion most predominantly are silences, particularly if one is examining emotional discourses within the history of the academy and higher education.[6] Within educational institutions, unacceptable/emotional behavior is defined by what it is not: namely, the prototype of the rational, curious, engaged, "balanced," well-behaved white male student. Why does a thesis of emotional epistemologies seem far-fetched within the disciplined academy? Why is it so outlandish to think that, as an educational community, we might benefit from emotional literacies, from learning how to articulate the ways in which the social realm defines the private and how our passions inform our desires for knowledge? Why, in our fear and resistance, do we "lock out" the possibility of an emotional literacy regarding, for example, our vulnerabilities as well as systems of denial with respect to the pain and joy we necessarily experience in each of our globalized private and classroom lives?

Instead of saying any of this to them, I affirm that "checking out" is an invaluable survival strategy commonly used by any sort of trauma survivors to enable them to withstand the horror of repeated abuse, shock, or invasions of boundaries. I tell them also that I feel an obligation to ask them to think about the war and particularly about how it is being represented in the dominant media. I establish that for each class two persons will bring in articles — preferably foreign or alternative press — and offer a quick analysis. I change their open-ended "creative" assignment, due the following week, to a "creative" response to some representation of the war. The next week, however, when they read their poems aloud and exhibit collages in class, I am dumbfounded: In my long experience with this particular assignment in its usual form, it has been profound and productive. The result of my imposed direction to respond to the war resulted in a handful of moving poems but for the most part some of the least impressive, uninspired "creative" work I have seen.

Now, several years after the Persian Gulf War, I experience a similar moment of entering the classroom desiring community and in this instance choose a very different path. This morning, I consciously choose silence (in no small part due to the general resistances to emotional epistemologies on the part of those with more power than I in the academic communities). I enter the hall at the University of Auckland and give my lecture to the classroom of seventy students without making reference to the fact that we are at this moment a vulnerable community that in the next day or so will suffer the effects of the French nuclear detonation of a 150-pound bomb in nearby Pacific waters New Zealand has declared nuclear-free. Why I choose silence disturbs me, for it is entirely complicitous with the dominant cultural constructions of complex silences to avoid anxiety in the face of international political power games.

That the academy persistently guards against productive solidarities leads me to ask: What is it about institutionalized power relations that constructs isolation and powerlessness? In his work *Becoming Somebody: Toward a Social Psychology of School* Philip Wexler writes, "Interaction, society and self are the lacking central elements of social relations. . . . Emotion, performance, and morality are the main constitutive dimensions of action underlying the institutional processes. Gender, class, and race are ways to understand class differentiated compensatory defenses against the absence of basic elements of social relations" (1992: 118). The fact that even a crisis such as a war does not allow us to reach across differences and establish community causes me to look beyond the individuals to understand the isolation. In the face of all manner of national and international horrors, we go about our business of education without consideration of the dynamics of community, identities, and emotional epistemologies that develop through the implicit values of our social interactions. Ideally, however ad hoc our community, we have a responsibility to develop emotional literacies that are part and parcel of community integrity.

What kind of community do we compose in our institutional settings? A classroom is in fact an extraordinarily "ad hoc" community. What we have in common may only be the students' shared administrative requirement for the course credit. Realistically, as an educator one is also responsible for being part of an apparatus that produces the next wave of workers and thinkers. In this minimal respect educators run the risk of dangerous hypocrisy in neglecting attention to emotional epistemologies. However, educational institutions have no commitment to community beyond the necessary behavioral requirements that enables bureaucracy. Neither are educational institutions committed to an examination of the emotional epistemologies that inform social dynamics, relations, and knowledge production. Institutions are inherently committed to maintaining silences (e.g., about emotion) and/or proliferating discourses that define emotion by negation. My aim here is to outline how institutionalized power relations thwart attempts to develop emotional epistemologies.

By emotional epistemologies I mean at minimum a public recognition of the ways in which the "social" defines the "interior" realm of experience, and vice versa. Clearly a central challenge in writing about discourses of emotion is that, particularly in Western thought, emotions have tended to occupy — in philosophy, sciences, and popular discourse — the status of "naturalized entities." Viewed as biological and fixed and essential experiences or givens, we run into serious problems of reference and explanation. What is clear from this conceptual challenge is in part the power of binaries and dualisms that define our imaginative capacities, as well as our experience. I am less interested in whether or not there are in fact universally similar emotional experiences or expressions and more interested in how the dominant discourses within a given local site determine what can and cannot be felt and/or expressed. For example, we can ask how education intersects with emotional epistemologies and how a student's cultural background informs his or her sense of entitlement to speak in the classroom. More specifically, how does a sexual abuse survivor's shame and his or her required silence about this experience inform his or her license to speak with authority? Another example of emotional epistemologies can be found in teaching students how to combine passionate response with critical analysis, to define and identify how and when particular emotions inform and define knowledge.

The crisis I faced discerning my responsibility and effective teaching strategies during the Persian Gulf War extends far beyond that winter and continues to haunt me. Like the boundaries of public and private, which have become increasingly blurred in the last decades, what counts as "inside" and "outside" the appropriate focus of knowledge and education becomes increasingly complex. As an intellectual worker, what responsibility do I have to local, national, or international social and political realities in which my citizenship and institution of affiliation are implicated? Is the classroom a sanctuary from the everyday, where educators and students alike can justify abdicating any direct responsibility for "outside" political events?

The pragmatic response to my alarmist worry is, quite simply, that given the time, subject, and commodified constraints of a classroom it is not possible to do justice to an entire social agenda. Furthermore, if the class is not in a position adequately to study the political and historical events leading up to the Persian Gulf War (or Central Intelligence Agency–backed military support of dictatorships, the destruction of East Timor, the Panama Invasion, or the drug war and trade in this country), then the gesture is empty. But more disturbing to me than any particular errors made in terms of curriculum is the phenomenon I witnessed in acute form during the Persian Gulf War: What accounts for the pervasive construction of a rampant feeling of powerlessness, which none of us were able to transcend on that fateful day? To answer this, I first sketch the "twilight zone" as the psychic terrain of emotion in the modern state of late capitalism and the students' predominant exhibitions of powerlessness and numbness, and I turn to an analysis of the repetitive trauma effected by the media, which constructs that twilight zone. Second, I draw on Michel Foucault's concept of pastoral power to explain the educator's limited capacity to contradict the numbness constructed during war. My analysis outlines the mutually interdependent ways in which feelings and reality construct one another, with an eye towards how emotion both informs and offers directions as well as limits possibilities.[8]

THE TWILIGHT ZONE OF POWERLESSNESS: Localized Sites of Global Shocks

TWILIGHT: "an intermediate state that is not clearly defined." Denial is the psyche's odd twilight zone: Sartre's "bad faith"; Rich's "lying"; Nietzsche's "forgetfulness." Denial can only be the product of human subjectivity, a unique feature of our species of consciousness, the space of neither knowing nor ignorance, awareness nor misinformation. The fact that our psyches abide to varying extents in this twilight zone arena with respect to the war, in the zone bordering powerlessness and denial, does not mean that some of us are not engaged in effective analysis, education, and/or resistance. An excavation of this phenomenon in relation to emotion reveals that the twilight zone syndrome feeds on our lack of awareness of how powerlessness functions, effects, feeds on, and drains our sense of agency and power as active creators of self- and world-representations. By powerlessness I mean a state that is usually silent and mutates into guilt and denial that gnaw at us; the latter especially are forms of internalized self-hatred, "internalized oppression" in the contemporary discourse — the poisonous by-products of powerlessness. As one student wrote, "With this war, I demonstrated in an anti-war rally for the first time in my life. I wrote writings and told everyone that this was wrong. But despite all that the war goes on and on. The politicians do not care at all. I have no power whatsoever to change the course of the Persian Gulf War. I am therefore powerless. Powerless to stop an event I think is unjust."

Powerlessness, however, is a more promising feeling and concept than denial or guilt, for beneath the numbness, which often signifies powerlessness, lies a force that can be transformed into an immediate source of power, "immediate vigorous action." Numbness is perhaps the most efficacious, postmodern survival strategy.[9] What other could possibly work as well to get us through either a glance or thorough reading of a newspaper — our awareness of all the occurrences and issues not represented in that newspaper; the dailiness of our work, its pressures, unexpected blows, and upsets; the massive contradiction of desiring peace and driving a car. Need I go on? As I said to my students, "checking out" — numbness — is perhaps most poignantly utilized by abuse survivors. The agency involved in numbness indicates that it is an intelligent psychic survival strategy — and no one can stop one from choosing it! But making this choice without educated consideration of our other options means that, at times, numbness may be the inadvertent effect of cultural illiteracy with respect to translating emotion into knowledge and action.[10]

What accounts for the construction of powerlessness, and how might it be interrupted within the classroom? One place to begin to understand the twilight zone of the representational psyche is an analysis of how media contributes to numbness.

THE REPETITIVE TRAUMA OF MEDIA

MEDIA CAN FUNCTION as a repetitive trauma, successfully so in terms of the fact that one effect of monopolized ideology is isolation and powerlessness. "Repetitive trauma" is generally opposed to "acute trauma." For example, an acute trauma is a car accident, which may involve all manner of emotional and physical pain, but observably survivors tend to remember the event quite well. Particularly in relation to memory, however, repetitive trauma has a quite different effect than acute trauma: It appears that a feature of repeated injury — to the body and/or psyche — is to forget, repress, and relegate the memory to what I call the twilight zone.[11]

In the case of an event like the Persian Gulf War, the repetition of "safe" images and rhetoric used in manufactured media has a guaranteed numbing effect. The repetition of any oft-repeated image or words might have that effect. But when the selected representation is deeply suspected as a "truth effect" rather than as a trusted source, a sense of repeated betrayal is added to the overstimulation. For example, the defusing representation of peace movements created the persistent illusion of isolation and freakishness in one's desire for peace. How do I engage with the classroom of diverse people in productive address of our distinct fears and terrors, when the language provided us consists of Pollyannish cartoon images?

Isolation in our moral existence is perpetuated through institutionalized silences as well as our own reluctances to acknowledge and discuss something so extreme as torture or war. Elaine Scarry's suggestions of the interrelations of flesh and language outline one aspect of how media functions as a repetitive trauma which becomes embodied and manifest as powerlessness. In *The Body in Pain*, she states that this reluctance increases "our vulnerability to power by ensuring that our moral intuitions and impulses which come forward so readily on behalf of human sentience, do not come forward far enough to be of any help. . . . The result of this is that the very moral intuitions that might act on behalf of the claims of sentience remain almost as interior and inarticulate as sentience itself" (1985: 60). What Scarry calls our sentient knowledge, our embodied emotion, is inextricably intertwined with the negotiation and enactment of justice.[12]

There is no doubt that the language of displaced meaning constructed to represent the Persian Gulf War as a benign event set the stage for the twilight zone I encountered in my classroom.[13] As a class, we discussed the images and language enough to share a laugh — albeit a painful one — about the irony not just of consistent understatement but point of view, for example the speaking voice maintaining fear to be the fear of crazy war resisters here in the United States rather than fear for the Iraqi casualties, or fear for Israel, or fear for U.S. soldiers.

Yet the globalized media repetitions cannot be distinguished from their severe local effect: A loss of community and hence loss of language within our classroom prevented us from transforming powerlessness we felt in the face of our government. There is a misnomer here, "our" government. The Filipina women in the classroom knew "our" government also as a presence in her country of origin. There was no unilateral concept of "our" government, of its concern for who counts as a citizen, or whose families had been transplanted and divided as a result of U.S. foreign military presence.

Indeed there are acute differences in the localized impact of U.S. foreign and domestic policies. During the war I visited a class conducted by Toni Cade Bambara and Buchi Emecheta,[14] and I heard two women students speak loud and clear: Those of you who chose to shut down this university haven't struggled to be allowed entrance to an education. Your peace movement is a self-serving product of privilege. And another who tells us that, as horrified as she is by this war, we didn't grow up where she grew up; she's used to bullets flying into houses from the street on favorite holidays.

These radically different meanings of signs and events explain in part how identity politics separates us even more acutely in a time of war, when the notion of "us" and "them" is put into sharp relief by national, class, and racial boundaries, and when the question, What counts as a political crisis? makes visible a multitude of crises not just overseas. The goal of challenging the psychic twilight zone is deeply threatened by the modes of administrative control available to me within the institution. An analysis of "pastoral power" helps illuminate the ways in which late-capitalist administrative power positions educators in a catch-22.

THE FACES OF PASTORAL POWER

FOUCAULT DEFINES pastoral power as "an old power technique which originated in Christian institutions" that "the modern Western state has integrated in a new political shape" ([1982] 1984: 421). Pastoral power is most notable for the fact that "[n]ever . . . in the history of human societies . . . has there been such a tricky combination in the same political structures of individualization techniques and of totalization procedures" (1984: 421).[15] Foucault traces the originary modes of pastoral power in its earlier association of a directly religious nature and its variations in the modern, secularized form. Both historical modes of pastoral power have in common several features, which relate to the site of education. Pastoral power's objective in its modern form is salvation in this life, salvation meaning "health, well-being . . . security, protection against accidents." The "officials of pastoral power" have multiplied greatly to include for example educators and social workers.

Within the classroom, pastoral power describes the educator's impotence in the institution. Because this is the form of power available to educators in an administrative setting and because within the instance of war I cannot deliver on the implied promise of salvation, the students rightly adopt a mode of resistance to my critical attempts to situate the war. They bear a relation of resistance to me as the embodiment of an authority who demands they address the war, thereby composing their attention to this "real" event as simply another assignment not of their choice. This role sets me up as a figure of authority the students will resist—in fact, a positive sign—but ironically in a time of war their constructive resistance simultaneously prevents me from effectively intervening in the media's traumatic impact on their sensibilities.

What does this mean in the classroom? In a "normal" state of affairs, what I assure them as the telos, the state of grace, of this process are tools for self-reflection and critical analysis. But the Persian Gulf War radically shifted my functionary position as pastor. What assurances could I offer them, after all? Clearly, what I wanted on that fateful morning was some kind of vulnerable confessions (or, I prefer to think, testimonies)[16] about their internal knowledge and response to the news. But in this case, do the repetitive trauma and consequence numbness that result from media images usurp my pastoral power and simultaneously castrate my power as it poses me as a pawn for the modern state.[17]

Thus we must ask, "To what degree do power relations in universities represent domination?" (Howley and Hatnett 1992: 281). If one accepts that the primary tools of power within the university have to do with prediction, control, and differentiation (more so than assimilation) as modes of constituting the normal and deviant, then we are faced with a disturbing answer: "As normalizing technologies, [these strategies] make use of differentiations that are essentially political, not intellectual. Such differentiations tend to support the transformation of power into domination by systematically limiting opportunities for recalcitrance" (282). In my classroom I witnessed increased differentiation of a political rather than intellectual character. The students' primary avenue for recalcitrance was — rightly — to resist my invocation of an intellectual and emotional discussion of the Persian Gulf War. Like it or not, as a pastor of the modern state by virtue of my position of power in the university setting, I enabled the "transformation of power into domination by systematically limiting opportunities for recalcitrance."

Pastoral power works especially effectively within institutions. For individuals to unite and express support for or opposition to the war outside of the classroom takes place in a climate less complex than the contradictory climate of a classroom. Public demonstration resists the totalizing intentions of media and Bush's unilateral offensive and resists the intention to isolate individuals from one another by bringing many bodies together in one location. It underscores the expression of individual differences as well, because in the face of a common "enemy" there can be united resistance yet extensive discussion of different strategies and intentions in resistance.

Why doesn't this mode of resistance translate to the classroom? The facile response is, first, that one must create a space for debate and analysis that calls for thoroughgoing critiques of media representations and political histories. Second, since in the classroom the teacher functions as an authority and pastor of power, there is a secondary resistance to this mode of administrative power that can stymie resistance to the wider net of power relations. It is this that caused my loneliness that morning: I felt us all to be in the same boat, as it were, as a result of our shared "victimization" by the mainstream media. But the students did not share that loneliness with me, partly because we had not all read the newspaper that morning, partly because they weren't facing the same ethical dilemma as I — trying to understand my role as teacher during the war, and partly because they entered that room with compulsory footsteps.

The resistance I did witness in the classroom took the form of the student's suspicion of the media's truths. Foucault lists "suspicion" as a central form of resistance to pastoral power.

> These struggles are not exactly for or against the "individual" but rather they are struggles against the "government of individualization." They are an opposition to the effects of power which are linked with knowledge, competence, and qualification: struggles against the privileges of knowledge. But they are also an opposition against secrecy, deformation, and mystifying representations imposed on people.
>
> There is nothing "scientistic" in this (that is, a dogmatic belief in the value of scientific knowledge), but neither is it a skeptical or relativistic refusal of all verified truth. What is questioned is the way in which knowledge circulates and functions, its relations to power. In short, the regime du savoir. (1984: 420)

Although the primary emotional tone I observed among my students was numbness, they also shared the more promising emotion of suspicion as evidenced by their responses to reports of a cease-fire declaration: "Well, I am so happy about this little news event. But who knows if we can believe it. They have censored everything up until now. How do we know they aren't lying? Is it really over or is this one of George Bush's schemes? The media makes it seem like they knew all along that we were going to win the war. . . ."

The suspicions posed by these eighteen-year-olds reveal a beginning critique of the regime du savoir. Suspicion indicates mistrust, a sense of previous betrayal, possible rational grounds for disbelief. Unlike other feelings, suspicion is linguistically active: It is also a verb, an activity. Suspicion, marking excellent progress from powerlessness, should encourage us to take emotional literacy seriously as part of the work of education.

THE CHALLENGES OF CRITICAL EMOTIONAL LITERACY

FOR MANY OF these students, their work in our classrooms may be one of their only forums for naming the emotions and the politics related to this war. Even if we are not willing as teachers to risk our own vulnerability, we must reevaluate what counts as knowledge for our students and whether or not emotional sensitivity and affective education represent crucial forms of epistemological awareness requisite to a transforming society. Simply stating that one does not express emotion in the classroom when in the role of authority is a culturally coded form of denial about what counts as "emotion." The classroom community, we are implicitly taught through discourses of negation, is not a place where emotional epistemology or literacy are part of the educational agenda. But in fact teachers' emotional needs are constantly attended to in the classroom: The interactions of authority, the effect of power on one's ego, the complex ways in which teachers take the last word, or use students' questions or insights to develop their own thinking cannot be separated from one's emotional needs. One can observe persistent patterns of male instructors, for example, controlling the sphere of rational discourse as an arena for their own very empassioned emotional articulation.[18]

Intervention at the level of representation does suggest a starting point for interrupting powerlessness. With respect to the repetitive trauma that helps to construct powerlessness, Walter Benjamin's straightforward direction for reading visual images is helpful on the issue of subversion. In a speech delivered in 1934, Benjamin addresses precisely how the artist/intellectual can transform or reappropriate the "means of production," as it were, rather than passively participating in the reproduction of the status quo. In his interrogation of the role of the intellectual/writer in relation to class struggle, Benjamin argues for a kind of authorship that transforms the means of production (in service to socialism) simultaneous with its production. He criticizes the New Matter-of-Fact photographers, who in one case "succeeded in transforming abject poverty, by recording it in a fashionably perfected manner, into an object of enjoyment" (1984: 304). He calls this "a flagrant example of what it means to supply a productive apparatus without changing it." Rather, he asserts, "What we require of the photographer is the ability to give his picture the caption that wrenches it from modish commerce and gives it a revolutionary useful value." By teaching skills of self-reflection and critical analysis that are available to students as they move beyond the walls of the university, we may enact Benjamin's suggestion of displacing meanings and shifting our relation to the world.

One alternative to numbness is to bridge the gap between the isolated internal life and the external visible life of "schoolwork." Elaine Scarry tells us that to articulate pain is an extraordinary challenge, for

> the moment [pain] is lifted out of the ironclad privacy of the body into speech, it immediately falls back in. Nothing sustains its image in the world. . . . From the inarticulate it half emerges into speech and then quickly recedes once more. Invisible in part because of its resistance to language, it is also invisible because its own powerfulness ensures its isolation, ensures that it will not be seen in the context of other events, that it will fall back from its new arrival into language and remain devastating. Its absolute claim for acknowledgment contributes to its being ultimately unacknowledged. (1985: 60–61)

In relation to the classroom, the ineffability of pain raises the challenge of discussing the "reality" of war effectively. What does it mean to learn to apply language to the critical articulation of anger, rage, grief, and pain? Emotion defies language, and education discursively denies language to emotion. To leap off this precipice into uncharted discursive space is an act of courage. Scarry's redefinition of "work" suggests articulate embodiment as part of education:

> Work and its "work" (or work and its object, its artifact) are the names that are given to the phenomena of pain and the imagination as they begin to move from being a self-contained loop within the body to becoming the equivalent loop now projected into the external world. It is through this movement out into the world that the extreme privacy of the occurrence (both pain and imagining are invisible to anyone outside the boundaries of the person's body) begins to be sharable, that sentience becomes social. (1985: 170)

"Work" as process and product are certainly familiar aspects of education. However, the public expression of this sentience represents a real risk. The extremely harsh prohibitions against vulnerability in academia circumscribe expression within these hallowed hails. Yet we are constantly engaged in this bridging and transformation of the internal and private into the public, although this process has not been fully legitimated as an educational goal.

To challenge pastoral power successfully involves an integration of structures of feeling with the work of education. The individual and collective work we engage in within academia is deeply etched with felt histories and meanings. We choose whether to turn away from these chasms and pulls to community or whether to learn to incorporate structures of feeling as the missing element for posttraumatic knowledges. The "controlled discomfort" Scarry describes as constituting some kinds of work is frequently avoided in the classroom, also attributable to the discourses of danger surrounding emotion.

Three strategic lessons emerge from pondering this crisis on the intersection of the global and the local. Students and educator are not and will never be equals or peers within the institutional setting; there are more and less effective strategies for encouraging debate on current events; and I am not alone in my frustration with the ethical crises provoked at that historical moment. Ideally, the work of developing emotional epistemologies and literacies, with an eye toward community, begins to occur even at the minimum level of self-reflective questions about representation and expression within circumscribed classroom norms and scripts. In sum, I am not willing to accept that emotional literacy and the aim of challenging powerlessness are not primary goals of education. The history and norms of classroom etiquette merely represent an institutional habit and do not justify systematic strictures against community.

Despite our complicated interactions and relationships fraught with power and desire, despite the longing for impossible connections and shared visions, we can model for students a form of world transformation and resistance to globalization by showing how pain and powerlessness are constructed and can be displaced into a notion of "work." Whether this means words, essays, collective projects, understandings of our ethical obligations in chemistry and biology, or recording dreams is undetermined. However, as long as we agree that this localized site is overshadowed by the ineffability of pain, and surrender to fears inculcated by the danger-discourse surrounding expression of emotion, as long as we continue to embody with docility the norms that appear so innocent and "apolitical," we offer students no better vision of how to transform either their own pain and rage or how to enact upon the world the alternative visions each carries.

The definitions of identity, the power relations, and persistent fears defined by discourses of negation and predominant silences tell us only that we are surviving the inscriptions of the modern institution. Whereas the Persian Gulf War brought this into sharp relief because of direct and offensive U.S. military action, the myriad versions of U.S. military action both inside and outside of the boundaries of this nation easily compel a sense of perpetual crisis that warrant calling educational aims into question at every historic moment. Although at times the relation between our interactions in the classroom feels hopelessly disconnected from what occurs halfway around the world, I recognize that this sense of futility intelligently is enacted through bodies, through local sites that interrupt the gloss of numb docility. In these bodies called students and teachers, within our very cells, abides an undiminishable source of energy always willing to be transformed into language, into marks upon unwilling walls.

I want to give special thanks to Ann Cvetkovich, Natasha Levinson, and Roz Spafford for their responses to this essay. I am also grateful to the Center for Cultural Studies, University of California, Santa Cruz, who published an earlier version of this essay through the Cultural Studies of Science and Technology Research Group. (Levinson's response to a version of this essay presented at the 1995 Philosophy of Education Society Meetings in San Francisco can be found in the Society's Proceedings.)

1 In their introduction to the collection *Colonial Discourses and Post Colonial Theory*, editors Patrick Williams and Laura Chrisman discuss how these literatures intersect with other contemporary theories (1994). Relevant to my arguments about refusing

false distinctions between discourses of the local and global, they define poststructuralism and postmodernism suggestively. The former refers to critiques of the self as conceived within bourgeois individualism; the latter challenges the notion of master narratives. While one might argue that globalization can be discussed without taking poststructuralism or postmodern theories into account, any critique of capitalism — particularly if following in Gramsci's shadow — is less than adequate without a critique of how the isolated self of pastoral power is one of the grandest master narratives of United States rhetoric.

2 For a fuller treatise of the media representations of the Persian Gulf War, see the recent anthology *Seeing Through the Media: The Persian Gulf War*, edited by Susan Jeffords and Lauren Rabinovitz; Douglas Kellner, *The Persian Gulf TV War*; and Les Levidow "The Gulf Massacre as Paranoid Reality." I composed this essay during the Persian Gulf War and am pleased that subsequent years have yielded significant analyses of media's new "globalized' role; as Jeffords states, "the primary functions the media served during the war [were]: reconstructing history, controlling the dissemination of information, creating social consensus, and solidifying national identity" (1994: 14). See also the pioneering work of Lynn Worsham, "Emotions and Pedagogic Violence" (1990–91).

3 In my essay "The Risks of Empathy: Interrogating Multiculturalism's Gaze" (1997a), I examine the contemporary faith in empathy and social imagination as a foundation for democratic communities and challenge this faith through an interdisciplinary analysis of the complexity of power relations that define reading, identification, and any "actions" that may result from empathy. In another essay, "Emotional Quotient: The Taming of the Alien" (forthcoming 1999), I examine the popularized sociobiological discourses regarding "emotional intelligence" and argue that altruism may play a new role in the globalized economy. imagination and community; see also Boler, "Review Essay of Benhabib's Situating the Self and Bogdan's Re-Educating the Imagination" (1995).

4 The ethnographic work of Lutz and Abu-Lughod (1990) provides international and cross-cultural research on cultural variation in emotional practices, expressions, rules, and codes. It is worth addressing the anticipated critique that a call for "emotional literacy" represents a practice most familiar through middle-class, white practices presently popular in distinct regions of the United States. It is certainly the case that "access" to the explicit discourses on emotions through the specific practices of psychotherapy are afforded by social class. Taking into account the gendered, racialized, and classed character of such popularized discourses on emotion, every one of us exists within a nexus of emotional discourses. In my larger project I have traced the dominant discourses in Western cultures: the pathological (medical, scientific, social scientific, and psychological); the romantic (as is permitted in the arts, the channeling of passions, etc.); the rational (emotion channeled into debate, argument within educational practices and politics); and the more recent emergence of sociopolitical discourses of emotion through the civil rights and feminist movements, in which emotions such as pride and anger take on new cultural meanings.

5 The negating discourses that determine when and how vulnerability is permitted between student and teacher is a subject I address in an essay titled "Medusa's Daughters" presented at the California Association of Philosophers of Education at Stanford University, April 1993. To develop emotional literacy and epistemology raises the central question: What are the ethics of requiring vulnerability given the power differential of student and teacher, and given vast cultural differences potentially represented in a classroom? Similarly, the codes circumscribing the different risks of vulnerability for male and female educators in higher education pose a genuine problem: For women to maintain authority, expressions of vulnerability risk denigration of women's authority in the classroom.

6 In the introduction to the winter 1990–1991 issue of *Discourse*: Kathleen Woodward

describes the work of the contributors/participants in the 1989–90 Center for Twentieth Century Studies who took as their theme "Discourses of the Emotions." Commenting on the missing discourses of emotion she writes, "The emotions are not dead, they are simply not present in academic discourse. Discourses of the emotions (even the emotions themselves) are everywhere, omnipresent in our everyday lives" (4). The work collected in two recent issues of *Discourse* represents excellent interdisciplinary analyses of emotion, and emotion and subjectivity, respectively: see *Discourse* 13 (1) (Fall–Winter 1990–1991); and 152 (Winter 1992–1993). It is not a coincidence that, particularly within classrooms, questions of identity politics and relations of powers are dynamics experienced and recognized. but generally not directly addressed. See for example, bell hooks's essays on pedagogy and class in *Talking Back*.

7 See for example Michael Katz, *Class, Bureaucracy, and Schools* (1971), in which he traces the historical development of the bureaucratic structures of North American schools, an analysis that dovetails with Foucault's understandings of administrative, pastoral power.

8 The literature that informs my research and study of emotion is drawn from several distinct fields. For analyses that combine ethnography with social and cultural critique, see Catherine Lutz and Lila Abu-Lughod (1990); in sociology, see for example Arlie Hochschild (1983). A few select interdisciplinary analyses relevant to thinking about such issues as war include Shoshana Felman and Dori Laub, (1992); Jennifer Gore and Carmen Luke (1992); Philip Wexler (1992); Henriques et al., Changing the Subject (1984); Megan Boler (1992). In the field of literature, see Ann Cvetkovich (1992). On the value of anger, see especially Peter Lyman (1991); Naomi Scheman, ([1980] 1993); in philosophy, see Elizabeth Spelman, (1980) and Lynne McFall, (1988).

9 The following student's written response to the cease-fire declaration evidences the double-edged function of numbness: "If you really want to know what I honestly think about this war being over. . . . I have no thoughts, feelings, or reactions towards it. . . . Yah I'm glad, but I really don't care at this point anymore about the war. . . . I'm happy that I know my best friend can come home safe and I don't have to worry about coming home each day and checking my machine to hear that he's dead and his body will be sent back on so and so a date. . . . Other than that I have no feeling about the war being over because I had no feeling toward the war in a very long time."

10 The phenomenon of powerlessness is experienced not only in response to an event such as war but is an everyday occurrence, bred within the walls of the university as this same student's writing continues on to say: "During my Jr. year when I was supposed to write down a classic 5-paragraph essay I did not get the format. I went through all of my notes, and listened to her when I was supposed to. Still, I could not get it together to write a better essay, no matter what I did, I felt powerless." The fact that a writing assignment engenders the same sense of powerlessness as that incurred by George Bush's military regime gives me great pause in my assumptions about liberatory education.

11 In *Desiring Identities* I examine identity as a form of repetitive trauma in order to assess the relation of silence and voice to modes of bearing witness. I analyze the relationship of narrative to identity, and to catharsis in turn. In the event of repeated (rather than acute) trauma, a "storytelling" frequently does not come easily, or can occur in fixed repetition that is not transformative. Questions that emerge in this study include: How are silence and voice related to the severity and extent of trauma in terms of its repetition? How is it that repetitive trauma becomes embodied and habituated such that it is "forgotten"?

12 Raymond Williams' notion of "structures of feelings"(1977) permits a bridge between these puzzles of language, and emotion.

13 In 1958 Hannah Arendt, for example, addresses with great foreshadowing the loss of

language as a casualty of science's language of mathematical symbols (*The Human Condition*, 4).

14 An African-American writer and a Nigerian-British writer, respectively authors of *The Salt Enters* and *The Joys of Motherhood*.

15 In "The Subject and Power," Foucault suggests that "to understand what power relations are about . . . we should investigate the forms of resistance and attempts made to dissociate these relations [of, for example, 'administration to how people live']" (1984: 419). Foucault focuses on pastoral power's individualizing techniques that make individuals "subjects," which assists in understanding how isolation and powerlessness get constructed.

16 I explore the difference between confession and testimony as modes of reading in "The Risks of Empathy: Interrogating Multiculturalism's Gaze" (1997a), Cultural Studies; an earlier version of this essay can be found in *Philosophy of Education Society Proceedings* (1994).

17 As Howley and Hatnett write, "Pastoral power represented a transaction: the individual revealed the truth about him or herself, and the pastor guaranteed the individual's salvation. By gaining knowledge of individuals in this way, the pastor gained power over them. The pastor exercised this power only insofar as it was necessary to restore individuals to a state of grace — or, in more contemporary parlance, to the state of being normal" (1992: 273).

18 In her article "On the Regulation of Speaking and Silence" (1985), Valerie Walkerdine provides an excellent analysis of how children are introduced into the use of white, middle-class rational discourse as the channel for their emotions, particularly expressions of conflict regarding those in authority. See also Kramarae and Treichler (1990).

CHAPTER SEVEN

THE RISKS OF EMPATHY

Interrogating Multiculturalism's Gaze

How old is the habit of denial? We keep secrets from ourselves that all along we know. The public was told that Dresden was bombed to destroy strategic railway lines. There were no railway lines in that part of the city. . . . I do not see my life as separate from history. In my mind my family secrets mingle with the secrets of statesmen and bombers. Nor is my life divided from the lives of others. . . . If I tell all the secrets I know, public and private, perhaps I will begin to see the way the old sometimes see, Monet, recording light and spirit in his paintings, or the way those see who have been trapped by circumstances — a death, a loss, a cataclysm of history.

— *Susan Griffin,* A Chorus of Stones

SOCIAL IMAGINATION AND ITS DISCONTENTS

UPON AN IVORY hill in central California another fall evening's garish red-hues announced my fourth year of teaching *MAUS*, the comic-book representation of author Art Spiegelman's father, Vladek, narrating his experience of surviving the Holocaust of the Second World War. Three hundred 18-year-olds—forty-seven of them charged to me — have been assigned this text, preceded by *The Joy Luck Club* by Amy Tan and quickly followed with *Zoot Suit* by Luis Valdez — the epitome of an introductory multicultural curriculum in the arts and humanities.

To all appearances, I should sleep well as a participant in this introduction to multiculturalism through the arts and literature; I should laud myself for taking up the liberatory potential outlined by forerunners John Dewey and Louise Rosenblatt. At the onset of the Second World War, the same moment that Vladek Spiegelman's story begins, progressive educational philosophers John Dewey and Louise Rosenblatt wrote optimistically of their faith in the "social imagination," developed in part through literature which allows the reader the possibility of identifying with the "other" and thereby developing modes of moral understanding thought to build democracy. In 1938 Louise

Rosenblatt wrote, "[i]t has been said that if our imaginations functioned actively, nowhere in the world would there be a child who was starving. Our vicarious suffering would force us to do something to alleviate it" (1938: 185). She describes the experience of reading a newspaper in a state of numbness, that all too familiar strategy for absorbing information without feeling it. "This habit of mind," she writes, "has its immediate value, of course, as a form of self-protection. . . . Because of the reluctance of the average mind to make this translation into human terms, the teacher must at times take the responsibility for stimulating it" (ibid.). Social imagination protects us, in this view, from Susan Griffin's above condemnation of the "habit of denial" that enables an occurrence like the bombing of Dresden. Thus faith is maintained today, for example, by Aristotelian philosopher Martha Nussbaum, who advocates "poetic justice" in which the student as "literary judge" comprehends the other through sympathy and fancy as well as rationality as the foundation for dignity, freedom and democracy (1995: 120–1).

Educators, philosophers of emotion and politicians have not abandoned this project of cultivating democracy through particular emotions, of which empathy is the most popular. Across the political and disciplinary spectrum, conservatives and liberals alike advocate variations of empathy as a solution to society's "ills." At a recent public lecture, Cornel West insisted that empathy is requisite to social justice.[1] Empathy is taught in legal and medical education under the rubric of 'narrative ethics'; there is now a journal entitled *Literature and Medicine*. Cognitive scientists claim empathy as a genetic attribute, and speculate on a neurological map of ethics (May et al. 1996). Empathy has been popularized recently through the bestselling book *Emotional Intelligence*, further publicized through *Oprah, Time* magazine and National Public Radio. Empathy, a primary component of "emotional intelligence quotient," is a product of genetic inheritance combined with self-control, Aristotelian fashion. This emotional literacy, essentially a behavioural modification program, is now taught in hundreds of public schools throughout the United States.[2] Finally, in the last fifteen years of Western "multiculturalism," empathy is promoted as a bridge between differences, the affective reason for engaging in democratic dialogue with the other.[3]

But who and what, I wonder, benefits from the production of empathy? What kinds of fantasy spaces do students come to occupy through the construction of particular types of emotions produced by certain readings?[4] In what ways does empathy risk decontextualizing particular moral problems?[5] In short, what is gained by the social imagination and empathy, and is this model possibly doing our social vision more harm than good?

While empathy may inspire action in particular lived contexts — it is largely empathy that motivates us to run to aid a woman screaming next door — I am not convinced that empathy leads to anything close to justice, to any shift in existing power relations. In fact, through modes of easy identification and flattened historical sensibility, the "passive empathy" represented by Nussbaum's faith in "poetic justice" may simply translate to reading practices that do not radically challenge the reader's world view.

I see education as a means to challenge rigid patterns of thinking that perpetuate injustice and instead encourage flexible analytic skills, which include the ability to self-reflectively evaluate the complex relations of power and emotion. As an educator I understand my role to be not merely to teach critical thinking, but to teach a critical thinking that seeks to transform consciousness in such a way that a Holocaust could never happen again. Ideally, multiculturalism widens what counts as theory, history, knowledge and value, rather than enabling modes of empathy that permit the reader's exon exoneration from privilege and complicities through the "ah-hah" experience.

Nussbaum admits that no matter how powerful a vision of social justice is gained by the empathetic reader, our habituated numbness is likely to prevent any action. "People are often too weak and confused and isolated," she says, "to carry out radical political changes" (1996: 57). One can only hope then that empathy is not the only viable route to inspiring change. As another colleague succinctly stated, these 'others' whose lives we imagine don't want empathy, they want justice.[6]

The untheorized gap between empathy and acting on another's behalf highlight my discomfort with the use of *MAUS* in an introductory "multicultural" curriculum. My students' readings of *MAUS* enabled them to enter "imaginatively into the lives of distant others and to have emotions related to that participation," Nussbaum's prescription for an "ethics of an impartial respect for human dignity" (1995: xvi). But passive empathy satisfies only the most benign multicultural agenda. *MAUS* could be taught, I recognize, within a curriculum in such a way as to avoid some of the risks of empathy.[7] Yet introductory multicultural curricula cannot be all things, and most often do not provide detailed histories as backdrop to the literature read. What are the risks of reading a text like *MAUS* in the absence of more complete historical accounts?[8] What kinds of histories are presented in the name of multiculturalism, and what kind of historical sensibility is associated with these democratic ideals?

In question is not the text itself, but what reading practices are taught, and how such texts function within educational objectives. I hope to complicate the concept of empathy as a "basic social emotion" produced through novel-reading. I invoke a "semiotics of empathy," which emphasizes the power and social hierarchies which complicate the relationship between reader/listener and text/speaker. I argue that educators need to encourage what I shall define as "testimonial reading." Testimonial reading involves empathy, but requires the reader's responsibility. Shoshana Felman asks, "Is the art of reading literary texts itself inherently related to the act of facing horror? If literature is the alignment between witnesses, what would this alignment mean?" (Felman and Laub, 1992: 2). Such readings are possible potentially not only with testimony, or with novels, but across genres. Ideally, testimonial reading inspires an empathetic response that motivates action: a "historicized ethics" engaged across genres, that radically shifts our self-reflective understanding of power relations.

THE RISKS OF PASSIVE EMPATHY

PHILOSOPHERS DO NOT agree on empathy's role in moral evaluation. Kant, for example, viewed emotions as far too unreliable a basis for moral action, and held that only a unified and rational moral principle could be the basis of right action. David Hume, on the other hand, saw emotions as central to our moral behavior. Nussbaum states in passing that her Aristotelian views could be "accommodated by a Kantianism modified so as to give emotions a . . . cognitive role" (1995: xvi). In a pivotal treatise on altruism (Blum 1980), a central unresolved question is the extent to which altruistic emotions must include being disposed to take *action* to improve the other's condition.

Empathy belongs to a class of "altruistic emotions" that go by different names. Nussbaum draws on Aristotle's "pity," but switches to "compassion" to avoid the contemporary connotations of pity that Aristotle doesn't intend. In our common usage, "pity" indicates a sense of concern, but more negatively a sense that the other is possibly inferiorized by virtue of their "pitiful" status. Sympathy commonly refers to a sense of concern based not on identical experiences but experiences sufficiently similar to evoke the feeling of "there but for the grace of God go I." Empathy is distinct from sympathy on the common sense that I can empathize only if I too have experienced what you are suffering.

Throughout the discussion that follows, a key question remains: What role does *identification with the other* play in definitions of altruistic emotions? Can we know the other's experience? Briefly I suggest that in the definitions above, pity does not require identification; sympathy employs a generalized identification as in "that could be me" or "I have experienced something that bears a family resemblance to your suffering"; and empathy implies a full identification. In the cases of sympathy and empathy, the identification between self and other also contains an irreducible difference — a recognition that I am not you, and that empathy is possible only by virtue of this distinction.

I elect to use the term "empathy" because it is the term most frequently used across the different literatures I detailed in the introduction. However, what I call empathy and Nussbaum calls compassion is probably best understood as our common-sense usage of "sympathy." I further distinguish "passive empathy" to refer to those instances where our concern is directed to a fairly distant other, whom we cannot directly help. Some philosophers have it that in such cases the sufficient expression of concern is to wish the other well. I shall argue that passive empathy is not a sufficient educational practice. At stake is not only the ability to empathize with the very distant other, but to recognize oneself as implicated in the social forces that create the climate of obstacles the other must confront.

In her latest work, *Poetic Justice* (1995) and in "Compassion: the Basic Social Emotion," recently published in *Social Philosophy and Policy* (1996), Nussbaum advocates a humanist, democratic vision in which educators successfully enable students to imagine others' lives through novel-reading. The "others" in her examples are the homosexual man, the African-American man and the working-class man. She summarizes Aristotle's definition of "pity," which Nussbaum calls 'compassion' and I call "passive empathy":[9]

> [Pity posits] (1) the belief that the suffering is serious rather than trivial; (2) the belief that the suffering was not caused primarily by the person's own culpable actions; and (3) the belief that the pitier's own possibilities are similar to those of the sufferer. (1996: 31)

The central strategy of Aristotelian pity is a faith in the value of "putting oneself in the other person's shoes." By imagining my own similar vulnerabilities I claim "I know what you are feeling because I fear that could happen to me." The agent of empathy, then, is a fear for oneself. This signals the first risk of empathy: Aristotle's pity is more a story and projection of myself than an understanding of you. I can hear the defensive cries: But how can we ever really know the other save through a projection of the self? While I share this question, our inability to answer it adequately is not a defense of passive pity. More to the point is to ask, What is gained and/or lost by advocating as a cure for social injustice an empathetic identification that is more about me than you?

Pity centrally posits the "other" as the secondary object of concern, known only because of the reader's fears about her own vulnerabilities. Pity's first and second defining aspects are supporting corollaries to this positioning of self/other: the reader is positioned as judge, evaluating the other's experience as "serious or trivial," and as "your fault/not your fault." The other's serious suffering is "rewarded" by the reader's pity, if not blamed on the sufferer's own actions.

The identification that occurs through compassion, Nussbaum claims, allows us also to judge what others need in order to flourish. Nussbaum emphasizes that "pity takes up the onlooker's point of view, informed *by the best judgment* the onlooker can make *about what is really happening to the person being observed* . . . implicit in pity itself is *a conception of human flourishing, the best one the pitier is able to form*" (1996: 32–3; emphasis added).

Nussbaum indicates that we can "know the other" through compassion. I have significantly less faith in our capacity to judge what is "really happening" to others. To judge what "others need in order to flourish" is an exceptionally complicated proposition not easily assumed in our cultures of difference. Feminist and post-colonial writers, from Fanon and W. E. B. Du Bois, to Irigaray and Levinas, have critiqued the self/other relationship assumed in Western and psychoanalytic models of identification. While there is much more to this question than can be pursued here, I wish to point out that the uninterrogated identification assumed by the faith in empathy is founded on a binary of self/other that situates the self/reader unproblematically as judge. This self is not required to identify with the oppressor, and not required to identify her complicity in structures of power relations mirrored by the text. Rather, to the extent that identification occurs in Nussbaum's model, this self feeds on a consumption of the other. To clarify: In popular and philosophical conceptions, empathy requires identification. I take up your perspective, and claim that I can know your experience through mine. By definition, empathy also recognizes our difference — not profoundly, but enough to distinguish that I am not in fact the one suffering at this moment. What is ignored is what has been called the "psychosis of our time": Empathetic identification requires the other's difference in order to consume it as sameness. The irony of identification is that the built-in consumption annihilates the other who is simultaneously required for our very existence. In sum, the social imagination reading model is a binary power relationship of self/other that threatens to consume and annihilate the very differences that permit empathy. Popular and scholarly (particularly in the analytic traditions of philosophy) definitions of empathy seem unwittingly founded on this ironic "psychosis" of consumptive objectification.[10]

The troublesome terrain of identification poses questions about empathy that must be pursued elsewhere. How do critiques of identification complicate Western models of empathy? What might empathy look like, and produce, when it doesn't require identification? What about more difficult cases in which the reader is required to empathize with the oppressor, or with more complicated protagonists? (Here I think of Marleen Gorris's film *A Question of Silence*; and of performances like Anna Deveare Smith's *Fires in the Mirror*, a representation of the Crown Heights conflicts in Brooklyn which permits the viewer to empathize with multiple points of view. Deveare Smith's performance exemplifies the potential for a disturbingly relativized ethics, while highlighting the vast historical and cultural ignorances that cause such moral conflicts.) Finally, the readers Nussbaum speaks of represent a largely homogenous group in terms of class and ethnicity. What would it mean to empathize across other differences; when and why, for example, should inner-city youths read Virginia Woolf or *Wuthering Heights*?[11]

For the time being I can confirm that the Aristotelian definition of pity can indeed be produced through reading literature, as it was when students read *MAUS*. Passive empathy produces no action towards justice but situates the powerful Western eye/I as the judging subject, never called upon to cast her gaze at her own reflection.

THE RISKS OF READING MAUS

ART SPIEGELMAN'S *MAUS* engages the social imagination precisely as progressive educators advocate: The reader easily identifies with the other, and easily occupies an emotional space that feels the other's experience. *MAUS* represents an additional effect of empathetic identification. While some students do read *MAUS* as a portrait of father/son dynamics rather than a story centrally about the Second World War, many come to the particularly dangerous conclusion that they have gained new insight into "history." The effect of this book on its audiences can be remarkable, literally beyond words: Few readers put the book down, once begun; students attest again and again how profoundly the reading affects them; and they state that for the first time they are able to "identify" with the experience of the Jewish people during the Second World War. The story takes the form of two narratives: Vladek's story of survival during the war, interrupted by present-moment interactions of Vladek, and the author, Art Spiegelman, living out their father-son relationship as Art interviews his father. Spiegelman enables a mixture of detachment and identification through his use of animal caricatures of Nazis, Jews and Polish people. Spiegelman stated in an interview that in writing this comic-book he had no intention of the work representing history. Rather, this comic—his unique artistic genre, first published as a comic-book series in *RAW* — was his way of coming to terms with his relationship with his father and his mother's suicide.[12]

MAUS is an appropriate representation of the incommensurability of histories and empathy: To read *MAUS* is to walk the border of mesmerizing pleasure, the apotheosis of the pleasure of the text, alongside absolute horror. Empathetic identification is not necessarily with the Holocaust survivor.

Pleasure is enabled by the easy identification with Art, the son, through whom we witness the father's story of the Holocaust. One can read through Art's veiled "survivor's guilt" (we too were excepted from this fate), a consequence of the fact that his brother, his parents' first child, was taken by the Nazis. Second, the depiction of characters through animal metaphor allows for pleasurable detachment. Finally, there is no doubt that reading pleasure stems from the unimaginable horror of the Holocaust being well contained in the genre of comic-book "frames."

This year one student commented that the device of representing people as animals — Spiegelman's technique of detachment, dehumanization and understatement — made the story all the more horrific; while another disagreed, saying that these devices are effective because the reader can learn about the Holocaust without guilt.

In a telling description of passive empathy, another student writes:

> A person unaccustomed to reading the kind of material presented in novels recounting the Holocaust might be more comfortable reading the easier flow of the comic-book-style used by Spiegelman. Spiegelman can ensnare readers into his book *MAUS* by sheer curiosity, and once they have begun it would be difficult to stop reading.
>
> . . . By not pulling any punches, he addresses the horrors that occurred without making the reader feel as though she or he has been bombarded by feelings of rage and guilt. Often, the story of the Holocaust is told from a standpoint of such emotional turmoil that factual information is lost. Although *MAUS* is filled with strong images and disturbing occurrences, the reader does not feel that blame and pity is being forced onto himself or herself, but rather that Spiegelman is just "telling his story."

This student's primary concern is for the reader's comfort: Spiegelman doesn't "pull any punches"; his representation does not "bombard" the reader with "feelings of rage and guilt." By "just telling his story" and through the "easier flow of the comic-book style," *MAUS* permits the reader not to feel attacked; the "reader does not feel that blame and pity is being forced onto herself." This "comfort" appears to rest in part on her classification of *MAUS* as an "unemotional" genre. Her account juxtaposes "just telling [a] story" and "factual information" on the one hand, with the emotionality of blame, pity, rage and guilt on the other. *MAUS* works effectively because unlike other genres it "just tells a story," she says, while "novels recounting the Holocaust" and "the story of the Holocaust" she classifies as too emotional thereby causing the reader discomfort. But this brings us directly to a risk of empathy: If this text allows the reader this sense of gripping and relatively "easy" reading, are we not faced precisely with an abdication of responsibility? The reader does not have to identify with the oppressors. Rather, one identifies with the son who was not present, and with the dehumanized animal metaphors. What does it mean to experience a pleasurable read and be spared the emotions of rage, blame and guilt? In what ways is passive empathy related to the dehumanization strategies used to justify and represent war?

Quite in line with Aristotle's ideal definition of empathy and with the ego's consuming desire for the distinctive other, the use of animal metaphor permitted students to feel relatively undisturbed, while simultaneously permitting them to easily "imagine the other" — too easily, with little self-reflective engagement. In a twist of Aristotle's shared vulnerabilities model, "being in the other's shoes" was possible not through identification with power relations, but through a floating animal metaphor that allows heightened detachment rather than intimacy as the basis for empathy. The identification with Art's witnessing of his father functioned both through reversibility ("I could be in your shoes"), and through a mode of passive empathy that not only frees the reader from blame, but in this case allows the voyeuristic pleasure of listening and judging the other from a position of power/safe distance. While in some cases the pleasurable reading of this text may inspire students to pursue study of Jewish history and culture, I am not at all convinced that this potential benefit outweighs the risk of readings that abdicate responsibility.

The readers' desire to occupy a particular space of empathic identification was challenged in a lecture on *MAUS* delivered to all three hundred students that semester.[13] The philosophy professor stated that the reader is utterly deceived if s/he feels they can imagine the Holocaust from reading *MAUS*. He argued that to learn successfully about the Holocaust required reading stories and statistics until it becomes, precisely, *unimaginable*. Since the primary response of students is a variation of "after reading *MAUS*, I feel for the first time that I understand the experience of those who survived," his challenge was appropriate. In our discussion some days later, the students expressed an almost unilateral offence at his statement that we could not imagine the Holocaust: They deeply wanted to believe that their identification was sufficient — a version of Rawls's (1972) commitment to "reversibility" as the abstracted universalization of moral situations.[14]

Students' reading of *MAUS* exonerated and redeemed them from the usual sense of guilt and numbing horror that they associate with histories of the Holocaust. Passive empathy does not engage an identification with the deeper implications of being a Holocaust survivor or child of a survivor; or of being excepted by virtue of WASP status; or of identifying with the contemporary climate of anti-Semitism. In some ways the relationship between reader and text is a shifting confessional: Passive empathy absolves the reader through the denial of power relations. The confessional relationship relies on a suffering that is not referred beyond the individual to the social.

To summarize my queries, I can entirely agree with Nussbaum's description that literature promotes "identification and emotional reaction" which "cut through those self-protective stratagems, requiring us to see . . . things that may be very difficult to confront — and they make this process palatable by giving us pleasure in the very act of confrontation" (1995:6). This palatable permission of pleasure motivates no consequent reflection or action, either about the production of meaning, or about one's complicit responsibility within historical and social conditions. Let off the hook, we are free to move on to the next consumption.

TOWARDS A SEMIOTICS OF EMPATHY

ALTHOUGH USED TO give the illusion of universalized experience, empathy cannot produce one kind of universal relation between reader and text. Empathy is produced within networks of power relations represented by reader and text, mediated by language, narratives, genres and metaphors. The missing paradigm in theories of emotion across disciplines is an account that shifts emotions from being seen as the property or idiosyncrasy of the individual, towards a collectivist account.[15] Who benefits from the production of empathy in what circumstances? Who should feel empathy for whom? If no change can be measured as a result of the production of empathy, what has been gained other than a "good brotherly feeling" on the part on the universal reader? As one small contribution to this project I propose "testimonial reading" as an alternative to passive empathy.

The primary difference between passive empathy and testimonial reading is the responsibility borne by the reader. Instead of a consumptive focus on the other, the reader accepts a commitment to rethink her own assumptions, and to confront the internal obstacles encountered as one's views are challenged. Shoshana Felman indicates that the "imperative of bearing witness . . . is itself somehow a philosophical and ethical correlative of a situation with no cure, and of a radical human condition of exposure and vulnerability" (Felman and Laub, 1992: 5). To share this burden, testimonial reading recognizes the correlative task of reading as a similarly exposed vulnerability. Rather than seeing reading as isolated acts of individual response to distant others, testimonial reading emphasizes a collective educational responsibility.

As we hear about and witness horrors, what calls for recognition is not "me" and the possibility of my misfortune, but a recognition of power relations that defines the interaction between reader and text and the conflicts represented within a text. Listening plays a central role in this semiotic understanding of any emotion. For example, in a discussion of the collaborative process through which an emotion like "bitterness" is named and takes shape, feminist philosopher Sue Cambell (1994) articulates how the "failure to listen" works alongside the recounting of injury to construct the accusation and thus experience of bitterness. In *The Drowned and the Saved* (1989), Primo Levi's discussion of shame exemplifies a structure of feeling that traces a listening to the residue of history.[16] Levi's question "Are you ashamed because you are alive in place of another?" demands an account of biography and history. In a similar vein, Roger Simon (1994) asks that we learn to "listen differently," through an integration of history and biography to establish what he calls "living memory" which depends in part on structures of feeling "that determine our relations to that history."

Minnie Bruce Pratt (1988) argues for such an alternative as she analyses her work integrating her biography with her history as a white Southern woman. "Sometimes we don't pretend to be the other, but we take something made by the other and use it for our own." She describes her identification experience listening to Black folk singing, and reflects her major turning point when she realized that

> I was using Black people to weep for me, to express my sorrow at my responsibility, and that of my people, for their oppression: and I was mourning because I felt they had something I didn't, a closeness, a hope, that I and my folks had lost because we tried to shut other people out of our hearts and lives.
>
> Finally I understood that I could feel sorrow . . . yet not confuse their sorrow with mine, or use their resistance for mine. . . . I could hear their songs like a trumpet to me: a startling . . . a challenge: but not take them as a replacement for my own work. (1988: 41)

The challenge to undertake "our own work" accepts a responsibility founded on the discrepancy of our experiences. There is no need to consume through empathetic identification, or to recognize the words from the speaker's perspective. Second, there is no need to "rank oppressions" in such a way that we are pitted against one another to produce guilt rather than empathy. Empathy offers a connection and communication we don't want to lose. It's possible to identify the sense in which we've all been hurt, but to do so without a reductive denial of specificities.

How might we read, not through the ethics of universal reversibility? What would a reading practice look like, if not founded on the consumptive binary self/other which threatens annihilation of the other's difference?

TESTIMONIAL READING

What is at stake is not only the ability to empathize with the very distant other, but to recognize oneself as implicated in the social forces that create the climate of obstacles the other must confront. What, then, distinguishes empathetic from testimonial reading? What might it mean for the reader to "take action"? I suggest that unlike passive empathy, testimonial reading requires a self-reflective participation: an awareness first of myself as reader, positioned in a relative position of power by virtue of the safe distance provided by the mediating text. Second, I recognize that reading potentially involves a task. This task is at minimum an active reading practice that involves challenging my own assumptions and world views.

In *Testimony: Crises of Witnessing in Literature, Psychoanalysis, and History,* Shoshana Felman analyses the role of testimony in relation to pedagogy to illustrate the crises of meaning and histories that mark education. Co-author Dori Laub outlines the obstacles encountered by testimony's audience. Their analyses suggest the preliminary characteristics of testimonial reading. I draw on two key areas to characterize testimonial reading: our political climate of crisis, which requires new representations of "truth" which are not static and fixed, but allow us to communicate trauma's "excess." Second, in response to crisis the reader accepts responsibility as a co-producer of "truth." This responsibility requires a committed interrogation of the reader's response as she faces the other's experience. To turn away, to refuse to engage, to deny complicity — each of these responses correlates with a passive empathy and risks annihilating the other.

The crisis of truth

FELMAN CHARACTERIZES our historical moment as marked by a "crisis of truth." The crisis is material and representational: the historical and social traumas which define our everyday and historical lives, and the crisis of representing these traumas. Testimony responds to the crisis of truth by "exceeding the facts." In the legal context, testimony is called for "when the facts upon which justice must pronounce its verdict are not clear, when historical accuracy is in doubt and when both the truth and its supporting elements of evidence are called into question" (Felman and Laub, 1992: 5–6). By definition, testimony challenges legal and historical claims to truth: Specifically, testimony challenges the call for "just the facts, ma'am."

What the testimony does not offer is . . . a completed statement, a totalizable account of those events. In the testimony, language is in process and in trial, it does not possess itself as a conclusion, as the constation of a verdict or the self-transparency of knowledge. Testimony is, in other words, a discursive practice, as opposed to a pure theory. To testify — to vow to tell, to promise and produce one's own speech as material evidence for truth — is to accomplish a speech act, rather than to simply formulate a statement. As a performative speech act, testimony in effect addresses what in history is action that exceeds any substantialized significance, and what in happenings is impact that dynamically explodes any conceptual reifications and any constative delimitations. (1992: 5)

Testimony in this definition does not claim a static "truth" or fixed "certainty." As a dynamic practice and promise (Felman details the sense in which she orhe who testifies carries their own unique obligation to speak), testimony contains the energy and life force that cannot be captured as content or conclusion. Testimony's own medium "is in process," and has no self-transparency.

Testimony is trauma's genre: The excess and the unimaginable attempts its own representation through testimony. As an artistic and literary genre, testimony portrays "our relation to the traumas of contemporary history . . . composed of bits and pieces of a memory that has been overwhelmed by occurrences that have not settled into understanding or remembrance, acts that cannot be constructed as knowledge nor assimilated into full cognition, events in excess of our frame of reference" (1992: 5). To listen to testimony is no simple process of identification. Rather, trauma as excess raises the question: What are the forces that brought about this crisis of truth? How have the speaker and her memories come to represent the "other"? To excavate the forces that constructed the unspeakable is a painful process for the speaker as well as for the listener, because those forces are about oppression.

How do we shift from an understanding of testimony as face-to-face relation, to understanding testimonial reading as a relationship between text and reader? Felman's extension of testimony to describe the process of teaching helps to define my concept of testimonial reading. Teaching, she ventures,

takes place precisely only through a crisis: if teaching does not . . . encounter either the vulnerability or the explosiveness of a . . . critical and unpredictable dimension, it has perhaps *not truly taught*: it has perhaps passed on some facts . . . with which the students . . . can for instance do what people during the occurrence of the Holocaust precisely did with information that kept coming forth but that no one could *recognize*, and that no one could therefore truly *learn*, *read*, or *put to use*. (1992: 53)

Testimony can describe, then, not only the face-to-face relation but a genre of communication that requires the reader to "encounter vulnerability" and the explosiveness of a "critical and unpredictable dimension." Our responsibility in testimonial reading lies in our response to the crises of truth: How to recognize and put to use the information offered by the text.

THE RESPONSIBILITY OF LISTENING

MOST SIGNIFICANT TO a critique of passive empathy, testimony calls for the listener's — and analogously the reader's — responsibility, invoked and engaged by virtue of testimony being an "action" and "promise," rather than a report, description or chronicle. In Dori Laub's analysis of the relationship between the Holocaust survivor who testifies and the listener, the listener's work is crucial: The absence of a listener, or a listener who turns away or who doubts, can shatter testimony's potential as a courageous act in truth's moment of crisis. As Laub warns, "the absence of an empathic listener, or more radically the absence of an addressable other, an other who can hear the anguish . . . and thus affirm and recognize their realness, annihilates the story" (1992: 68). The listener plays a tremendous role in the production of truth, and relations of power are thus foregrounded.

Laub describes empathetic identification when he writes that the "listener to trauma comes to be a participant and co-owner of the traumatic event . . . comes to feel the bewilderment, injury, confusion, dread, and conflicts." Laub's description so far fits with empathy as a form of identification, of recognition that one is as vulnerable as the speaker — and that the listener "is also a separate human being and will experience hazards and struggles of his own" (58). Here again we see the irony of empathy: that it is only our separation — I/not I — that permits empathy. But Laub projects this separation as a place of connection as well: "[the listener] nonetheless does not become the victim — he preserves his own separate place, position, and perspective; a battleground for forces raging in himself, to which he has to pay attention if he is to properly carry out his task" (ibid.).

We arrive finally at the key distinction between passive empathy and testimonial reading: in testimonial reading, the reader recognizes herself as a "battleground for forces raging . . . to which [she] must pay attention . . . to properly carry out [her] task" (ibid.). "[T]o properly carry out her task," the testimonial reader must attend to herself as much as to the other — not in terms of "fears for one's own vulnerabilities," but rather in terms of the affective obstacles that prevent the reader's acute attention to the power relations guiding her response and judgements. For example, to experience a surge of irritation at the text allows the reader to examine potential analyses: Does she dismiss the text or protagonist on some count, or examine her own safeguarded investment that desires to dismiss the text out of irritation? Might irritation, for example, indicate the reader's desire to avoid confronting the articulated pain?

Expanding this point of responsibility, Laub identifies the "listening defenses that may interfere with carrying out the task of bearing witness." These include a "paralysis" from "fear of merger with the atrocities being recounted"; "anger unwittingly directed at the narrator"; "a sense of total withdrawal and numbness"; and an "obsession with fact-finding" that shuts off the human dynamic (1992: 72–3). By allowing these affective obstacles to interfere with testimonial reading, the reader risks "annihilating the story" (68). The ultimate risk of passive empathy may be the annihilation of the text into an object of easy consumption.

Testimony resonates with poststructuralist crises of truth: Testimony denies the reader's desires for certainty; the emphasis on language as practice, as action, replaces coherence and resolution with vulnerability and ambiguity. One of Felman's pedagogical objectives in using testimony was to

> make the class feel . . . how the texts that testify do not simply report facts but, in different ways, encounter — and make us encounter — strangeness; how the concept of testimony . . . is in fact quite unfamiliar and estranging, and how, the more we look closely at texts, the more they show us that, unwittingly, we do not even know what testimony is and that, in any case, it is not simply what we thought we knew it was. (1992: 7)

The notion of testimony as an attempt to represent, as Felman says, "events in excess of our frame of reference" refers back to the idea that such histories as the Holocaust must retain an unimaginable status. This abiding definition of testimony as a discursive process in defiance of closure underscored my discomfort with the risks of reading *MAUS* in isolation from a fuller historicization of surrounding events. My students' readings of *MAUS* seemed to defy the definition of testimony at each turn. Passive empathy did not engage them in an encounter with strangeness, with the uncanny; did not throw into question what they felt they knew. The readers experienced an untroubled identification that did not create estrangement or unfamiliarity. Rather, passive empathy allowed them familiarity, "insight", and "clear imagination" of historical occurrences — and finally, a cathartic, innocent, and I would argue voyeuristic sense of closure.

At minimum testimonial reading will call on us to analyze the historical genealogy of emotional consciousness as part of the structure that forms and accounts for the other's testimony. Testimonial reading leaves for the reader "no hiding place intact. As one comes to know the survivor, one really comes to know oneself" (72). Testimony calls for empathy as necessary to the comprehension of trauma, and necessary to extend cognition to its limits through historical consciousness. Through testimonial reading, then, one may recognize that I may imagine/feel the speaker's anguish (as my own). However, I also recognize that I cannot know the other (by virtue of historical difference, and/or through recognition that one speaker cannot embody and represent the six million unquantifiable traumas of this historical epoch). Testimonial reading recognizes its own limits, obstacles, ignorances, and zones of numbness, and in so doing offers an ally to truth's representational crisis.

To experience rage and shame on Bigger Thomas's behalf is not sufficient; nor is it sufficient to see racism as a "stain" and "infection" that prevents a common humanity (Nussbaum 1995: 96). Recognizing my position as "judge" granted through the reading privilege, I must learn to question the genealogy of any particular emotional response: My scorn, my evaluation of others' behavior as good or bad, my irritation — each provides a site for interrogation of how the text challenges my investments in familiar cultural values. As I examine the history of a particular emotion, I can identify the taken-for-granted social values and structures of my own historical moment which mirror those encountered by the protagonist. Testimonial reading pushes us to recognize that a novel or biography reflects not merely a distant other, but analogous social relations in our own environment, in which our economic and social positions are implicated.

Nussbaum focuses solely on the novel; Felman addresses literature, and Laub addresses the actual testimony of Holocaust survivors. I intend testimonial reading to be applicable across genres.[17] Empathy, argues Nussbaum, is a product of the "disturbing power" of "good" novels, an effect less common with histories or social sciences (5). This may reflect a symptom of our cultural numbness more than a genre distinction. Nussbaum's quick distinctions between genres reflects traditional disciplinary axioms: "history simply records what in fact occurred, whether or not it represents a general possibility for human lives. Literature focuses on the possible, inviting its readers to wonder about themselves" (5). In fact, historiographers have long debated history's ability to help us compare who we were and who we want to be.

As the nearly quintessential postmodern genre — comic-book, literature, history, testimonial, biography — *MAUS* represents an excellent example of the empathies produced not only through novels but through increasingly cross-disciplinary genres. It is beyond the scope of this article to analyse what testimonial reading will look like across different genres. But since texts are historically situated in power relationships, all texts can potentially be read testimonially. To enquire about these reading tasks, we might ask, what crisis of truth does this text speak to, and what mass of contradictions and struggles do I become as a result?

While "face-to-face" testimony and listening might seem another order from reading, in our fragmented, globalized, and technological culture communication becomes increasingly indirect in terms of face-to-face interaction. Schooling itself continues to take form through "distance education." Intimate relations are begun and borne out through electronic communications. We may come to redefine "face-to-face," as we also redefine the genres and forms of testimony. To reconceptualize the task of reading, as text replaces human speech, provides an ethical groundwork for post-modern interaction.

THE PROMISES OF TESTIMONIAL READING

LET ME CONCLUDE with a hopeful example in which a student seemed to move from a decontextualized, empathetic reading of *MAUS* to a testimonial reading. Her first essay expresses a classic example of social imagination at work:

> Spiegelman uses mice and cats to assign Jews and Germans specific characteristics that we usually attribute to these animals. . . . For example, if we imagine a town of mice, running everywhere with nowhere to go, always cautious and afraid, scampering to hide, it gives us a clear picture of what it must have been like for the Jews to be attacked by the Germans.

We had a lengthy and careful discussion about this troubling reading of *MAUS*—a conversation in which I took risks, and pushed her to think deeply about her relationship to the text, to her own audience, and to her experience. In the following excerpt of her revised essay she seems not only to locate herself, but to consider this text in the broadest sense of history and responsibility. "I used to look at history with a sense of guilt," she begins, and lists Native American and African-American history and white supremacy, "and I hated to think that I might be distantly related to some of these [oppressors]. This way of thinking led me to reject some aspects of history. I felt that I should not dwell on the past. . . . I rid myself of any sense of responsibility for what these people had done to other races. . . ." She then recounts a turning point in high school after viewing *Farewell to Manzanar*, a documentary about the internment of Japanese Americans during the Second World War. The issue was not guilt, she realizes: "it was more a question of discovering how things like concentration camps were started, and how it was that people came to think along these lines. It was a matter of examining their mistakes and our own mistakes so that we could move on . . . [Spiegelman]. . . . wants us to find an alternative to guilt." Strikingly different from her earlier notion that by imagining the Holocaust as a cat-and-mouse chase we understand history, one of her revised conclusions states: "The collective guilt that overpowers many of us should not be the reason for examining the Holocaust. We need to explore the origin of the cruelty of it."

"To explore the origins of this cruelty" requires not only multifaceted historical studies, but testimonial reading. Neither empathy nor historical knowledge alone suffices to shoulder the responsibility of this task. To excavate the structures of feeling that mediate testimonial reading is, in a sense, a labor of love. This work represents the obligation of witnessing truth's crisis, and accepting a responsibility to carry out the ethical relations implicit in languages that exceed the facts. In a sense, the reader is called upon to meet the text with her own testimony, rather than using the other as a catalyst or a substitute for oneself.

The call for testimonial reading is situated within a greater need for new conceptions of the relation of emotions and power. As we develop alternatives to privatized and naturalized models of emotion, I offer two concepts of the analysis of emotion and power relations: "economies of mind," which refers to emotion and affect as models of currency in social relations; and as an alternative to theories of depth unconscious, I suggest we consider emotions as "inscribed habits of inattention."

In a historical epoch of saturated communications, there is every temptation to turn our backs, to maintain the habit of denial, and to keep secrets from ourselves through the numb consumption of another's suffering, grateful for distances that seem to confirm our safety. Yet, at best, this illusion of safety and distance in which most live is precarious. Audre Lorde reminds us that our silence shall not protect us, nor does passive empathy protect the other from the forces of cataclysmic history that are made of each of our actions and choices. Aristotle also claimed that virtue is a matter of habit: We choose our ignorances, just as we choose our challenges.

I am grateful to many people whose readings have refined this article: Stephen Appel, Betsan Martin, Karen Jones, Mary Leach, Jennifer McKnight, Frank Margonis, Audrey Thomas, Roger Simon, Hayden White, and members of the Philosophy of Education Society.

1 Dr. West, author of *Race Matters* (1993), delivered this inaugural W. E. B. Du Bois Lecture and Film Series sponsored by the Ebony Museum in Oakland, 14 January 1994.

2 In "Emotional Quotient: The Taming of the Alien," I argue that contemporary constructions of empathy, and the new curricula of "emotional literacy," represent metaphorical and ideological shifts that may reflect capitalism's changed conceptions for human resource capital within globalization. (Conference paper delivered at "Narrative and Metaphor Across the Disciplines," University of Auckland, New Zealand, 10 July 1995.)

3 The social relations and democratic ideals embedded in articulations of "multi-culturalism" are by no means uniform, given its diverse appropriations. For historical treatments, see McCarthy (1990); McCarthy and Crichlow (1993). For a valuable collection of essays examining the radical practices of education (from W. E. B. Du Bois, to John Dewey, to bell hooks), see Perry and Fraser (1993); also Hull et al. (1982). Toni Morrison (1992) offers a stunning analysis of racialized identities mapped through the literary imagination.

4 From a conversation with Karen Jones in 1992.

5 From a conversation with Michael Katz in 1993.

6 A comment made by Ron Glass at the California Association of Philosophers of Education, Stanford University, May 1993.

7 In response to this article's critique of the risks of empathy with *MAUS*, Roger Simon offered an important counterexample regarding the use of *MAUS* in a course he teaches, in which he states "at least half.my class" undertook "the refusal of the possibility of an empathetic reading. This was generated as a self-conscious moral response by the reader/viewers and was a stance taken in regards to *MAUS*, the film version of *Schindler's List*, Morrison's *Beloved*, and a visit to the Toronto AIDS memorial. . . . This is a big improvement on any simple assumption of an empathetic identification and this refusal did lead to interesting discussions of the problematics of voyeurism and the possibilities and obligations of 'ethical tourism' (helped along I might add by students reading the original version of your paper)" (correspondence, 28 July 1994). In defence of the course I taught, each year our reading of *MAUS* was supplemented by speakers — one year Art Spiegelman himself, which strongly contextualized the work as "art" and "his own story" rather than as a history; another year, a Holocaust survivor testified; at other times, scholars of Holocaust literature and/or history addressed the students.

8 I am grateful for comments from Hayden White in response to this article about what would count as the 'histories' that complicated a reading of *MAUS*. See also, for example, Barzun (1950); White (1978).

9 Aristotle's philosophical portrait represents, of course, one among several; his model is frequently referenced in addition by feminist philosophers, and in popular texts. My rationale for selecting Aristotle is that the risks I see present in his definition represent what are in fact real risks we encounter in political solidarity work and learning to think about differences.

10 In a chapter entitled "Ethnology, Affect, and Intensifies: The Prediscursive Zone of Infant Feeling," of my forthcoming book, I explore contemporary psychoanalytic theorizing of affect and social relations. As Theresa Brennan describes in *History After Lacan*, "the ego can only make the world over in its own image by reducing the lively heterogeneity of living nature and diverse cultural orders to a gray mirror of sameness" (1993: 4). (See also Fuss 1995) who details the illusions built into the processes of identification; Robert Young (1990) who details the political violence wrought through imperialism as a kind of consumption through reduction of differences.) For further refigurings of the ethical relation, see, for example, Levinas (1989), and Irigaray (1977). On Irigaray and education see Martin (1997); on

Deleuze and education, see Leach and Boler (1997).

11 See, for example, "Tim Rollins and the Kids of Survival" in Paley (1995), a different interpretation of classic literature used by a project in the South Bronx that might be called "transgressive" and reappropriative readings.

12 For example, in contrast to Vladek's understated narrative of the war, the centerfold of *MAUS* is an inlaid cartoon depicting Art Spiegelman's highly emotional experience of his mother's suicide, his guilt, and the tension between Art and his father and the father's regulation of Art's emotional response, all of which puts into relief the deep structures of shame that accompany surviving a suicide or genocide. The presence of history and erasure is evidenced throughout the father/son relationship. The book ends, for example, with Art calling his father a "murderer," because Vladek confesses that he burned all the journals Art's mother had kept before, during, and following her survival of the concentration camps. For further reading on comicbooks in relation to history, and commentary on *MAUS*, see Hirsch (1992–93), and Witek (1987). See also Simon (1994); Zuckerman (1988); and Appelfeld (1993).

13 A lecture to the Porter Core Course students delivered by Professor Robert Goff, November 1993, University of California, Santa Cruz.

14 I have reviewed related questions of ethics, community, and imagination in relation to reading and political communities in Boler (1995).

15 Feminist analyses of emotion provide the most consistent political analyses of emotion (as opposed to what I call the three dominant paradigms of emotion). The other three dominant discourses of emotion I have identified as the rational, pathological, and romantic. See Sandra Bartky's invaluable political study of shame (1990). On anger, see especially Peter Lyman (1981); Scheman ([1977] 1983); and Spelman (1989). For a pioneering critique of emotions conceived in relation to the individual, see Scheman (1993). In philosophy, two essays on bitterness suggest promising routes towards a politicized philosophical theory of emotions: McFall (1991) and Campbell (1994); on trust, see Jones (1996). For interdisciplinary feminist and media studies, two issues of *Discourse* (1990–91) and (1992–93); and especially the work of Woodward in both issues. See also Grossberg (1992) for discussions of affect and agency within cultural studies. In feminist ethnography, see Lutz and Abu-Lughod (1990). Martin (1998) details Levinas's influence on Irigaray, with particular attention to the ethical "face-to-face" relation that outlines an alternative to the objectification of the other. She quotes John Wild, who suggests that the revolutionary potential of Levinas's 'face-to-face' ethical relation is that it is a 'third' way between individualism and collectivism" (30).

16 Raymond Williams (1961, 1977) introduced the term "structures of feeling" to describe the least understood aspect of cultural transmission of ideology. In a paper, "Affecting Assemblages," presented at Deleuze: A Symposium (6 December 1996), the University of Western Australia, Perth, I suggest the model "Economies of mind," to refer to emotion and affect as modes of currency in social relations; and I challenge psychoanalytic models to consider emotions inscribed "habits of inattention" as an alternative to theories of depth unconscious. On gossip and flight as rhizomatic pedagogies, see Leach and Boler (1998).

17 For an interesting discussion of "bearing witness" in relation to popular culture, in this case an *Oprah* episode on incest survivors, see Champagne (1994–95).

CHAPTER EIGHT

A PEDAGOGY OF DISCOMFORT

Witnessing and the Politics of Anger and Fear

What we commonly mean by "understand" coincides with "simplify": without a profound simplification the world around us would be an infinite, undefined tangle that would defy our ability to orient ourselves and decide upon our actions. In short, we are compelled to reduce the knowable to a schema.

—Primo Levi, *The Drowned and the Saved* [1]

For Descartes, there are only two possibilities: absolute certainty or epistemological chaos; that is, purity or corruption. ... When the universe becomes unmanageable, human beings become absolutists. We create a world without ambiguity in order to escape, as Dewey puts it, "from the vicissitudes of experience", to impose order on what is experienced as without organic order of its own.

— Susan Bordo, *The Flight to Objectivity* [2]

In every era the attempt must be made anew to wrest tradition away from a conformism that is about to overpower it.

— Walter Benjamin, *Illuminations* [3]

INTRODUCTION

WHAT WE ARE faced with in the course of the most ordinary lifetime is terrifying. The desire to order chaos through simplified schemas, to ward off the felt dangers of ambiguity, seems perhaps more "human" a characteristic than any other. The educator who endeavors to rattle complacent cages, who attempts to "wrest us anew" from the threat of conformism, undoubtedly faces the treacherous ghosts of the other's fears and terrors, which in turn evoke one's own demons. The path of understanding, if it is not to "simplify," must be tread gently. Yet if one believes in alternatives to the reductive binaries of good and evil, "purity and corruption," one is challenged to invite the other, with compassion and fortitude, to learn to see things differently, no matter how perilous the course for all involved.

I opened *Feeling Power* with examples of Bob Marley's and Calvin's different forms of resistance to education. In this chapter I explore in greater depth what we stand to gain from learning to "see differently." Exemplifying a refusal to see things differently, we will recall, in the *Calvin and Hobbes* cartoon Calvin hands back to his mother a book that she had given him and he had read. Calvin says, "It really made me see things differently. It's given me a lot to think about." Walking away, Calvin says, "It's complicating my life. Don't get me any more." Calvin represents one of those whom Maxine Greene notes when she comments, "relatively few people are . . . courageous enough actually to 'see'" (1988: 131). What helps us to develop, collectively, the courage to see things differently?

I outline a pedagogy of discomfort to foreground the question, What do we — educators and students — stand to gain by engaging in the discomforting process of questioning cherished beliefs and assumptions? I begin by defining a pedagogy of discomfort as both an invitation to inquiry as well as a call to action. As inquiry, a pedagogy of discomfort emphasizes "collective witnessing" as opposed to individualized self-reflection. I distinguish *witnessing* from *spectating* as one entrée into a collectivized engagement in learning to see differently. A central focus of my discussion is the emotions that often arise in the process of examining cherished beliefs and assumptions. I address defensive anger, fear of change, and fears of losing our personal and cultural identities. An ethical aim of a pedagogy of discomfort is willingly to inhabit a more ambiguous and flexible sense of self. My hope is that we are able to extend our ethical language and sense of possibilities beyond a reductive model of "guilt vs. innocence."

In this chapter I focus on how the dominant culture has taught us to view differences of race and sexual orientation. I choose these examples because in my teaching experience it is consistently questions of race and sexuality that are the most "discomforting" to educators and to students. I want to understand how *collectively* it is possible to step into this murky minefield and come out as allies and without severe injury to any party.

A PEDAGOGY OF DISCOMFORT AS CRITICAL INQUIRY

A PEDAGOGY OF DISCOMFORT begins by inviting educators and students to engage in critical inquiry regarding values and cherished beliefs, and to examine constructed self-images in relation to how one has learned to perceive others. Within this culture of inquiry and flexibility, a central focus is to recognize how emotions define how and what one chooses to see, and conversely, not to see.

This inquiry is a collective, not an individualized, process. As Greene notes, searching for freedom

> never occurs in a vacuum. Freedom cannot be conceived apart from a matrix of social, economic, cultural, and psychological conditions. It is within the matrix that selves take shape or are created through choice of action in the changing situations of life. The degree and quality of whatever freedom is achieved are functions of the perspectives available, and the reflectiveness on the choices made. (1988: 80)

In addition to being a collective process, this inquiry requires that educators and students learn to notice how one's sense of self and perspectives are shifting and contingent.

The call for "critical inquiry" in the liberal tradition is easily subsumed within the hollow invocations of values of dialogue, democracy, and rationality. Deeply rooted in Western conceptions of liberal individualism,[4] this common rhetoric threatens to reduce genuine inquiry to an individualized process with no collective accountability. Instead we are challenged to distinguish collective witnessing, for example, from the familiar notions of critical inquiry. I explore one version of educational individualism: the *risks of self-reflection*.[5]

The Risks of Self-Reflection

Self-reflection, like passive empathy, runs the risk of reducing historical complexities to an overly tidy package that ignores our mutual responsibility to one another. Empathy, as I argued in the previous chapter, often works through reducing the other to a mirror-identification of oneself, a means of rendering the discomforting other familiar and non threatening. In the example discussed in the previous chapter, students experienced a deceptive "ah-hah!" moment while reading Art Spiegelman's *MAUS*: "Now I know what it feels like to be the son of a Holocaust survivor/to be a survivor of the Nazi regime!" The simple identifications and passive empathy produced through this "confessional reading" assures no actual change. "Testimonial reading," I argued, carries with it a responsibility for the "forces raging within us"[6] — we are asked to turn the gaze equally upon our own historical moment and upon ourselves.

The Socratic admonition to "know thyself" may not lead to self-transformation. Like passive empathy, self-reflection in and of itself may result in no measurable change or good to others or oneself. The familiar call for critical self-reflection can easily be reduced to a form of solipsism, a kind of "new age," liberal navel-gazing. Upon self-reflection I may tell you, "I feel defensively angry when you suggest that I examine my privilege; this is how I feel when I think about racism/sexism/homophobia. It's too scary and hard and I don't want to change." This statement appears to take responsibility but in fact changes nothing, other than perhaps permitting the well-meaning white liberal to "feel better" having provided a self-critique. Thus "self-critique" easily functions as a form of "confession."

In contrast to the admonition to "know thyself," collective witnessing is always understood in relation to others, and in relation to personal and cultural histories and material conditions. To honor these complexities requires learning to develop *genealogies* of one's positionalities and emotional resistances. As Barbara Houston notes, "whatever pedagogy we use has to be one that directs us to something larger and other than ourselves and constantly and effectively reminds us that we are *more* than what is currently under scrutiny."[7] In order to achieve a vision beyond the isolated self, I am guided by Minnie Bruce Pratt's suggestions of "what we stand to gain" from this process of scrutiny. Put in slightly different terms she notes that "[t]o understand the complexity of another's existence is not to deny the complexity of our own" (1984: 18).

The demand for a genealogy of one's experience resonates with Joan Scott's argument regarding the evidence of experience. "When the evidence offered is the evidence of 'experience,' the claim for referentiality is further buttressed — what could be truer, after all, than a subject's own account of what he or she has lived through? It is precisely this kind of appeal to experience as uncontestable evidence and as an original point of explanation . . . that weakens the critical thrust of histories of difference" (1991: 777). However, as I have argued throughout *Feeling Power*, to believe we need to choose between *either* experience *or* history reflects the embedded binary oppositions of Western thought and not a necessary either/or choice.

To avoid an oversimplified version of self-reflection or an uncontestable invocation of "experience," pedagogical strategies must push beyond the usual Western conceptions of the liberal individual. Instead, the process of "becoming" may be understood as an undertaking that is both

(1) collective: "who we feel ourselves to be," how we see ourselves and want to see ourselves, is inextricably intertwined with others. To evidence this I examine how our identities, frail and precarious, are bound up with "popular history,"

with self-images, investments, and beliefs reiterated through the mass media, school textbooks, and dominant cultural values.
(2) flexible: leading to a willingness to reconsider and undergo possible transformation of our self-identity in relation to others and to history.

Any rigid belief is potentially "miseducative," and I do not exempt my own beliefs from this inquiry. Indeed one of the enriching and fulfilling aspects of being an educator, which is simultaneously difficult and painful, is that on a daily basis students may challenge me to question my own aims, ideas, and assumptions. I frequently encounter my own defensive anger and fears. Like Calvin, I am often tempted to dismiss views that I don't want to hear. Listening is fraught with emotional landmines. An ethical pedagogy would seem to require listening with equal attention to all views and perspectives. But some perspectives, particularly those I feel are reiterated throughout the dominant culture in harmful ways, are difficult, even dangerous, for me to hear.[8] I perpetually reevaluate and struggle to develop a pedagogy that calls on each of us to be responsible, and particularly calls for me to be extremely sensitive in how I pose my invitation to discomfort. Shifting views and questioning assumptions likely encounters emotional vicissitudes, such as defensive anger and fears. A pedagogy of discomfort, then, aims to invite students and educators to examine how our modes of seeing have been shaped specifically by the dominant culture of the historical moment.

A PEDAGOGY OF DISCOMFORT AS A CALL TO ACTION

A PEDAGOGY OF DISCOMFORT calls not only for inquiry but also, at critical junctures, for action — action hopefully catalyzed as a result of learning to bear witness. Just as self-reflection and passive empathy do not assure any change, so the safe project of inquiry represents only the first step of a transformative journey.

I anticipate the reader who believes that a call to action lies beyond the appropriate bounds of education. From the starting premises of *Feeling Power* I have argued that education always involves a political or social agenda. A pedagogy of discomfort is not a demand to take one particular road of action. The purpose is not to enforce a particular political agenda, or to evaluate students on what agenda they choose to carry out, if any. Further, given the "constraints" of educational settings, we may not always see or know what actions follow from a pedagogy of discomfort. But ethically speaking, the telos of inquiry does not provide sufficient response to a system of differential privileges built upon arbitrary social hierarchies.

EMOTIONAL SELECTIVITY AND LEARNING TO SEE

IN AN ASTUTE DESCRIPTION of the interrelationship between habit, sense of self, and what we do and do not wish to see or feel, John Dewey writes:

> Habit reaches . . . down into the very structure of the self; it signifies a building up and solidifying of certain desires; an increased sensitiveness and responsiveness . . . or an impaired capacity to attend to and think about certain things. Habit covers . . . the very makeup of desire, intent, choice, disposition which gives an act its voluntary quality. (quoted in Garrison 1997: 139)

Some philosophers call this emotional selectivity, "patterns of moral salience." Like Aristotle, John Dewey analyzed "selective emphasis" and argued for the ethical importance of seeing the "whole context."[9]

With Aristotle and Dewey, I emphasize the ways in which our emotional selectivity is shaped in particular political ways. If they did not think some degree of indoctrination inevitable, they should have.[10] I cannot imagine an education that is in any way uncontestable or neutral. One's learned emotional selectivity inevitably reflects the effects of specific cultural agendas.

Aristotle's ideas regarding the "habituation of character" as part of education entails bringing "the child to more critical discriminations. . . . What is required is a shifting of beliefs and perspectives through the guidance of an outside instructor" (Sherman 1989: 172). This is not a one-time event of shifting vision, but rather a "continuous and consistent instruction which will allow for the formation of patterns and trends in what the child notices and sees" (ibid.). The ability to see one's own foibles requires, according to Aristotle, dialogue and audience (Sherman 1989: 27).

I call this emotional selectivity *inscribed habits of (in)attention.* Aristotle and Dewey both stressed the importance of attending to our emotional selectivity as part of learning to choose "right actions," to "habituate character" towards a good.[11] The extraordinarily challenging question, never to be comfortably resolved, is who decides what counts as the "good"? What gives the "outside instructor" the authority to tell a child or student that their vision is "too selective," their emotions not properly habituated?

Some will argue that this conundrum is simply a "moral loggerheads": It is my view against yours, and on what basis can we possibly claim that one view is better than another, or that any action or transformation is required? Often it is at this juncture that educational philosophies retreat to rhetoric of pluralism, freedom of belief and speech, dialogue, and democracy. While these invocations are comforting and sometimes useful practices, the history of the Western world confirms that these democratic practices by no means assure justice, freedom, or a world free from violence. Once we examine the particulars, we may discover that we need more nuanced ways to speak about justice and injustice: *an historicized ethics.* A pedagogy of discomfort invites students to leave the familiar shores of learned beliefs and habits, and swim further out into the "foreign" and risky depths of the sea of ethical and moral differences.

WHAT WE STAND TO GAIN

IN HER ESSAY "Identity: Skin/Blood/Heart," Minnie Bruce Pratt (1984) addresses those born into privilege and asks, Why and when does a person willingly undertake change, especially if one is materially and ideologically safe and comfortable? What does one stand to gain from questioning one's cherished beliefs and changing fundamental ways of thinking?[12]

Pratt offers a unique example of a historicized analysis of "consciousness" and emotions. She examines her experience through different genealogical lenses: She maps her learned ways of seeing; her family history; her own particular investments and disinvestments; and the emotions that motivate her to change and which also make change discomforting and something to be resisted.

Pratt offers three answers to "what we gain" by setting on the frightening path of change. Each of her answers addresses *structures of feeling* (Williams 1977): the ways in which ideologies reflect emotional investments that by and large remain unexamined during our lifetimes, because they have been insidiously woven into the everyday fabric of common sense.

The first gain Pratt lists evidences how epistemology, emotions, and ethics are intertwined:

> I learn a way of looking at the world that is more accurate, complex, multi-layered, multi-dimensioned, more truthful. . . . I gain truth when I expand my constricted eye, an eye that has only let in what I have been taught to see. But there have been other constructions: the clutch of fear around my heart . . . kin to a terror that has been in my birth culture for years, for centuries: the terror of a people who have set themselves apart and above, who have wronged others, and

> feel they are about to be found out and punished. (1984: 17)

Pratt's second gain might be seen as a method that enables us to move beyond fear. What is required is the willingness to be "at the edge between fear and outside, on the edge of my skin, listening, asking what new thing will I hear, will I see, will I let myself feel. . . . I try to say to myself: To acknowledge the complexity of another's existence is not to deny my own" (18).

The third gain, she argues, is the relief afforded through the opportunity to move beyond the pain inherent to "separation" and distance from others. It is "painful," she states, "to keep understanding this separation within myself and the world. Sometimes this pain feels only like despair: yet I have felt it also to be another kind of pain, where the need to be with [others . . . breaks] through the shell around me . . . where with understanding and change, the loneliness won't be necessary" (1984: 19). As Houston summarizes, "At the heart of Pratt's discussion of each of the rewards or gains we might attain is her conviction that it is only when we are willing to recognize our fear, and how our fear is integral to why and how we have learned to separate ourselves from others, that we can achieve these rewards."[13]

Pratt emphasizes how what we learn *not* to see is shaped by fear, and how learning to see differently requires a willingness to live with new fears — what I call learning to inhabit a morally ambiguous self. As we learn to see differently, she encourages, we may actually gain relief from the pain of separateness.

I have used Pratt's work as an invitation to students for many years, at several universities, and I find that her narrative is an exceptionally powerful catalyst for many students. Here is an example from a graduate student in one of my seminars:

> [Pratt] made me think of my own life, and how I "view the world with my lenses." I want to have the knowledge and understanding to see the complexity and patterns of life. I want to be able to understand the layering of circles. . . . I feel the same way as Pratt, that when I begin to feel as if I had gained some truth, I discover that it is only partially the truth, or even a lie. I am confused by the contradictions from what I was brought up believing and what I am now starting to learn.

To explore what we stand to gain requires, then, a pedagogy that emphasizes the interrelationships of how we see as well as the emotional selectivity that shapes what and how we see.

TOWARD AN HISTORICIZED ETHICS

TO DEVELOP AN historicized ethics depends upon recognizing the selectivity of one's vision and emotional attention. As one learns to recognize patterns of emotional selectivity, one also learns to recognize when one "spectates" vs. when one "bears witness." I have chosen to focus on examples of how issues of racism and homophobia spark especially challenging forms of discomfort. Given my underlying premise that education is never a neutral activity, but is inevitably political and never disinterested, I feel compelled to explore territories that evoke some of the most challenging investments and resistances. Readers may feel "imposed" upon, may feel that my suggestions are extreme, "too political," and represent unfair calls to action. I suggest that, even in our engagement here between text and reader, we are experiencing a pedagogy of discomfort. And I remind again that a call to action is not a demand or requirement, but an invitation. Given my definition of education as always an ethical undertaking, any pedagogy or curricula potentially evokes resistance, fear, and anger.

Racism and homophobia in our culture manifest in similar forms of bias, institutionalized discrimination, and marginalization. Concretely, racism and homophobia are effective insofar as they successfully deny access, publicly shame and humiliate, and subject individuals and communities to violence. However, they are also significantly different in their historical origins, trajectories, and contemporary manifestations. Arguably, questions of race are viewed as appropriate curriculum topics and pedagogical concerns, but this was not always the case. The gains that have been made, specifically within education and in the wider cultural climate with respect to discourses about racism, didn't happen "naturally." It is not the case that white supremacists decided racism was a terrible injustice and decided to work to change it. Neither do oppressions right themselves "naturally." The change in curricula over the last two decades, and the change in school climates since 1954, is part of a long, and ongoing, historical struggle against racist injustice, a struggle that is by no means over.[14]

Lesbian and gay rights and equity issues are arguably more volatile in contemporary classrooms than is race. At present, "lesbian and gay pride/ history month" is not celebrated in many public schools. Debates over how and when and what to teach about sexuality, from middle to high schools, are fraught with controversy and contested — contraception and abortion are most often not discussed, along with resounding silences, or condemnation, of lesbian and gay lifestyle. Although most university classrooms do not face the same forms of censure, college-age students' sexuality also renders these issues difficult. For those becoming teachers, these questions are a

Pandora's box. Sexuality, from abortion to sexual preference, is pervasively viewed as a "private" matter. Race, gender, and social class, on the other hand, have come to be viewed as viable topics for public educational discussion.

All of these issues of oppression are frequently dealt with by silence and omission, and sexuality issues perhaps more so. Silence and omission are by no means neutral. One of the central manifestations of racism, sexism, and homophobia is "erasure": omissions and silences that often stem from ignorance and not necessarily from intentional desires to hurt or oppress.

SPECTATING VS. WITNESSING

SPECTATING SIGNIFIES learned and chosen modes of visual omission and erasure. To spectate, to be a voyeur, takes many forms: pleasurable Hollywood experience, "cinematic diversion", "carries" us into the narrative, and rather than critically analyze the images we permit ourselves easy identification with dominant representations of good and evil. Spectating permits a gaping distance between self and other. A photo printed in *Life* magazine of a black man who had been lynched exemplifies an example of spectating with potentially more severe consequences than Hollywood. In her use of this image, artist Pat Ward Williams writes, "WHO took this picture?" and "Can you be BLACK and look at this?" The "reappropriation" of this photograph juxtaposed with Williams's questions scrawled beneath the photo powerfully shatters students' assumption of the objectivity of photojournalism. Students recognize the unspoken ethical question embedded in spectating: Why didn't that photographer *do* something? We can then ask: Who is permitted the luxury of spectating; and what is the cost to others when we choose the comfortable safety of distance?

Spectating thus signifies a privilege: allowing oneself to inhabit a position of distance and separation, to remain in the "anonymous" spectating crowd and abdicate any possible responsibility. By contrast, in an essay titled "Can I Be BLACK and Look at This?" author Elizabeth Alexander offers a genealogy of witnessing, specific to the black male African-American watching the televised beating of Rodney King. To witness this event is but one example of how "black bodies in pain" have been made available for "[d]aily consumption [as] an American national spectacle for centuries" (1995: 82).[15] Alexander argues that the "white-authored national narrative deliberately contradicts the histories our [black] bodies know" (1995: 84).

Alexander's example of the historically shaped, collective bodily memories through which "her people" witness violence against black bodies, suggests that members of the dominant culture necessarily "see" these images very differently. In learning to see, one is challenged to disrupt the oversimplifications of "popular history." Rigorously learning the "untold" histories enables a recognition of how truths have been constructed in relation to particular silences.

The spectating or witnessing subject comes to recognize him/herself in relation to dominant cultural representation and to "popular history." The quote from Primo Levi with which I opened speaks to the simplification of popular history. Levi writes further,

> perhaps for reasons that go back to our origins as social animals, the need to divide the field into 'we' and 'they' is so strong that this pattern, this bipartition — friend/enemy — prevails over all others. Popular history, and also the history taught in schools, is influenced by this Manichean tendency, which shuns half-tints and complexities: it is prone to reduce the river of human occurrences to conflicts. (1988, 36–7)

Historiographer Jacques Barzun (1950) also identifies this phenomenon of "shunned complexities," and decries what he terms "popular history." Popular history is the "history which lives in the minds of men," its primary sources school textbooks and mass media. The risks of popular history include that it is (1) discontinuous, and represents historical events as singularities decontextualized from their complex, ongoing processes; (2) "reductive" and oversimplifying; and (3) inevitably partisan, reflecting specific national interests.

Through an examination of popular histories one can trace how and which fears are systematically learned, reiterated, and perpetuated through a constant barrage of images and connotations, increasingly through *visual* symbols and representations.[16] The mass media plays with our dominant cultural constructions of feelings and symbols on a daily basis.[17] Glancing at the newspaper today, I find the president's trip to Africa billed as necessary to demystify "the deep dark Africa." In Western cultures, steeped in long histories of colonization and slavery, fear of the "other" functions as a powerful social symbol and spur to the national psyche.[18] Fear of the other, fear of difference, need not be a racist fear. *Xenophobia* describes a more generalized fear of difference. But the media representations of what the dominant culture needs to fear (1) reflects the *dominant culture's* fears;[19] (2) fuels stereotypes regarding what "we" need to fear.[20]

The aim of discomfort is for each person, myself included, to explore beliefs and values; to examine when visual "habits" and emotional selectivity have become rigid and immune to flexibility; and to identify when and how our habits harm ourselves and others.[21] Responding to Alexander's point that, upon watching the Rodney King beating and trial, "sympathetic white colleagues . . . exempt themselves from the category of oppressor . . . by saying they too were nauseated. . . ." (Alexander, 1995: 85), one of my students corroborates, "I myself often fall into the trap of being defensive and trying to separate myself from the situation."

Another example of spectating is reflected in students' reaction to an independently produced tape by Not Channel Zero on the Los Angeles rebellion. Some of the white students in my seminar express that they are more deeply disturbed by the frequently-televised images of the truck driver being beaten than by the beating of Rodney King. They state that they view the beating of the truck-driver as entirely "unprovoked" and the victim entirely "innocent." I urge them to explore what they mean by "unprovoked" and "innocent." One could argue, I point out, that the beating of Rodney King is more unjust because it is condoned by the state and police force, and represents a long history of the accepted, everyday occurrence of police brutality. The point here is not to rank injustices but to ask, as a teacher, how we can unsettle learned modes of spectating and witnessing. (For example I may ask my students: Is it possible that the truck driver's image was repeatedly aired in the dominant mass media in part to erase or distract from police brutality?)

Witnessing, in contrast to spectating, is a process in which we do not have the luxury of seeing a static truth or fixed certainty. As a medium of perception, witnessing is a dynamic process, and cannot capture meaning as conclusion (Felman 1992: 5). Rather than falling into easy identification, as a witness we undertake our historical responsibilities and co-implication: What are the forces that bring about this "crisis?" As discussed at length in the previous chapter, we can recognize ourselves as a "battleground for forces raging," and by attending to these forces we may "properly carry out our task" (Laub 1992: 68).[22]

By tracing genealogies of particular emotional investments one can come to recognize the emotional selectivity that I call inscribed habits of (in)attention. This approach can be applied to our listening habits, to how we see ourselves and our attachments to personal and cultural identities, and to how we view representations of difference — for example, in film, video, and popular culture, and how we "read" our own experiences.

However, the invitation to question cherished beliefs is not one all students readily accept. A number of my white students' responses explicitly stated they felt "angry and confused and blamed." One student writes, "I felt that Pratt's approach and her tone are full of blame. To be honest, I felt as though she was pointing a finger at me." Another writes, "Our culture is one of blame-placing, so it is very difficult to hold up a mirror to anyone without them feeling like they are being accused."

These students' comments reflect the discomfort encountered when attempting to inhabit a morally ambiguous self. It is easier to retreat to defensive anger, or fall into the "guilt" side of the binary trap. This brings us to another central risk of a pedagogy of discomfort: the reductive model of "innocence vs. guilt." I make a brief segueway to outline the risks and moral reductiveness of either/or thinking.

AVOIDING THE BINARY TRAP OF INNOCENCE AND GUILT

EVEN THE MOST inviting approach to mapping genealogies of one's emotions, in relation to historical legacies of privilege and injustice, often puts one in the no-win trap of "guilt vs. innocence." A model of binary morality severely constrains educational possibilities. Many educators express their frustration that, as they teach social issues such as histories of racism, they encounter white students' unproductive guilt. On the one hand, the student who assumes the "guilty" position often stops participating in discussion, feels blamed, possible defensively angry, and may refuse to engage in further complex self-reflection or critical inquiry. At the same time, guilt cannot be done away with altogether. Not all actions are acceptable or ethical. The challenge within educational environments is to create a space for honest and collective self-reflection and inquiry rather than closing off discussion. At the same time, such inquiry needs to avoid letting ourselves "off the hook" from responsibilities and ethical complexities.

This moral binary reflects the shortcoming of ethical discourses. Ethical language is impoverished by the pitfalls of Western binary, either/or thinking.[23] How can one maintain processes of moral and ethical evaluation, while also pushing ethical evaluative systems beyond reductive versions of good and evil?

Spectating vs. witnessing provides a useful tool for learning how positionalities shift and slip in complex, unpredictable, and precarious ways. Through learning to see how and when one spectates or bears witness it becomes possible, at least provisionally, to inhabit a more ambiguous sense of self not reduced to either guilt or innocence. In this process one acknowledges profound interconnections with others, and how emotions, beliefs, and actions are collaboratively co-implicated.[24] Beyond good and evil lies the possibility, at least in educational transactions, to inhabit an ambiguous sense of self, and this may be deeply discomforting.

A pedagogy of discomfort does not intentionally seek to provoke, or to cause anger or fear. However, as educators and students engage in a collective self-reflection and develop accountability for how we see ourselves, and as we question cherished beliefs, we are likely to encounter such emotions as fear and anger — as well as joy, passion, new hopes and a sense of possibility—in Garrison's words, a "rhythm of loss and reintegration" (1997: 49). Again I emphasize "educators and students" because a pedagogy of discomfort is a mutual transaction.[25] The educator's own beliefs and assumptions are by no means immune to the process of questioning and "shattering." Similarly, it is important that the educator explore what it means to "share" the students' vulnerability and suffering.

Aristotelian and other cognitive accounts of emotions permit one to trace the "phenomenology" of a particularly reaction. To respond in anger does not "mean" the same thing in every circumstance. The reasons for the anger, its etiology, differs and these differences matter. In educational settings, a historicized ethics offers a more complex lens than that offered by the reductive model of innocence vs. guilt. I turn now to explore the phenomenon of anger.

ARISTOTLE'S MORAL ANGER

ANGER IS UNDERSTOOD as a "moral" emotion, one of the ways we measure transgression and injustices. Yet the moral evaluation that anger provides does not issue from the "feel" of anger — increased heartbeat, adrenaline, the "sweet pleasure and rush." No, in fact the sensations of anger are indistinguishable from other possible emotions: arousal, excitement. The distinctions between emotions, and between different shades or types of one emotion such as anger, are not located simply in the feel but rather in the social values, cultural rules, linguistic framing, self-reflective introspection, and an emotion's relation to perception and belief.[26]

This view is often traced to Aristotle, whose analyses of emotions have been widely adopted by feminists and others.[27] Aristotle offers a cognitivist theory of emotion which understands emotions not simply as a feeling or sensation, but rather as intricately intertwined with beliefs and reasons: emotions are about something. The significance of the cognitivist theory of emotions is that we can distinguish the different reasons or kinds of an emotion only through an analysis of the social context.

In a frequently-quoted maxim Aristotle asserts: "anyone one who does not get angry when there is reason to be angry, or does not get angry in the right way at the right time and with the right people, is a dolt." Anger is bound up with a perception or a belief that I have been slighted; and if I do not respond to this slight with anger, I am a dolt.

Aristotle's particular anger, "orge," he defines as a response to a sense of being slighted, a slighting of men's "sense of importance, their dignity, respect and honor . . . and anger arousing slight strikes at, and may well harm, their moral core. It is shaming" (Stocker 1996: 267). On Aristotle's view, anger is the appropriate reaction to feeling shamed when one perceives that one's honor and dignity have been slighted.

Aristotle's maxim seems right: He is describing those instances in which, for example, we have been wrongly accused — and, in such instances, it is preferable that the accused respond to such disrespect with anger, rather than internalize a sense of inferiority. It seems true that in any case in which we feel slighted, we are likely to respond with the feeling of anger: a sense of righteousness and outrage, of having been offended or shamed. We feel angry in cases where we have been wrongly accused. We may also feel outrage on behalf of injustice done to others (though this version of anger is debated extensively within philosophical analyses of Aristotle's conception). Finally, we may feel anger when someone suggests that we bear responsibility in a given situation. Think for example if we complain to a friend about how our beloved has treated us poorly. If our friend suggests that we too may have behaved poorly, we may react with defensive anger: "How dare you suggest I have some responsibility when they are the one at fault!" This is an example where we want or need to protect a particular image of ourselves as good or innocent. Likewise, to suggest that white privilege is unjust, or that by virtue of growing up in our culture we are all "racists," may well encounter defensive anger.

But I want to inquire: Does Aristotle's definition adequately describe all of the different instances of anger? Or, might it be helpful to distinguish different kinds of anger that may represent different forms of moral evaluation?

Philosophers have critiqued Aristotle's account of anger. To begin with, as several contemporary philosophers persuasively demonstrate, Aristotle was referring to a *man's* anger — and not to *any* man's anger, at that: not to a male slave's or a woman's anger. Aristotle's analyses must then be understood as describing the reasons why an *ancient Greek man* should feel angry. Accordingly, in his analysis of Aristotelian anger philosopher Michael Stocker does not invoke "all people" but insistently uses the phase "*Aristotle's man* feels slighted when," etc. In a landmark essay titled "Anger and Insubordination," philosopher Elizabeth Spelman (1989) demonstrates how women's anger has been controlled to maintain women's subordinate status.[28]

Once power relations muddy the waters, evaluating a person's perception of feeling slighted becomes exceptionally complex. One's sense of "dignity," respect and honor is not an objectively measurable fact. Social status is by no means a fixed given, but rather a shifting relation intricately bound up with the hierarchies of one's particular society and culture. One's sense of importance and honor vary tremendously, depending as well on one's internalized values, self-perception, and sense of self-worth.[29] Calvin's "refusal," for example, may represent less an instance of Aristotle's man's wounded honor and more an instance of defensive anger.

At the level of *feeling*, Aristotle's definition of anger as a response to being shamed, to being slighted, accurately describes any angry reaction. However, the phenomenological description of the reasons for our anger matters, and makes a difference to the ethical implications of the situation. Instances where I am simply wrongly accused, and am not culpable in any way, are quite different than cases where in fact I may be partially culpable but do not wish to recognize my implication.

Thus I wish to explore how defensive anger differs from Aristotle's anger, insofar as it is a defense against a felt threat to our precarious identities. I characterize this as "moral" vs. "defensive" anger. After searching high and low for other philosophers who make this distinction, I have thus far found only one instance, described in a 1997 book titled *Emotional Literacy: Keeping Your Heart*, subtitled "How to Educate Your Emotions and Let Them Educate You," by philosopher Francis Seeburger.[30]

In a chapter titled "The Ethics of Anger," Seeburger introduces an example from his local church, in which a three-day discussion/workshop centered on the screening of a video about the experience of several gay people. He describes the video as including the gay people's "expressions of anger" about injustice they had suffered. The context set for the discussion by the bishop was "not to judge anyone's emotions as right or wrong." Seeburger then describes one audience member's angry reaction: "He was angry because what the interviewees had said implied that he . . . was himself bigoted, intolerant, prejudiced, and ignorant. . . . He was, by implication, being called all of those things simply because of the view he held about homosexuality — the view, namely, that homosexuality was a sin condemned repeatedly in the Bible" (1997: 35–6).

Seeburger analyzes the different forms of anger that were expressed, questioning the context suggested by the Bishop that "no emotion was to be judged right or wrong." Seeburger distinguishes, to my surprise, a distinction precisely between the two forms of anger I had recognized in my students: what he calls the "anger of indignation" vs. "the anger of defensiveness." "The anger of indignation is what I feel when I perceive something as an *injustice,* either against myself or some other person. . . . The anger of defensiveness, in contrast, is what I feel when I perceive myself or some other person with whom I . . . have a personal connection to be threatened by something" (44). He goes on to describe the source of the defensive anger as part of the "'fight' half of the 'flight or fight' response triggered by fear. It masks fear, in effect. . ." (45) He analyses the sensitive "ego" that feels threatened, and states that the angry reaction to gay interviewees "added to the injustice originally perpetrated against them because it denied them the right to protest against that initial perceived injustice" (1997: 46). In this way, he states, "victims are made to accept blame for their own victimization" (47).[31] Seeburger concludes, "what's wrong in the case of the anger of the oppressors is precisely the anger that the oppressors feel. . . . Instead, they should feel guilt — a guilt inviting them to cease acting oppressively. . . . Their anger tells the oppressors that what's wrong is in themselves. It is they who need changing, not the world" (49).

Defensive anger can be interpreted as a protection of beliefs, a protection of one's precarious sense of identity. To challenge a student's (or educator's) cherished assumptions may be felt as a threat to their very identity. This reaction of anger should be interpreted not so much as a righteous objection to one's honor, but more as a defense of one's investments in the values of the dominant culture. To respond in defensive anger is to defend one's stake (whether or not one consciously acknowledges that stake). So although this defensive anger may *feel* like Aristotle's Greek man's anger, may *feel* like a response to being shamed, with more nuanced reflection one may come to recognize defensive anger as the protection of precarious identities.

Although Seeburger's analysis resonates with my own analysis of the different instances of anger considered within the actual context of power relations, the question of the philosophical viability of this distinction remains. Seeburger's conviction regarding the viability of the distinction between defensive and indignant anger may seem implausible to some. First, actual felt experiences of anger are not distinguishable in this way. Second, one could argue that every instance of anger is in some sense justified on the same grounds. Anger, in every case, is a sense of being offended or wronged. On this view, even if I express blatant homophobia I have a right to my moral conviction, and your challenge to the "rightness" of my beliefs is just cause for my angry reaction.

Finally, even if we accept a distinction between different reasons for anger, we face the thorny dilemma: Who gets to decide what counts as appropriate anger, and what is rather a defensive masking of one's fear and guilt?[32]

Seeburger implies that there are clear-cut cases in which one should feel guilty. But as I argued earlier, I am wary of falling into the either/or trap of guilt and innocence, especially in educational spaces dedicated to critical inquiry and transformative possibilities.[33] The question of who gets to decide, and how educational inquiry can cultivate this evaluation as part of collective witnessing, poses a genuine challenge.

There are no easy answers to these dilemmas. But it is possible to trace different phenomenologies of anger which offer insight into one's personal and cultural histories. Such emotional genealogies also make visible what we have and have not learned, or chosen, to see. Rather than view this as a "moral loggerheads," a pedagogy of discomfort invites students and educators to engage in collective self-reflection regarding the reasons for our emotions.

Assuming, at least provisionally, that the distinction between defensive and moral anger is plausible, I turn now to examine the fears that underlie defensive anger, fears that go hand-in-hand with the fragility of identity.

DEFENSIVE ANGER AND FEAR

Two key features seem to underlie defensive anger: fear as a response to change, and a fear of loss. Fear of loss may be a fear of losing personal or cultural identities, or a literal, material loss.[34] In most cases of fear, it is often easier to react angrily rather than feel one's vulnerability. Hurt is a painful and passive, even victimized, emotion; anger can feel much more "bittersweet." As Toni Morrison writes, "anger is better. There's a sense of being in anger, an awareness of worth. It is a lovely surging" (quoted in Culley 1985: 216). Fear is not usually analyzed as a moral emotion, but more often categorized as an instinctual and "universal" response of flight or fight. Two classic philosophical depictions of fear as motives for action are: fleeing from a bear; or, the mother fighting to protect her child when she fears it will be harmed. Both cases of fear are categorized as survival instincts.[35]

Of course, in daily life one rarely encounters bears and only some have occasion to protect biological progeny. In most cases of fear, one must examine other sources. What one is taught to fear will vary considerably depending on family, culture, and religion. Idiosyncratic personality differences also play a role. Having grown up in poverty, I may not be afraid of running out of money as I have learned that I will survive in spite of this lack; while another who grew up in similar circumstance may live in fear of returning to that poverty.

In Dewey's analysis of educational contexts, adult habits are systematically taught to children and in fact are intended to shore up the culturally familiar and safe. As a result, natural curiosity and impulses become increasingly rigid.

> Habit reaches . . . down into the very structure of the self; it signifies a building up and solidifying of certain desires; an increased sensitiveness and responsiveness . . . or an impaired capacity to attend to and think about certain things. Habit covers . . . the very makeup of desire, intent, choice, disposition which gives an act its voluntary quality. (quoted in Garrison 1997: 139)

To "break" these habits that constitute the "very structure of the self" necessarily faces one with fears of loss, both felt losses (of personal and cultural identities) and literal losses. "Loss is our human lot. . . . The rhythm of expansive growth [is] a way of learning to cope with the paradoxical relation between expansive growth and loss" (48–9). Dewey states that "adults have given training rather than education" (1932: 92). He argues that "fixed patterns of adult habits of thought and affection" lead to "an impatient, premature mechanization of impulsive activity. . . . The combined effects of love of power, timidity in the face of the novel and a self-admiring complacency has been too strong" to allow young people to "reorganize potentialities" (ibid.). Alice Miller (1983) defines "poisonous pedagogy" as the systematic ways we teach young people *not to notice* the cruelties and injustices inflicted upon them, a point which resonates with Dewey's analysis of rigidities and flexibilities in education. As with poisonous pedagogy, Dewey notes that "The younger generation has hardly even knocked frankly at the door of adult customs, much less been invited in to rectify through better education the brutalities and inequities established in adult habits" (1932: 92).[36]

Dewey speaks of "moral habits" instilled in part through a "maximum of emotional empressement and adamantine hold with a minimum of understanding" (94). "These habitudes," he continues, "deeply ingrained before thought is awake and even before the day of experiences which can later be recalled, govern conscious later thought. They are usually deepest and most unget-at-able just where critical thought is most needed — in morals, religion and politics" (ibid.). Consistent with Dewey, Greene (1973, 1988) argues throughout her work that educators are challenged to discover creative means of disturbing the most familiar habits and assumptions.

In educational contexts, "felt" and "literal" losses frequently manifest as resistance to change. The entrenched character of our (emotional, habitual) investments Dewey calls "personal 'hang-overs'" (ibid.), as "survivals." This speaks to the emotional vicissitudes encountered in a pedagogy of discomfort. While an educator may see herself as simply urging critical inquiry, the other may feel this call as profoundly threatening to their very survival.

An educator's invitation to transformative action and change may well be perceived either as a threat of felt or literal loss. For example, I use the video *It's Elementary* (Chasnoff, 1996) to evidence how lesbian and gay issues can be incorporated into elementary and middle school curricula. This tape documents several public schools where teachers both heterosexual and gay have courageously introduced curriculum addressing lesbian and gay issues.

Some of the students who view this tape express their resistance to taking any risks (not just regarding sex education) in terms of fear of parental reprisal and losing their jobs. Here the loss is overt and visible as a potentially literal loss. But the fears are not always literal; jobs may or may not be lost. Further, these issues are volatile even in educational contexts where the call to action is not about creating curricula but simply evaluating beliefs.[37] In these instances, the call to inquiry and action touches on the deepest core of social and moral and religious values. These fears also reflect the felt loss of an individual's personal identity and the dominant culture's customary fueling of deeply religious, and culturally-specific, "moral panic."[38]

It is important to note that moral panics regarding lesbian and gay lifestyle in education are not always traceable to religious beliefs. For example, holding Christian beliefs does not necessarily lead to resisting such curricula. Students' responses in this class varied; one student wrote about the strength of her Christian beliefs as entirely compatible with her desire to create an inclusive curriculum that addressed lesbian and gay issues. Another student told the class of attending a public event featuring "a proud mother of a lesbian daughter," and reported the impact on him when this speaker said that her interpretation of the Bible was not that gay people should be ostracized but rather embraced with love. The volatility of these issues in our class was remarkable, a heated and contested debate. Students did not seem hesitant to express their resistances and fears, and the tone of exchange reflected impassioned anger from all sides. Regardless of the source of one's beliefs, the call to examine questions of sexuality evokes strong fears and defensive anger.

The precariousness and frailty of identity confirms the myriad ways in which subjectivity exists in complex relation to others. This phenomenon has been explored by numerous philosophers for many decades: Hegel's analysis of the relation of master/slave; Sartre's articulation of self in relation to the other's gaze; psychoanalyst Jessica Benjamin's description of the "bonds of love"; or Virginia Woolf 's witty analysis of how men's anger at women can be traced to his vulnerability: That in fact he is not so much angry as afraid, and afraid because his sense of superiority rests on woman's assigned inferiority.[39]

A great deal more could be said regarding the fragility of identities—think simply of the fact that the identity associated with white privilege, for example, is an identity based not on individually earned merit but rather on an arbitrary social status. Despite the power of the dominant cultural hierarchy, white privilege may be felt as a precarious identity, for on some level the white person recognizes their privileged identity as having little to do with one's actual accomplishments and actions.[40]

In sum, cultural identities and "selves" are founded on vastly frail identities. National identities rest upon complex fictions and investments; students' identities are invested as well in the dominant paradigm. Students and educators may feel a sense of threat to our precarious identities as we learn to bear witness. Witnessing involves recognizing moral relations not simply as a "perspectival" difference — "we all see things differently" — but rather, that how we see or choose not to see has ethical implications and may even cause others to suffer.

The impact of how student resistance to learning to see differently affected one of the students in the class is evident in this e-mail. The letter was sent to me by a student who had participated in a collaborative presentation to our class. This student was one of a collaborative group of four students who had presented a possible "curricula unit" for use with high school-age students, addressing issues ranging from abortion, lesbian and gay issues, and racism in science. Admittedly, I particularly appreciated this letter because the student, having stood in front of our class in essence in my role as the teacher, expressed some of my own feelings. Part of the student's letter to me reads,

> While we were presenting I saw people shaking their heads as if the things that we were suggesting could never be done, and we were ridiculous to suggest that abortion or homosexuality even be taught in the classroom. I have seen this happen during class on other occasions also and I often leave frustrated because no one even wants to consider bringing up difficult issues in their own classrooms. This is something that I would like to be able to do and after class yesterday I was very discouraged. . . . No one would say anything against teaching African-American history and culture even if they did have a problem with it. . . . I am trying to take this as a learning experience about the difficulty that people face when they try to teach something different. I was wondering what you thought about the class reaction on this occasion and others and I was hoping you could offer some suggestions on better ways to teach this material, because after yesterday it did not seem like our plan would be accepted by other teachers or administration. I just wish they would listen and consider options.

The issue of students' resistance to teaching "sensitive" curricula requires enormous sensitivity on my part. I am not in the same boat as they are: My job is not necessarily "threatened" in the same way as theirs may be. However, as an educator committed to social justice, as are many of my students, I find myself in a bind. What are my choices about how to approach the volatile question of sexuality? Do I "omit and erase," choose not to address the question at all in my work in educational foundations? Do I raise the issue, and say, "I realize how difficult this is for you, and that you fear losing your jobs, so never mind — don't think about incorporating this?" Or do I raise these issues and create a space in which we can examine the risks, the call to action, the needs of lesbian and gay youth, as well as children raised in lesbian and gay families; do we debate how we might offer students information about abortion? To raise the issues seems the only ethical path to me. I cannot demand that they choose to address these issues when they go into their classrooms. But, as part of the pedagogy of discomfort, I can hope that they examine their emotional investments and beliefs, evaluate how the actions that follow from their beliefs and strong feelings may affect others, and as a result, become able to evaluate their teaching philosophy and understand when and why other teachers choose different curricula.

Expressions of anger and resistance to change may well be justified — students may be angry at me for suggesting they take a risk that I don't share; they may be angry at me if they feel I am implying they are "hypocritical" by not teaching lesbian and gay issues, when they otherwise express "tolerant" values. But their defensive anger may also reflect fears that have to do with fear of loss that is not material — and one might argue, if we accept a distinction between moral and defensive anger, the latter kind of fear is not about a loss of justice. The question of homosexuality is deeply threatening to all who identify as heterosexual in a culture that thrives on homophobia as a way of shoring up heterosexuality.[41] In short, even identities that are shaped by dominant cultural values are precarious. Thus I would argue that in many instances, whether one faces a felt or material loss, the right thing to do is risk one's own comfort for the sake of others' freedom. However, it cannot be up to the educator, for example, to push a particular path of action.

A SPACE BETWEEN BINARIES
Learning to Inhabit Ambiguous Selves

A PEDAGOGY OF DISCOMFORT is about bodies, about particulars, about the "real" material world we live in. Beliefs are "embodied habits," dispositions to act in a certain way in a given context. Such a view is by now familiar especially through the work of feminist epistemologies, and through concepts such as "situated knowledge."[42] Those who are seeking transcendental rules, a science of morality, or even prescriptions may not be satisfied with this insistence on historical, embodied specificity. The insistence on the importance of the particulars need not lead to moral relativism, or to an infinite "deconstruction" that only "shatters" habits without replacing them. The recognition of our ethical dilemmas as "intrinsically paradoxical," the recognition that contradictory beliefs and desires may coexist, provides creative spaces to inhabit.

However, living with ambiguity is discomforting: In Bordo's words, "[w]hen the universe becomes unmanageable, human beings become absolutists. We create a world without ambiguity in order to escape, as Dewey puts it, 'from the vicissitudes of experience'" (1987: 17). To tolerate ambiguity is as challenging as finding alternatives to the Cartesian binary of "purity and corruption." How are we to decide which "good" habits are to replace the old? Genuine ethical dilemmas arise: What about the student whose worldview and relation to their community is perhaps so shattered that the pieces don't fall back into comfortable harmony?

Two positive approaches provide some "comfort," a means of offering stability in this rough terrain. Minnie Bruce Pratt emphasizes "what we, together, stand to gain." Just as this is not a question of someone having to be a "loser," to question the familiar may lead to greater sense of connection, a fuller sense of meaning, and in the end a greater sense of "comfort" with who we have "chosen" to be and how we act in our lives. Second, the conceptual tool of learning to bear witness to ourselves allows a breathing space. Rather than feel immersed in a torn, excavated, gutted sense of self we can undertake discomfort as an approach: an approach to how we see. Through the capacity to shift our positionality and modes of seeing, we can allow ourselves to inhabit the "old, familiar" spaces and begin our process of inquiry by noticing where we are presently situated.

Throughout *Feeling Power* I have argued that the ethical project of education requires better accounts of the emotional vicissitudes that infuse the classroom. At present, our ethical language and modes of discussion are impoverished by such reductive binary positions as simple "guilt" vs. "innocence" — only one of us can be right. If just one of us isn't right, we are trapped in moral relativism. Before jumping to that response, I suggest we develop a more complex ethical language that recognizes the ambiguous complexity of ethical interrelations. To raise the specter of racism does not mean for the white person that "guilt" is the permanent or only option. A pedagogy of discomfort offers an entrée to learn to in-habit positions and identities that are ambiguous. Once engaged in the discomfort of ambiguity, it is possible to explore the emotional dimensions and investments—angers and fears, and the histories in which these are rooted. We can explore how our identities are precariously constructed in relation to one another, so that to suggest change may feel like a threat to our survival. At minimum, one might offer a responsible accountability for how these emotional investments shape one's actions, and evaluate how one's actions affect others. Learning to live with ambiguity, discomfort, and uncertainty is a worthy educational ideal.

"WHAT NOW?": *The Call to Action*

AS STUDENTS BECOME willing to learn to see differently, they frequently raise the question: "What now?" Numerous times students have expressed that their critical inquiry has brought them to a crossroads of determining for themselves what kinds of action make sense for them to take given their own ethical vision. For example, some tell me how they intervene in conversations with their peers, and take risks by expressing alternative perspectives. Others describe how they will choose to reformulate their curricula and pedagogies.

One student responds to Alexander(1995), "We are obligated not simply to see what goes on in the world, but to witness — to cry out against that which is wrong." The student continues, "I loved how she included Williams's spreading of the guilt from the subjects of the *Life* photograph to the person holding the camera. Similarly, the responsibility for the L.A. riots rests with anyone who watched the videotape and was not outraged, and with all of us who were outraged and still haven't done anything about it." Another student responds by asking: "What do people do with their history of horror? What does it mean to bear witness in the act of watching a retelling? Why [do] such images need to be remembered? I would like to answer [these] questions: 'We cannot repeat the same mistake.'" This student's desire not to repeat the same mistake echoes Walter Benjamin's hope that each generation attempt to "wrest tradition away from . . . conformism" (1969: 255).

These examples reflect students' willingness to examine what they are and are not able to hear, when and why they are able to bear witness vs. when and why they choose the comfortable distance of spectating. Their comments reflect that they have elected a path that considers the complexity of ethical relations, in which they are aware of how we are taught to "see" in historically specific ways. Further, a number of students described in clear terms what path of action they were choosing as a result of learning to see differently.

THE ETHICAL RESPONSIBILITY OF THE EDUCATOR

Those who engage a pedagogy of discomfort need to clarify for themselves and for the students their own ethical responsibilities.

- It matters a great deal how the educator invites students to engage in collective witnessing. It may be that an educator needs to "share" the suffering and vulnerability, to explicitly discuss the pedagogies and one's own emotional challenges. How we speak, how we listen, when and how we "confront" one another matters a great deal. To further understand a pedagogy of discomfort, we need analyses of the "politics of listening."[43] One fear I have is that we don't, systematically, learn to listen very well to one another. Thus we risk creating pain within the pedagogical process, layered on top of what is already a difficult and vulnerable enterprise. The best antiracist and antisexist work I have studied and seen in action is not about confrontation but rather a mutual exploration.
- It must be made clear to students that they are not being graded or evaluated on whether or how they choose to "transform," or whether they undertake "radical" pedagogies of their own. This is not to deny that every educator has particular investments and hopes, and may be disappointed when students "refuse" or "dismiss." My minimal hope is that students examine their values, and analyze how they came to hold those values. If, following such collective self-reflection, they assert: "I am not changing," my work may be done: I have encouraged them to come to an understanding of their educational philosophy. At minimum they may be in a position to explain their rationale, and to understand the other ethical positions of others and the possible harmful effects of their own choices on others. (It is of course extremely difficult to estimate when and how someone may have undergone this kind of self-reflection.) But at a certain point, out of a pragmatic and ethical respect — as well as a concern for the resilience of the educator — one must recognize that the revolution (however envisioned) will not be accomplished by educators per se. The goal is greater clarity of our emotional investments and the ability to account historically for our values and their effects of others.
- Finally, as distance education increasingly replaces the physical classroom, how do our ethical resonsibilities change in the absence of face-to-face

> interaction? How can emotions inform a pedagogy of discomfort as we experience each other through computer-mediated communication, and in virtually disembodied ways?[44]

A pedagogy of discomfort does not assert one right ideology or resolution. Rather, it is a mode of inquiry and invitation that emphasizes a historicized ethics and testimonial witnessing. But this is to delve into the most challenging vicissitudes of human fears. As Primo Levi notes, in the process of "understanding" we desire to "simplify." To inhabit an ambiguous self requires courage.

I have tried to show that Aristotle's ancient Greek man's anger, and the righteous response to a perceived slight and shaming, do not adequately describe the complexities of the fears of change encountered within educational transactions. To conceive of angry resistance to change as simply a justified "moral" response is to subscribe to a culture built on binaries of good and evil, either/or: There can be only one winner, one truth. The first sign of the success of a pedagogy of discomfort is, quite simply, the ability to recognize what it is that one doesn't want to know, and how one has developed emotional investments to protect oneself from this knowing. This process may require facing the "tragic loss" inherent to educational inquiry; facing demons and a precarious sense of self. But in so doing one gains a new sense of interconnection with others. Ideally, a pedagogy of discomfort represents an engaged and mutual exchange, a historicized exploration of emotional investments. Through education we invite one another to risk "living at the edge of our skin," where we find the greatest hope of revisioning ourselves.

---

1 1989: 36.
2 1987: 17.
3 1955/1969: 255.
4 See Chapter 1 and 2.
5 Granted, a perhaps insurmountable challenge is that within educational settings one may never be able to evaluate whether another person has thoroughly interrogated their own cherished beliefs and values.
6 See Laub (1992) discussed in previous chapter.
7 From a written response (April 1998) to an earlier draft of this essay.
8 See Garrison (1996) for an insightful discussion of the dangers and promises of listening in relation to the philosophies of Dewey and Gadamer.
9 "Purposeful selective interests, arising out of need, care, and concern, develop the intuition and continue to determine the context of later thought" (Garrison 1997: 109).
10 I refer the readers to Ross (1964) and to a close reading of Dewey (1932) for exam-

ple, to discern the philosophies of education as involving social and political agendas.

11 See Ross (1964) for a classic analysis of Aristotle's political vision of education. For Aristotle, unlike Dewey, education was explicitly designed to serve the explicit and even absolute interests of the state while Dewey sees education of individuals to be pluralist democrats.

12 These questions are widely addressed by social theorists, from Fanon (1967) to Freire (1973). In *White Women, Race Matters*, Ruth Frankenberg discusses the prevalence of "fear" as a part of the "social geography" of white women's racism. Frankenberg concludes her brief discussion of this fear stating that is crucial to ask what "'interrupts' or changes white people's fear of people of color: for those who are not afraid, what made, or makes, the difference? I do not know the answer to this question, but I register it here as an important one for us as white women to address" (1993: 61).

13 From correspondence, April 1998.

14 Sociology of education details the ongoing challenges of issues of racism, sexism, social class divisions, and homophobia in schools. See for example Fine and Weis (1993); Fine et al (1997); Williams (1991).

15 By taking us through a recounting of historical representations of the black body in pain, and how black writers have documented the experiences of witnessing these, Alexander makes a case for how witnessing is not only an "experienced bodily trauma" but a "collective cultural trauma. . . come to reside in the flesh as forms of memory reactivated and articulated at moments of collective" witnessing (1995: 84).

16 In cultural and media studies see for example Fiske (1987, 1989); Buckingham and Sefton-Greene (1994); Hebdige (1979).

17 I refer to the fact that, within dominant cultural institutions where white privilege is at stake, encouraging fear of black men helps to justify a whole raft of exclusions and penalizations that maintain social stratifications. Yet this is not always an intentionally supremacist act on the part of news publishers; it is not always easy to place "individualized" intention of malicious intent. Racism is institutionalized: for example, individual journalists are writing a story at deadline regarding homeless shelters. They need visual footage for the last minute deadline; archival footage available happens to show black people at a shelter. The journalist's story is about the fact that homelessness and poverty affect both white and black persons. But under time pressure the journalist uses the misleading footage; and, perhaps thinks to themselves, "after all there are black people in shelters." However, this partially "innocent," partially "racist" decision then perpetuates the false image of black people as the only ones populating homeless shelters.

18 See Fanon (1967); West (1992); Memmi (1965); Bhabha (1992); Hall (1994); Patricia Williams (1991).

19 A particularly powerful example of this is the coverage of the Los Angeles Rebellion. View any of the TV news coverage and it is blatantly apparent that the camera and "point of view" are located behind the eyes of the white middle-class person, who is situated outside of the geographical area where the riots occurred. Two articles in the *Washington Post* on the anniversary of these events in 1998 portrayed a disturbing and lengthy defense of the beating of Rodney King: January 25, 1998, A1; January 26, 1998, A1. See also Not Channel Zero's Independent video production on the L.A. rebellion titled "The Nation Erupts."

20 By "need to fear" I refer, for example, to particular fears fueled by the dominant culture. There are fears evoked to stimulate the economy (fear of scarcity, the Protestant work ethic, shame, etc.); to maintain white supremacy (fear of the "black" other, the "yellow" peril, the "immigrant alien"); and to perpetuate male privilege (fear of women challenging male power, girls' success in school threaten-

ing boys' success). These fears have been analyzed from numerous perspectives; within feminist studies, for example, psychoanalysis has been used to explore men's fear of women; in postcolonial studies, relations of race and colonizer/colonized are often studies through discourses of nationalism and social imagination. One valuable analysis of young people's fears surrounding gender reform is explored in Kenway and Willis (1997).

21 These questions present long-standing dilemmas: How are we to judge when our habits harm others and ourselves? How are we to know when we are complying with subjugation? When is one acting against our own best interest or others best interests?

22 See discussion in previous chapter.

23 Primo Levi explores powerful examples of historicizing ethics in his analysis of the experience of Holocaust survivors (1989).

24 On the interrelationship of subjective positions, see for example Bartky (1990); Benjamin (1988); Fanon (1967); Memmi (1965); Sartre (1956); Levinas (1989).

25 Garrison writes, "Teachers are moral artists. They, too, have their potentials actualized by the students and by the creative activities in which they engage . . . " (1997: 45)

26 For a discussion of how our "Sociocultural narratives reinterpret our own experience to us," see Garrison 1997: 139 ff.

27 See Chapter 1 and Chapter 5.

28 I describe Spelman's account of anger in greater detail in Chapter 1.

29 See Fanon (1967) on language and identity in colonized subjectivities.

30 This text is a combination of lay person's philosophy, drawing on Aristotle and Spelman, as well as different philosophies of religion and the author's experiences in what might be called "self-help" movements.

31 This analysis resonated with Campbell's analysis of bitterness; see Chapter 1 and Chapter 5.

32 However, it is interesting to note that the Aristotelian and Dewey conceptions of practical wisdom and the habituation of right character do indeed see some emotions as "better" than others; not all emotions are equally appropriate. For fuller discussion see Sherman (1989,1997); Nussbaum (1995); Garrison (1997); Stocker (1996); Ross (1964).

33 Given more time, I would attempt to argue that in outlining an historicized ethics, we will need to account for differentials in anger and guilt: not all forms of anger are "moral" in the same sense. Affirmative action presents such a case: affirmative action functions to "correct" historical justice; it does not function as a transcendental principle of how to treat all people at all times. I would strongly advocate for these kinds of historical ethics, but, once one acknowledges the question, "Who gets to decide what counts as moral?", one runs the risk of the tables being turned. However, one could argue that, given the myth of equal opportunity, marginalized persons have little left lose so it's worth the risk.

34 Defensive anger may also be channeled into dismissal, pure and simple. Such dismissal is well-described by Rene Arcilla's characterization of the "misanthrope," whose "mood and conduct swings from rude righteousness to stony withdrawal to unguarded naiveté. . . . whatever state he is in, he does not want to learn anymore. He refuses to listen, he says again and again, because he does not respect either the worth of what you are teaching or your worthiness to teach" (1995: 346).

35 In the second case, the act of altruism perpetually fascinates philosophers, as it appears the only predictable altruism in our society. In most cultures altruism is tied to the mother through discourses regarding her natural maternal instincts. I find it troubling that motherhood is persistently naturalized through this discourse of altruism, and that the only altruism or apparently "unselfish" acts we can find in Western culture are those of biological "mothers." It is in part because of

the pervasiveness of this discourse that discourses regarding care as a model for ethics and teaching disturbs me and seems at times too fraught with cultural connotations to extend beyond those connotations.

36 One hopes that in the nearly eighty years since Dewey wrote this, that the younger generation has been invited to "rectify the brutalities and inequities." In any event it is certainly true that radical social movements have transformed education, though whether pastoral power continues to appropriate and subvert the radical tendencies is an open question.

37 For excellent discussions of different curricula and pedagogies addressing sexual orientation, see Linda Garber (Ed.) *Tilting the Tower* (1994).

38 Like Larry Grossberg's example of an "affective epidemic," the charged issues that magnetize around an issue such as lesbian and gay lifestyle are woven so deeply into the cultural fabric that their causes are invisible and slippery. Affective epidemics "most important function is to proliferate wildly so that, like a moral panic, once an affective epidemic is put into place, it is seen everywhere, displacing every other possible investment" (Grossberg 1992: 284).

39 See *A Room of One's Own* (1937). Woolf's analysis of her own anger, and her ensuing analysis of the subtext of anger and vulnerability she discovers in the misogynist writing of Professors during her famous library visit, offering an exemplary example of tracing the genealogy of an emotion.

40 Given this sense of the fragility of white supremacy, perhaps one can begin to make sense of the intensity of the violently defensive anger characteristic of backlash against affirmative action.

41 See Friend (1993) for an argument that homophobia is a key source of sexism.

42 Haraway (1990).

43 For analyses related to politics of listening, see for example Garrison (1996); Levinas (1989); Martin (1998); Irigaray (1996); Miller (1983).

44 My next research project explores how the shift from face-to-face to computer-mediated education shapes how we teach about diversity and gender on-line.

BIBLIOGRAPHY

Acker, Sandra. 1994. "Feminist Theory and the Study of Gender and Education." In *Gendered Education*. Buckingham, England: Open University Press.

Aisenberg, N., and M. Harrington. 1988. *Women of Academe: Outsiders in the Sacred Grove*. Amherst: University of Massachusetts Press.

Alcoff, Linda, and Potter, Elizabeth, eds. 1993. *Feminist Epistemologies*. New York: Routledge.

Alexander, Elizabeth. 1995. "'Can You Be BLACK and Look at This?': Reading the Rodney King Video(s)." In *The Black Public Sphere*. Eds. the Black Public Sphere Collective. Chicago: University of Chicago Press.

All Things Considered. 1995. National Public Radio. 10 December.

Alston, Kal. 1991. "Teaching Philosophy and Eros: Love as a Relation to Truth." *Educational Theory* (Fall).

Althusser, Louis. 1971. *Lenin and Philosophy*. Trans. Ben Brewster. New York: Monthly Review Press.

Anzaldúa, Gloria. 1987. *Borderlands/La Frontera*. San Francisco: Spinsters/Aunt Lute Foundation Books.

———ed. 1990. *Making Face, Making Soul: Haciendo Caras*. San Francisco: Aunt Lute Foundation Books.

Appadurai, Arjun. 1994. "Disjuncture and Difference in the Global Cultural Economy." In *Colonial Discourse and Post-Colonial Theory*. New York: Columbia University Press.

Appel, Stephen W. D. 1996. *Positioning Subjects: Psychoanalysis and Critical Educational Studies*. Westport, Conn. and London: Bergin & Garvey.

Appelfeld, Aharon. 1993. *Unto the Soul*. New York: Random House.

Apple, Michael. 1990. *Ideology and Curriculum*. 2d Ed. New York: Routledge.

———. 1993. "Constructing the 'Other': Rightist Reconstructions of Common Sense." *In Race, Identity, and Representation in Education*. New York: Routledge.

Aptheker, Herbert, ed. 1973. *A Documentary History of the Negro People in the United States*, 1910–1932. Secaucus, New Jersey: Citadel Press.

———. 1974. *A Documentary History of the Negro People in the United States, 1933–45*. Secausus, New Jersey: Citadel Press.

Arcilla, Rene. 1995. "How Can the Misanthrope Learn?" In *Philosophy of Education 1994*. Ed. Michael S. Katz. Urbana, Illinois: Philosophy of Education Society.

Aries, Phillipe. 1962. *Centuries of Childhood: A Social History of Family Life*. New York: Alfred A. Knopf.

Averill, James. 1982. *Anger and Aggression: An Essay on Emotion*. Springer Series in Social Psychology. New York: Springer-Verlag.

Ayers, William, and Janet Miller, eds. 1998. *A Light in Dark Times: Maxine Greene and the Unfinished Conversation*. New York: Teachers College Press.

Baier, Annette C. 1991. "Whom Can Women Trust?" In *Feminist Ethics*. Ed. Claudia Card. Lawrence, KS: University Press of Kansas.

Ball, Stephen J., ed. 1990. *Foucault and Education*. New York: Routledge.

Barrington, J., and T. Beaglehole. 1974. *Maori Schools in a Changing Society*. Wellington: New Zealand Council for Educational Research.

Bartky, Sandra. 1990. *Femininity and Domination*. New York: Routledge.

Barzun, Jacques. 1950. "History — Popular and Unpopular." In *Interpretation in History*. Ed. J. Strayer. New York: Peter Smith.

Beane, James. 1990. *Affect in the Curriculum: Toward Democracy, Dignity, and Diversity*. New York: Teachers College Press.

Bee, Barbara. 1993. "Critical Literacy and the Politics of Gender." In *Critical Literacy: Politics, Praxis, and the Postmodern*. Eds. Colin Lankshear and Peter McLaren. Albany: State University of New York Press.

Belenky, M. F., B. V. Clinchy, N. R. Goldberger, and J. M.Tarule. 1986. *Women's Ways of Knowing*. New York: Basic Books.

Benhabib, Seyla. 1992. *Situating the Self*. New York: Routledge.

Benjamin, Jessica. 1988. *The Bonds of Love: Psychoanalysis, Feminism, and the Problem of Domination*. New York: Pantheon Books.

Benjamin, Walter. [1955] 1969. *Illuminations* New York: Schoken Books.

Berlak, Ann. 1989. "Teaching for Outrage and Empathy in the Liberal Arts". *Educational Foundations* 3 (2): 69–91.

Bernstein, Basil. 1975. *Class, Codes, and Control*. Vol. 3 of *Towards a Theory of Educational Transmissions*. Boston: Routledge and Kegan Paul.

———. 1990. *The Structuring of Pedagogic Discourse*. Vol. 4. New York: Routledge.

Bernstein, Richard. 1993. *Beyond Objectivism and Relativism*. Philadelphia: University of Pennsylvania Press.

Bhabha, Homi. 1992. "Postcolonial Authority and Postmodern Guilt." In *Cultural Studies*. Eds. Grossberg et al. New York: Routledge.

Bick, Ilsa J. 1992–93. "To Be Real: Shame, Envy, and the Reflections of Self in Masquerade." *Discourse: Journal for Theoretical Studies in Media and Culture* 15 (2) (Winter): 80–93.

Bird, W. W. 1928. "The Education of the Maori." In *Fifty Years of National Education in New Zealand: 1878–1928*. Ed. R. Davey. New Zealand: Whitcombe & Tombs.

Bledstein, Burton. 1976. *The Culture of Professionalism*. New York: W. W. Norton & Co.

Blount, Jackie. 1996. "Manly Men and Womanly Women: Deviance, Gender Role Polarization, and the Shift in Women's School Employment, 1900–1976." *Harvard Educational Review* 66 (2) (Summer): 318–338.

Blum, Lawrence. 1980. *Friendship, Altruism, and Morality*. London: Routledge.

Bogdan, Deanne. 1992. *Re-Educating the Imagination: Towards a Poetics, Politics, and Pedagogy of Literary Engagement*. Portsmouth: Boynton/Cook Publishers.

Boler, Megan 1993. "Feeling Power: The Discourses of Emotion in United States Esucation." Ph. D. dissertation. University of California, Santa Cruz.

———. 1994. "Teaching for Diversity." *Concerns* (Publication of Modern Language Association) (Spring).

———. 1995. "Review Essay of Benhabib's *Situating the Self* and Bogdan's *Re-Educating the Imagination.*" *Hypatia* 10 (4) (Fall): 130–142.

———. 1996. "License to Feel: Teaching in the Context of War." *Articulating the Global and Local*. Ed. Douglas Kellner and Ann Cvetkovich. *Politics and Culture Series*. Boulder: Westview Press.

———. 1996b. "Affecting Assemblages: Towards a Feminist Theory of Emotion." Conference paper delivered at Deleuze: A Symposium, University of Western Australia, 6 December 1996.

———. 1997a "The Risks of Empathy: Interrogating Multiculturalism's Gaze." *Cultural Studies* 11 (2): 253–273.

———. 1997b "Disciplined Emotions: Philosophies of Educated Feelings." *Educational Theory* 47 (3) (Summer): 226–246.

———. 1997c. "Taming the Labile Other," Philosophy of Education Society Yearbook.

———. Forthcoming.1999 "Posing Feminist Questions to Freire." In *Paolo Freire and Education: Voices from New Zealand.* Ed. Peter Roberts. Auckland: Dunmore Press.

———. Forthcoming 1999 "Disciplined Absence: Cultural Studies and the Missing Discourse of a Feminist Politics of Emotion." In *After the Disciplines: The Emergence of Cultural Studies.* Ed. Michael Peters. South Hadley, MA: Bergin and Garvey Press.

———. Forthcoming "Capitalizing on Emotion: The Taming of the EQ Alien," *Discourse: Journal for the Theoretical Studies in Media and Culture* 21(2) 1999.

Bordo, Susan. 1987. *The Flight to Objectivity: Essays on Cartesianism and Culture.* Albany: State University of New York Press.

Boscagli, Maurizia. 1992–93. "A Moving Story: Masculine Tears and the Humanity of Televised Emotions." *Discourse: Journal for Theoretical Studies in Media and Culture* 15 (2) (Winter): 64–79.

Bosshart, John. 1939. "Learning to Direct and Control the Emotions." *Harvard Educational Review* 9 (4) (October).452–458.

Bourdieu, Pierre. 1984. *Distinction: A Social Critique of the Judgment of Taste.* Cambridge: Harvard University Press.

Bow, Leslie, Margaret Villanueva, Mary E. John, Bob Anderson, and Raul Homero Villa. 1990. *Towards a "Multi-Cultural" Pedagogy.* Santa Cruz: University of California, The Center for Cultural Studies.

Bowles, Gloria, and Renate D. Klein, eds. 1983. *Theories of Women's Studies.* Boston: Routledge and Kegan Paul.

Braidotti, Rosi. 1994 "Of Bugs and Women: Irigaray and Deleuze on the Becoming Woman." In *Engaging with Irigaray.* Eds. Carolyn Burke, Naomi Schor, and Margaret Whitford. New York: Columbia University Press.

———. (date) "Towards a New Nomadism: Feminist Deleuzian Tracks; Or, Metaphysics and Metabolism." In *Gilles Deleuze and the Theatre of Philosophy.* Ed. Constantin Boundas and Dorothea Olkowski. New York: Routledge.

Brennan, Teresa. 1993. *History after Lacan.* New York: Routledge.

Brigham, Amariah. [1833] 1973. "Remarks on the Influence of Mental Cultivation and Mental Excitement Upon Health." 2d ed. 1833. In *The Beginnings of Mental Hygiene in America.* Ed. Gerald Grob. New York: Arno Press.

Briskin, Alan. 1996. *The Stirring of the Soul in the Workplace.* San Francisco: Jossey-Bass Publishers.

Britzman, Deborah P. 1991a. "Decentering Discourses in Teacher Education: Or, The Unleashing of Unpopular Things." *Journal of Education* 173 (3): 60–80.

———. 1991b. *Practice Makes Practice: A Critical Study of Learning to Teach.* Albany: State University of New York Press.

———. 1992. "The Terrible Problem of Knowing Thyself: Toward a Poststructural Account of Teacher Identity." *Journal of Curriculum Theorizing* 9 (3): 23–46.

———. 1998. *Lost Subjects, Contested Objects.* Albany: State University of New York Press.

Brooks, Barbara, Charlotte Macdonald, and Marget Tennant. 1992. *Women in History* 2. New Zealand: Bridgette Williams Books Limited.

Brown, Wendy. 1995. *States of Injury.* Princeton: Princeton University Press.

Buckingham, David, and Julian Sefton-Green. 1994. *Cultural Studies Goes to School: Reading and Teaching Popular Media.* Bristol, PA: Taylor & Francis Publishers.

Bunch, Charlotte. 1983. "Not By Degrees: Feminist Theory and Education" In *Learning Our Way: Essays in Feminist Education.* Eds. Charlotte Bunch and Sandra Pollack. New York: The Crossing Press.

Bunch, C. and S. Pollack, eds. 1983. *Learning Our Way: Essays in Feminist Education.* New York: The Crossing Press.

Burbules, Nicholas. 1997. "Aporia: Webs, Passages, Getting Lost, Learning to Go On,"

Philosophy of Education Society Proceedings.

Burbules, Nicholas, and Suzanne Rice. 1992. "Can We Be Heard? A Reply to Leach." *Harvard Educational Review* 62 (2) (Summer): 264–272.

Butler, Judith. 1989. *Gender Trouble: Feminism and the Subversion of Identity*. New York: Routledge.

Calhoun, Cheshire, and Robert Solomon, eds. 1984. *What Is an Emotion? Classic Readings in Philosophical Psychology*. New York: Oxford University Press.

Callahan, Raymond. 1962. *Education and the Cult of Efficiency*. Chicago: University of Chicago Press.

Campbell, Susan. 1994. "Being Dismissed: The Politics of Emotional Expression." *Hypatia* 9 (3): 46–65.

———. 1997. *Interpreting the Personal: Expression and the Formation of Feeling*. Ithaca: Cornell University Press.

Cantor, M., and M. Glucksman, eds. 1983. *Affect: Psychoanalytic Theory and Practice*. New York: John Wiley & Sons.

Card, Claudia. ed. 1991. *Feminist Ethics*. Kansas City: University Press of Kansas.

Cassell, Joan. 1977. *A Group Called Women*. New York: David McKay Co., Inc.

Champagne, Rosaria. 1994–95. "Oprah Winfrey's Scared Silent and the Spectatorship of Incest." *Discourse* 17 (2): 123–38.

Chasnoff, Debra. 1996. *It's Elementary*. Videorecording. San Francisco: Women's Educational Media.

Cheshire, Aileen, and Dorothea Lewis. 1996. "The Journey: A Narrative Approach to Adventure-based Therapy." *Dulwich Centre Newsletter* (4): 7–16.

Christian, Barbara. 1988. "The Race for Theory." *Feminist Studies* 14 (1) (Spring): 67–80.

Churchill, Ward. 1992. *Fantasies of the Master Race: Literature, Cinema and the Colonization of American Indians*. Monroe, ME: Common Courage Press.

———. 1993. *Struggle for the Land*. Monroe, ME: Common Courage Press.

Clark, Suzanne, and Kathleen Hulley. "An Interview with Julia Kristeva: Cultural Strangeness and the Subjects in Crisis." In *Discourse* 13 (1): 149–80.

Cleverley, John, and D. C. Phillips. 1986. *Visions of Childhood*. New York: Teachers College Press.

Clifford, James. 1988. *The Predicament of Culture*. Cambridge: Harvard University Press.

Cocks, Joan. 1985. "Suspicious Pleasures: On Teaching Feminist Theory." In *Gendered Subjects*. Ed. Marge Culley and Catherine Portuges. Boston: Routledge & Kegan Paul.

Code, Lorraine. 1988. "Credibility: A Double Standard." In *Feminist Perspectives*. Ed. L. Code, S. Mullett, C. Overall. Buffalo: University of Toronto Press.

———. 1988b. "Experience, Knowledge, and Responsibility." In *Feminist Perspectives in Philosophy*. Ed. M. Griffiths and M. Whitford. London: The Macmillan Press.

———. 1996. "What Is Natural about Epistemology Naturalized?" *American Philosophical Quarterly* 33 (1) (January): 1–22.

Cohen, Sol 1979. "In the Name of the Prevention of Neurosis: The Search for a Psychoanalytic Pedagogy in Europe, 1905–1938."In *Regulated Children/Liberated Children: Education in Psychohistorical Perspective*. Ed. B. Finkelstein. New York: Psychohistory Press.

———. 1993. "The Mental Hygiene Movement, The Development of Personality and the School: The Medicalization of American Education." *History of Education Quarterly* (Summer): 123–49.

Cohn, Carol. 1987. "Sex and Death in the Rational World of Defense Intellectuals." *Signs* 12 (4): 687–718.

Coleman, Peter and Morton Deutsch. 1998. "Mediation of Interethnic Conflict in Schools," in Eugene Weiner Ed., *Handbook of Interethnic Conflict*. NY: Conpinum

Press.
Collins, P. H. 1990. *Black Feminist Thought*. Boston: Unwin Hyman.
Connell, R. W. 1993. "Disruptions: Improper Masculinities and Schooling." In *Beyond Silenced Voices*. Eds. Lois Weis and Michelle Fine. Albany: State University of New York Press.
Cook-Gumperz, Jenny, ed. 1986. *The Social Construction of Literacy*. New York: Cambridge University Press.
Cott, Nancy. 1987. *The Grounding of Modern Feminism*. New Haven, CT: Yale University Press.
Cremin, Lawrence. 1988. *American Education: The Metropolitan Experience 1876–1980*. New York: Harper & Row Publishers.
Cross, Barbara, Ed. 1965. *The Educated Woman in America: Selected Writings of Catherine Beecher, Margaret Fuller, and M. Carey Thomas*. NY: Teachers College Press.
Cruikshank, Margaret, ed. 1982. *Lesbian Studies: Present and Future*. New York: The Feminist Press.
Culley Margo. 1985. "Anger and Authority in the Introductory Women's Studies Classroom." In *Gendered Subject*. Ed. Margo Culley and Catherine Portuges. Boston: Routledge and Kegan Paul.
Culley, Margo, et al. 1985. "The Politics of Nurturance." In *Gendered Subject*. Eds. Margo Culley and Catherine Portuges. Boston: Routledge and Kegan Paul.
Culley, Margo, and Catherine Portuges, eds. 1985. *Gendered Subjects: The Dynamics of Feminist Teaching*. Boston: Routledge and Kegan Paul.
Cvetkovich, Ann, and Douglas Kellner 1996.. *Articulating the Global and the Local*. Boulder, CO: Westview Press.
Dale, Roger. 1989. *The State and Education Policy*. Philadelphia: Open University Press.
Damasio, Antonio R. 1995. *Descartes' Error: Emotion, Reason, and the Human Brain*. New York: Avon Books.
Davis, Angela. 1983. *Women, Race, and Class*. New York: Vintage Books.
de Certeau, Michel. 1984. *The Practice of Everyday Life*. Trans. Steven F. Randall. Berkeley: University of California Press.
de Lauretis, Teresa, ed. 1986. *Feminist Studies/Critical Studies*. Bloomington: Indiana University Press.
———. 1987. *Technologies of Gender*. Bloomington: Indiana University Press.
———. 1990. "Eccentric Subjects: Feminist Theory and Historical Consciousness." *Feminist Studies* 16 (1).
Deleuze, Gilles, and Felix Guattari. 1983. *Anti-Oedipus: Capitalism and Schizophrenia*. Trans. Robert Hurley, Mark Seem, Helen R. Lane. Minneapolis: University of Minnesota Press.
———. 1987. *A Thousand Plateaus*. Ed. and trans. Brian Massumi. Minneapolis: University of Minnesota Press.
Deleuze, Gilles. 1990–95. *Negotiations 1972–1990*. Trans. Martin Joughin. New York: Columbia University Press.
Delpit, Lisa. 1993. "The Silenced Dialogue: Power and Pedagogy in Educating Other People's Children." In *Beyond Silenced Voices: Class, Race, and Gender in United States Schools*. Ed. Lois Weis and Michelle Fine. Albany: State University of New York Press.
Depaepe, Marc, and Frank Simon. 1995. "Is There Any Place for the History of 'Education' in the 'History of Education'? A Plea for the History of Everyday Reality In and Outside Schools." *Paedagogica Historica* 33 (1): 9–16.
Deutsch, Morton. 1993."Education for a Peaceful World." *American Psychologist* 48 (5) (May): 510–6.
Developmental Studies Center. *Dedicated to Children's Intellectual, Ethical and Social*

Development. Handout. Oakland, California.

DeVitis, J. L. ed. 1987. *Women, Culture, and Morality*. New York: Peter Lang Publishing, Inc.

Dewey, John. [1922] 1983. *Human Nature and Conduct*. Carbondale: Southern Illinois University Press.

———. [1934] 1987. *John Dewey: The Later Works, 1925–1953*. Ed. JoAnn Boydston. Carbondale: Southern Illinois University Press.

———. [1938] 1963. *Experience and Education*. New York: Collier Books.

———. [1963.] *Philosophy, Psychology, and Social Practice*. Ed. Joseph Ratner. (date) New York: G. P. Putnam's Sons.

Diller, Ann, Barbara Houston, Kathryn Pauly Morgan, and Maryann Ayim. 1996. *The Gender Question in Education: Theory, Pedagogy, and Politics*. Boulder, CO: Westview Press.

Dirks, Nicholas. 1994. "Introduction." In *Culture/Power/History: Readings in Contemporary Social Theory*. Ed. Dirks et al. Princeton: Princeton University Press.

Dirks, Nicholas, Geoff Eley, and Sherry Ortner. Eds. 1994. *Culture/Power/History: Readings in Contemporary Social Theory*. Princeton: Princeton University Press.

Domestic Economy Reader Standard IV. 1898. New York: Longmans, Green and Co.

Dreifus, Claudia. 1973. *Woman's Fate: Raps From a Consciousness-Raising Group*. New York: Bantam Books.

DuBois, Rachel. 1945. *Build Together Americans*. New York: Hinds, Hayden, and Eldregde, Inc.

———. 1963. *The Art of Group Conversation*. New York: National Board of Young Men's Christian Associations.

———. 1971. *Reducing Social Tension and Conflict*. New York: Association Press.

———. 1984. *All This and Something More: Pioneering in Intercultural Education*. Bryn Mawr, PA: Dorrance and Co.

Du Bois, W. E. B. [1903] 1989. *The Souls of Black Folk*. New York: Bantam Books.

Echols, Alice. 1989. *Daring to be Bad*. Minneapolis: University of Minnesota.

Eisenstein, Hester. 1983. *Contemporary Feminist Thought*. Boston: G. K. Hall and Co.

Eisner, Elliott, ed. 1985. *Learning and Teaching the Ways of Knowing*. Chicago: University of Chicago Press.

Elias, Norbert. [1939] 1978. *The History of Manners*. Trans. E. Jephcott. New York: Pantheon.

Ellsworth, Elizabeth 1989. "Why Doesn't This Feel Empowering? Working Through the Repressive Myths of Critical Pedagogy." *Harvard Educational Review* 59 (3).297–324.

Fanon, Frantz. 1967. *Black Skin, White Masks*. New York: Grove Press.

Feinberg, Walter. 1975. *Reason and Rhetoric: The Intellectual Foundations of 20th Century Liberal Educational Policy*. New York: John Wiley & Sons.

Felman, Shoshana and Dori Laub. 1992. *Testimony: Crises of Witnessing in Literature, Psychoanalysis, and History*. New York: Routledge.

Ferguson, Ann. 1982. "Feminist Teaching: A Practice Developed in Undergraduate Courses." *Radical Teacher* (20). 27–30.

———. 1991. *Sexual Democracy, Women, Oppression and Revolution*. Boulder, CO: Westview Press.

Fine, Michelle. 1993. "Sexuality, Schooling, and Adolescent Females: The Missing Discourse of Desire," In *Beyond Silenced Voices*. Ed. Lois Weis and Michelle Fine. Albany: State University of New York Press.

———. 1987. "Silencing in Public Schools." *Language Arts* 64 (2).

Fine, Michelle, Lois Weis, Linda Powell, and L. Mun Wong. Eds. 1997. *Off White*. New York: Routledge.

Finkelstein, Barbara. 1992. "Education Historians as Mythmakers," *Review of Research of Education* 18: 255–97.

Fisher, Berenice. 1981. "What is Feminist Pedagogy?" *Radical Teacher* (18) 20–24.
———. 1987. "The Heart Has Its Reasons: Feelings, Thinking, and Community-Building in Feminist Education." *Women's Studies Quarterly* xv: 3–4.
Fiske, John. 1987. *Reading the Popular*. Boston: Unwin Hyman.
———. 1989a. *Television Culture*. London: Routledge.
———. 1989b. *Understanding Popular Culture*. Boston: Unwin Hyman.
Flannagan, Owen, and Amelie Rorty, eds. 1990. *Identity, Character, and Morality*. Cambridge: MIT Press.
Flax, Jane. 1993. *Disputed Essays on Psychoanalysis, Subjects Politics and Philosophy*. New York: Routledge.
Foucault, Michel. 1972a. *The Archaeology of Knowledge*. New York: Pantheon Books.
———. 1972b. *The Archaeology of Knowledge, the Discourse on Language*. New York: Tavistock Publishing Limited.
———. 1976. *Mental Illness and Psychology*. New York: Harper & Row Publishing.
———. 1978. *The History of Sexuality. Volume 1: An Introduction*. New York: Vintage.
———. 1979. *Discipline and Punish*. New York: Vintage Books.
———. 1980. *Power/Knowledge*. Brighton, Sussex: Harvester Press.
———. [1982] 1984. "The Subject and Power." In *Art After Modernism*. Boston: David R. Godine.
———. 1984. *Foucault Reader*. New York: Random House.
Frankenberg, Ruth. 1993. *White Women, Race Matters: The Social Construction of Whiteness*. Minneapolis: Minnesota Press.
Frazer, Nancy. 1989. *Unruly Practices*. Minneapolis:University of Minnesota Press.
Freedman, Estelle. 1994. "Small-Group Pedagogy: Consciousness Raising in Conservative Times." In *Tilting the Tower*. Ed. Linda Garber. New York: Routledge.
Freire, Paolo. 1973. *Pedagogy of the Oppressed*. New York: The Seabury Press.
Freire, P., and I. Shor, eds. 1987. *A Pedagogy for Liberation: Dialogues on Transforming Education*. South Hadley: Bergin and Garvey.
———. 1987. "What Are the Fears and Risks of Transformation?" In *A Pedagogy for Liberation*. London: Macmillan.
Freud, Sigmund. [1939] 1961. *Civilization and Its Discontents*. New York: Norton and Company.
Friedman, Susan. 1985. "Authority in the Feminist Classroom: A Contradiction in Terms?" In *Gendered Subjects*. Eds. Margo Culley and Catherine Portuges. Boston: Routledge and Kegan Paul.
Friend, Richard. 1993. "Choices, Not Closets: Heterosexism and Homophobia in Schools." In *Beyond Silenced Voices*. Ed. Lois Weis and Michelle Fine. Albany: State University of New York Press.
Frye, Marilyn. 1983. *The Politics of Reality*. New York: The Crossing Press.
Fuss, Diana. 1989. "Essentialism in the Classroom," In *Essentially Speaking: Feminism, Nature, and Difference*. New York: Routledge.
———. Ed. 1991. *Inside/Out*. New York: Routledge.
———. 1995. *Identification Papers*. New York: Routledge.
Gabriel, Susan, and Isaiah Smithson, eds. 1990. *Gender in the Classroom: Power and Pedagogy*. Urbana: University of Illinois Press.
Game, Ann, and A. Metcalfe. 1996. *Passionate Sociology*. London: Sage.
Garber, Linda. Ed. 1994. *Tilting the Tower: Lesbians, Teaching, Queer Subjects*. New York: Routledge.
Gardner, Howard. 1985. *The Mind's New Science*. New York: Basic Books.
Garlick, A. H. [1897] 1907. *A New Manual of Method*. Seventh. New York: Longmans, Green and Co.
Garrison, Jim. 1996. "A Deweyan Theory of Democratic Listening." *Educational Theory* 46 (4) (Fall): 429–52.
———. 1997. *Dewey and Eros: Wisdom and Desire in the Art of Teaching*. New York:

Teachers College Press.

Garry, Ann, and Marilyn Pearsall, eds. 1989. *Women, Knowledge, and Reality: Explorations in Feminist Philosophy*. Boston: Unwin Hyman.

Gatens, Moira. 1996a. *Imaginary Bodies, Ethics, Power, and Corporeality*. New York: Routledge.

———. 1996b. "Through a Spinozist Lens: Ethology, Difference, Power." In *Deleuze: A Critical Reader*. Ed. Paul Patton. Oxford, UK Blackwell Publishers.

Gay, Peter. 1974. "Introduction: Style from Manner to Matter." In *Style in History*, London: Jonathan Cape Ltd.

Geiger, Susan. 1986. "Women's Life Histories: Method and Content." In *Signs* 11, (2) (Winter): 334–51.

Genovese, Eugene. 1968. "In Red and Black." *Marxian Explorations in Southern and Afro American History*. New York Pantheon.

———. 1972. *Roll Jordan Roll: The World the Slaves Made*. New York: Vintage Books.

Gibbs, Nancy. 1995. "The EQ Factor." *Time*. 2 October: 60–8.

Giddens, Anthony. 1994. *Beyond Left and Right: The Future of Radical Politics*. Stanford: Stanford University Press.

Giddings, Paula. 1984. *When and Where I Enter: The Impact of Black Women on Race and Sex in America*. New York: Bantam Books.

Gilligan, Carol. 1982. *In a Different Voice*. Cambridge: Harvard University Press.

———. 1993. "Joining the Resistance: Psychology, Politics, Girls, and Women." In *Beyond Silenced Voices*. Ed. Lois Weis and Michelle Fine. Albany: State University of New York Press.

Gingrich, Newt. *To Renew America*. 1996. New York: HarperCollins.

Giroux, Henry. 1981. *Ideology, Culture, and the Process of Schooling*. Philadelphia: Temple University Press.

———. 1983. *Theory and Resistance in Education*. Boston: Bergin and Garvey.

Giroux, Henry, and D. Purpel, eds. 1983. *The Hidden Curriculum and Moral Education*. Berkeley: McCutchan Publishing Corporation.

Giroux, Henry, and R. Simon. 1988. "Schooling, Popular Culture, and a Pedagogy of Possibility." *Journal of Education* 170 (1).

Gluck, Sherna Berger, and Daphne Patai, eds. 1991. *Women's Words: The Feminist Practice of Oral History*. New York: Routledge.

Goldman, David, ed. 1990. *Anatomy of Racism*. Minneapolis: University of Minnesota Press.

Goleman, Daniel. 1995. *Emotional Intelligence: Why it Can Matter More Than IQ*. New York: Bantam.

———. 1992. "Pioneering Schools Teach Lessons of Emotional Life." *New York Times*. 3 March: Science Times.

———. 1993. "Managing Your Feelings 101." *New York Times*. 7 November: 4A (Education Life).

Goodman, Nelson. 1978. *Ways of Worldmaking*. Indianapolis: Hackett Publishing. Co.

Gordon, Lynn. 1990. *Gender and Higher Education in the Progressive Era*. New Haven, CT: Yale University Press.

Gordon, Robert. 1987. *The Structure of Emotions*. New York: Cambridge University Press.

Gore, Jennifer M. 1990. "What Can We Do for You! What Can 'We' Do for 'You'?: Struggling over Empowerment in Critical and Feminist Pedagogy." *Educational Foundations* 4 (3): 5–25.

———. 1993. *The Struggle for Pedagogies*. New York: Routledge.

Gorsline, Gerry, ed. 1992. *Shadows of our Ancestors*. Port Townsend, WA: Empty Bowl Press.

Gould, Stephen. 1981. *The Mismeasure of Man*. New York: W. W. Norton & Co.

Graebner, William. 1987. *The Engineering of Consent: Democracy and Authority in*

Twentieth-Century America. Madison: University of Wisconsin Press.

Gramsci, Antonio. 1992. *Prison Notebooks*. Trans. and ed. Quintin Hoare and Geoffrey Smith. New York: International Publishers.

Green, Bill, and Alison Lee. 1995. "Theorising Postgraduate Pedagogy." *Australian Universities' Review* 2: 40–45.

Greenberg, Mark T. et al. 1995. "Promoting Emotional Competence in School-Aged Children: The Effects of the PATHS Curriculum." *Development and Psychopathology* 7: 117–36.

Greene, Maxine. 1965. *The Public School and the Private Vision*. New York: Random House.

———. 1973. *Teacher as Stranger*. Belmont CA: Wadsworth Publishing Company, Inc.

———. 1986. "Landscapes and Meanings." *Language Arts* 63: 8.

———. 1988. *The Dialectic of Freedom*. New York: Teachers College Press.

Greenspan, Patricia. 1988. *Emotions and Reasons: An Inquiry into Emotional Justication*. New York: Routledge

Gregoriou, Zelia. 1995. "Derrida's Responsibility: Autobiographies, the Teaching of the Vulnerable, and Diary Fragments." *Educational Theory* 45 (3).

Griffin, Susan. 1992. *A Chorus of Stones*. New York: Doubleday.

Griffiths, Morwenna. 1988. "Feminism, Feelings, and Philosophy." In *Feminist Perspectives in Philosophy*. Ed. M. Griffiths and M. Whitford. London: Macmillan Press.

———. 1995. *Feminism and the Self: The Web of Identity*. New York: Routledge.

Gross, Bertram. 1980. *Friendly Fascism: The New Face of Power in America*. Boston: South End Press.

Grossberg, Lawrence. 1992. *We Gotta Get Out of This Place*. New York: Routledge.

———.1997. *Bringing it All Back Home*. Durham, NC: Duke University Press.

Grossberg, Lawrence, and Cary Nelson, and Paula Treichler, eds. 1992. *Cultural Studies*. New York: Routledge.

Grosz, Elizabeth. 1989. *Sexual Subversions*. Australia: Allen and Unwin.

———. 1993. "A Thousand Tiny Sexes." In *Gilles Deleuze and the Theatre of Philosophy*. Minneapolis: University of Minnesota Press.

Grumet, Madeline. 1988. *Bitter Milk*. Amherst: University of Massachusetts Press.

Guerrero, Annette Jaimes. 1996. "Academic Apartheid: American Indian Studies and Multiculturalism." In *Mapping Multiculturalism*. Ed. Avery Gordon and S. Newfield. Minneapolis: University of Minnesota Press.

Hale, Nathan, Jr. 1971. *Freud in America: The Beginnings of Psychoanlysis in the United States, 1876–1917*. New York: Oxford University Press.

Hall, Stuart. 1994. "Cultural Studies: Two Paradigms." *In Culture/Power/History: A Reader* in *Contemporary Social Theory*. Ed. Nicholas Dirks, Geoff Eley, Sherry Ortner. Princeton: Princeton University Press.

Haraway, Donna. 1991. *Simians, Cyborgs, and Women: The Reinvention of Nature*. New York: Routledge.

———. 1992. "The Promises of Monsters: A Regenerative Politics for Inappropriate/d Others." In *Cultural Studies*. Ed. Grossberg et al. New York: Routledge.

———. 1997. *Modest Witness @ Second Millennium. FemaleMan Meets OncoMouse*. New York: Routledge.

Harding, Sandra. 1986. *The Science Question in Feminism*. Ithaca, NY: Cornell University Press.

Harding, Sandra, and Merrill B. Hintikka. 1983. *Discovering Reality*. Boston: D. Reidel Publishing Co.

Harre, Rom, ed. 1986. *The Social Construction of Emotions*. New York: Basil Blackwell Ltd.

Hartsock, Nancy. 1983. "Political Change: Two Perspectives on Power." In *Building*

Feminist Theory. Essay from Quest. New York: Longman, Inc..
———. 1981. "The Feminist Standpoint: Developing the Ground for a Specifically Feminist Historical Materialism." In *Discovering Reality*. Ed. Sandra Harding and Merrill B. Hintikka. Boston: D. Reidel Publishing Co.
———. 1988. *Epistemology and Politics: Developing Alternatives to Western Political Thought*. Delivered at International Political Science Association meetings.
Hayles, N. Katherine. 1993. "Virtual Bodies and Flickering Signifiers." *OCTOBER* 66 (Fall): 69–61.
Hebdige, Dick. 1979. *Subculture: The Meaning of Style*. New York: Methuen Press.
Henriques, Julian, 1984. "Social Psychology and the Politics of Racism." In *Changing the Subject*. Ed. Julian Henriques et al. New York: Methuen Press.
Henriques, Julian, Wendy Hollway, Cathy Urwin, Couze Venn, and Valerie Walkerdine. eds. 1984. *Changing the Subject*. New York: Methuen Press.
Herman, Barbara. 1993. *The Practice of Moral Judgement*. Cambridge: Harvard University Press.
Herman, Edward, and Noam Chomsky. 1988. "A Propaganda Model." In *Manufacturing Consent*. New York: Pantheon Books.
Higgins, Chris. 1998. "Transference Love from the Couch to the Classroom: A Psychoanalytic Perspective on the Ethics of Teacher-Student Romance." *Philosophy of Education Society Yearbook*.
Hirsch, Marianne. 1992–93. "Family Pictures: MAUS, Mourning, and Post Memory." *Discourse* 15 (2): 3–29.
Hirsch, Marianne, and Evelyn Keller. 1990. *Conflicts in Feminism*. New York: Routledge.
Hirschfelder, Arlene, ed. 1995. *Native Heritage: Personal Accounts by American Indians 1790–present*. New York: Macmillan.
Hochschild, Arlie Russell. 1983. *The Managed Heart: The Commercialization of Human Feeling*. Berkeley: University of California Press.
Hoffman, Nancy. 1985. "Breaking Silences: Life in the Feminist Classroom." In *Gendered Subjects*. Ed. Margo Culley and Catherine Portuges. Boston: Routledge and Kegan Paul.
hooks, bell. 1989. *Talking Back: Thinking Feminist, Thinking Black*. Boston: South End Press.
———. 1992. *Black Looks: Race and Representation*. Boston: South End Press.
———. 1994. *Teaching to Transgress*. New York: Routledge.
———. 1995. "Teaching Resistance: Racial Politics of Mass Media." In *Killing Rage*. New York: Holt.
Houston, Barbara. 1992. "In Praise of Blame." *Hypatia* 7 (4) (Fall): 128–47.
Hull, G., P. B. Scott, and B. Smith, eds. 1982. *All the Women Are White, All the Blacks Are Men, But Some of Us Are Brave*. New York: The Feminist Press.
Hull, Gloria, and Barbara Smith. 1983. "The Politics of Black Women's Studies." In *Learning Our Way: Essays in Feminist Education*. Ed. Charlotte Bunch and Sandra Pollack. New York: The Crossing Press.
Ihle, E., ed. 1992. *Black Women in Higher Education: An Anthology of Essays, Studies, and Documents*. New York: Garland.
Irigaray, Luce. 1996. *I Love to You*. New York: Routledge.
Jack, Christine. 1995. "School History: Reconstructing the Lived Experience." Australia and New Zealand History of Education Society. Collected Papers of the 24th Annual Conference, Sydney 1995. 131–143.
Jacoby, Russell, and Naomi Glauberman. 1995. *The Bell Curve Debate: History, Documents, Opinions*. New York: Times Books.
Jaggar, Alison. 1989. "Love and Knowledge: Emotion in Feminist Epistemology." In *Gender/Body/Knowledge*. Ed. Alison Jaggar and Susan Bordo. New Brunswick: Rutgers University Press.

Jaggar, Alison and Susan Bordo, eds. 1989. *Gender/Body/Knowledge*. New Brunswick: Rutgers University Press.

Jarrett, James. 1972. "Countering Alienation," *Journal of Aesthetic Education*. 6(1) 179-91.

Jenkins, Kuni, and Kay Morris Matthews. 1995. *Hukarere and the Politics of Maori Girls' Schooling 1875–1995*. Auckland: Dunmore Press.

Johnston, Basil. 1993. "A Day in the Life of Spanish." In *Growing up Native American*. Ed. Patricia Riley. New York: Avon Books.

Jones, Alison. 1991. *At School, I've Got a Chance*. New Zealand: Dunmore Press Ltd.

———. 1998a *Surveillance and Student Handwriting: Tracing the Body*. American Educational Research Association Conference. San Diego, April 1998.

———. 1998b. *Pedagogical Desires at the Border: Absolution and Difference in the University Classroom*. Winds of Change: Women and the Culture of the Universities International Conference. Sydney, Australia, 13–17 July 1998.

Jones, Karen. 1996. "Trust as an Affective Attitude." *Ethics* 107 (October): 4–25.

Jones, Seth. 1996. "Schools Try Conflict Resolution to Help Students Stay Focused on Facts, Not Fights." *Christian Science Monitor*. 21 October.

Jordan, June. 1985. *On Call: Political Essays*. Boston: South End Press.

Judis, John B. 1991. "Why Bush Voucher Plan Would be a Poor Choice." *In These Times*. (September): 18–24.

Katz, Michael. 1971. *Class, Bureaucracy, and School*. New York: Praeger.

Katz, M., M. Doucet, and M. Stern. 1982. "Early Industrial Capitalism: Public Education and Social Problems." *The Social Organization of Early Industrial Capitalism*. Ed. Katz et al. Cambridge: Harvard University Press.

Keller, Evelyn Fox. 1985. *Reflections on Gender and Science*. New Haven, CT: Yale University Press.

Kenway, Jane, and Helen Modra. 1992. "Feminist Pedagogy and Emancipatory Possibilities." In *Feminisms and Critical Pedagogy*. Ed. Carmen Luke and Jennifer Gore. New York: Routledge.

Kenway, Jane, and Sue Willis. 1997. *Answering Back, Girls, Boys, and Feminism in Schools*. New York: Allen & Unwin.

Klein, Julie Thompson. 1993. "Blurring, Cracking, and Crossing: Permeation and the Fracturing of Discipline." *Knowledges: Historical and Critical Studies in Disciplinarity*. Ed. Ellen Messer-Davidow, David Shumway, David Sylvan. Charlottesville: University Press of Virginia.

Kohli, Wendy. 1995. *Critical Conversations in Philosophy of Education*. New York: Routledge.

Konradi, Amanda. 1993. "Teaching about Sexual Assault: Problematic Silences and Solutions." *Teaching Sociology* 21 (13–25).

Kramarae, Cheris, and Paula Treichler. 1990. "Power Relationships in the Classroom." In *Gender in the Classroom: Power and Pedagogy*. Ed. Gabriel, Susan, and Isaiah Smithson. Urbana: University of Illinois Press.

Kristeva, Julia. 1982. *Powers of Horror*. New York: Columbia University Press.

Kuhn, Thomas. 1962. *The Structure of Scientific Revolutions*. Chicago: Chicago University Press.

Ladson-Billings, Gloria. 1994. *The Dreamkeepers: Successful Teachers of African American Children*. San Francisco: Jossey-Bass Inc.

Lange, Carl, and William James. [1922] 1967. *The Emotions*. New York: Hafner Publishing Co.

Lankshear, Colin, and McLaren, Peter. 1993. *Critical Literacy, Politics, Praxis, and the Postmodern*. Albany: State University of New York,

Lantieri, Linda, and Janet Patti. 1996. *Waging Peace in Our Schools*. Boston: Beacon Press.

Lantieri, Linda, with Janet Patti. 1996. "The Road to Peace in Our Schools," *Educational Leadership* (September): 28–31.

Lasch, Christopher. 1978. *The Culture of Narcissism*. New York: Norton.

Laslett, Barbara. 1990. "Unfeeling Knowledge: Emotion and Objectivity in the History of Sociology." *Sociological Forum* 5 (3) 413–434.

Lather, Patti. 1990. *Getting Smart: Feminist Research and Pedagogy With/in the Postmodern*. New York: Routledge.

Laub, Dori. 1992a. "Bearing Witness, or the Vicissitudes of Listening". In *Testimony: Crises of Witnessing in Literature, Psychoanalysis, and History*. Ed. Shoshana Felman and Dori Laub. New York: Routledge.

———. 1992b. "An Event Without a Witness: Truth, Testimony, and Survival". In *Testimony: Crises of Witnessing in Literature, Psychoanalysis, and History*. Ed. Shoshana Felman and Dori Laub. New York: Routledge.

Lawn, Martin, Ian Grosvenor, and Kate Rousmaniere, eds. *Silences and Images: The Social History of the Classroom* Forthcoming.

Lazreg, Marnie. 1988. "Feminism and Difference: The Perils of Writing as a Woman on Women in Algeria." In *Feminist Studies* 14 (1).

Leach, Mary S. 1992. "Can We Talk? A Response to Burbules and Rice." In *Harvard Educational Review* 62 (2): 257–271.

Leach, Mary, and Megan Boler. 1998. "Gilles Deleuze: Practicing Education Through Flight and Gossip." In *Naming the Multiple: Poststructuralism and Education*. Ed. M. Peters. New York: Bergin and Garvey.

Lemert, Charles, ed. 1993. *Social Theory. The Multicultural and Classic Readings*. Boulder, CO: Westview Press.

Lerner, G., ed. 1972. *Black Women in White America: A Documentary History*. New York: Vintage Books.

Lerner, Gerder. 1979. "The Lady and the Mill Girl: Changes in the Status of Women in the Age of Jackson 1800–1840." In *A Heritage of Her Own*. Ed. N. Cott and E. Pleck. New York: Simon & Schuster.

Lesko, Nancy. 1996. "Past, Present, And Future Conceptions of Adolescence." *Educational Theory* 46 (4) (Fall): 453–72.

Levi, Primo. 1989. *The Drowned and the Saved*. New York: Vintage Books.

Levinas, Emmanuel. 1989. *The Levinas Reader*. Cambridge: Basil Blackwell.

Lewis, Magda. 1992. "Interrupting Patriarchy: Politics, Resistance and Transformation in the Feminist Classroom." In *Feminisms and Critical Pedagogy*. Ed. Carmen Luke and Jennifer Gore. New York: Routledge.

Lippmann, Walter. [1922]1997. *Public Opinion*. New York: Free Press.

Lloyd, Genevieve. 1984. *The Man of Reason: "Male" and "Female" in Western Philosophy*. Minneapolis: University of Minnesota Press.

Longino, Helen. 1995. "To See Feelingly: Reason, Passion, and Dialogue in Feminist Philosophy." In *Feminisms in the Academy*. Ed. Donna Stanton and Abigail Stewart. Ann Arbor: University of Michigan Press.

Lorde, Audre. 1984. *Sister/Outsider*. New York: Crossing Press.

Lugones, Maria. 1987. "Playfulness, 'World-Traveling, and Loving Perception." *Hypatia* 2(2) 3–19.

Luke, Carmen. 1989. *Pedagogy, Printing, and Protestantism. The Discourse on Childhood*. New York: State University of New York.

———. 1992. "Feminist Politics in Radical Pedagogy." In *Feminisms and Critical Pedagogy*. Ed. Carmen Luke and Jennifer Gore. New York: Routledge.

Luke, Carmen, and Jennifer Gore. 1992. "Women in the Academy: Strategy, Struggle and Survival." In *Feminisms and Critical Pedagogy*. Ed. Carmen Luke and Jennifer Gore. New York: Routledge.

Lund, Frederick H. 1939. *Emotions: Their Psychological, Physiological, and Educative Implications*. New York: Ronald Press.

Lunsford, Andrea, Helene Moglen, and James Slevin, eds. 1990. *The Right to Literacy*. New York: The Modern Language Association of America.

Lutz, Catherine. 1988. *Unnatural Emotions*. Chicago: University of Chicago Press.

Lutz, Catherine, and Lila Abu-Lughod. 1990. *Language and the Politics of Emotion.* Cambridge: Cambridge University Press.

Lyman, Peter. 1981. "The Politics of Anger: On Silence, Resentment, and Political Speech." *Socialist Review* 11 (3) (May–June).

Macdonald, Charlotte. 1984. "What Makes Feminist History Different from 'Ordinary' History?" *Women's Studies Conference Papers*, 43–6.

MacKinnon, Catherine. 1989. *Toward a Feminist Theory of the State.* Cambridge: Harvard University Press.

Maher, Frances. 1985. "Classroom Pedagogy and the New Scholarship on Women." In *Gendered Subjects.* Ed. Margo Culley and Catherine Portuges. Boston: Routledge and Kegan Paul.

———. 1987a. "Inquiry Teaching and Feminist Pedagogy." *Social Education* 51 (3).

———. 1987b. "Toward a Richer Theory of Feminist Pedagogy: A Comparison of 'Liberation' and 'Gender' Models for Teaching and Learning." *Journal of Education* 169 (3).

Manicom, Ann. 1984. "Feminist Frameworks and Teacher Education." *Journal of Education* 166 (1).

Marshall, James. 1996. "The Autonomous Chooser and 'Reforms' in Education." *Studies in Philosophy and Education* 15 (1): 89–96.

Martin, Jane Roland. 1985a. "Becoming Educated: A Journey of Alienation or Integration?" *Journal of Education* 167 (3).

———. 1985b. *Reclaiming a Conversation: The Ideal of the Educated Woman.* New Haven, CT: Yale University Press.

———. 1994. *Changing the Educational Landscape.* New York: Routledge.

Martin, Betsan. 1998. "Luce Irigaray: Introducing Time for Two/ Education and the Face-to-Face Relation." In *Naming the Multiple: Poststructuralism and Education.* Ed. M. Peters. New York: Bergin and Garvey.

Martino, Wayne. 1998. "Powerful People Aren't Usually Real Kind, Friendly, Open People!: Adolescent Boys Interrogating Masculinities at School." AERA Conference. San Diego, 13–17 April.

Massumi, Brian. 1996. "The Autonomy of Affect." In *Deleuze: A Critical Reader.* Ed. Paul Patton. Oxford, UK: Blackwell.

———. 1996b. "The Bleed: Where Body Meets Image." In *Rethinking Borders.* Ed. John Welchman. London: Macmillan.

May, Larry, M. Friedman, and A. Clark. 1996. *Mind and Morals: Essays on Ethics and Cognitive Science.* Cambridge: MIT Press.

Mayo, Cris. 1998. "Gagged and Bound: Sex Education, Secondary Virginity and the Welfare Reform Act." Philosophy of Education Society Conference.

McCarthy, Cameron. 1990. *Race and Curriculum: Social Inequality and the Theories and Politics of Difference in Contemporary Research on Schooling.* New York: The Falmer Press.

McCarthy, Cameron, and Warren Crichlow, Eds. 1993. *Race, Identity, and Representation in Education.* New York: Routledge.

McFall, Lynne. 1991. "What's Wrong with Bitterness?" In *Feminist Ethics.* Ed. C. Card. Lawrence: University Press of Kansas.

McIntosh, Peggy. 1992. "White Privilege and Male Privilege: A Personal Account of Coming to See Correspondences Through Work in Women's Studies." In *Race, Class and Gender: An Anthology.* Ed. Andersen and Collins. Belmont, CA: Wadsworth.

McLaren, Peter L. 1991. "Schooling the Postmodern Body: Critical Pedagogy and the Politics of Enfleshment." In *Postmodernism, Feminism, and Cultural Politics.* Ed. Henry A. Giroux. Albany: State University of New York Press.

Mead, Margaret. 1963. *Sex and Temperament.* New York: William Morrow.

Meese, Elizabeth. 1986. *Crossing the Double-Cross.* Chapel Hill: University of North Carolina Press.

Meisner, Jane. 1998. "Emotional Intelligence." *Better Homes and Gardens* (May):

102–6.

Memmi, A. 1965. *The Colonizer and the Colonized.* (Expanded ed.) Boston: Beacon Press.

Menninger, Karl M. D. 1930. *The Human Mind.* New York: The Literary Guild of America.

Messer-Davidow, Ellen, David Shumway, and David Sylvan. 1993. *Knowledges: Historical and Critical Studies in Disciplinarity.* Charlottesville: University Press of Virginia.

Michaelman, Stephen. 1994. *From Affect to Symbol: A Philosophical Critique of the Concept of Emotion.* New York: State University of New York at Stony Brook.

Michaels, Sarah. 1986. "Narrative Presentations: An Oral Preparation for Literacy with First Graders." In *The Social Construction of Literacy.* Ed. Jenny Cook-Gumperz. New York: Cambridge University Press.

Middleton, Sue, and Alison Jones . 1992. *Women and Education in Aotearoa.* New Zealand: Bridget Williams Books Ltd.

Miller, Alice. 1983. *For Her Own Good: Hidden Cruelty in Child-Rearing and the Roots of Violence.* Trans. Hildegarde and Hunter Hannum. New York: Farrar, Straus & Giroux.

Minh-ha, Trinh T. 1989. *Woman, Native, Other: Writing Postcoloniality and Feminism.* Bloomington: Indiana University Press.

Moglen, Helene, and Evelyn Fox Keller. 1987. "Competition: A Problem for Academic Women." In *Competition: a Feminist Taboo?* Ed. Valerie Miner and Helen Longino. New York: Feminist Press at the City University of New York.

Mohanty, Chandra Talpade. 1988. "Under Western Eyes: Feminist Scholarship and Colonial Discourse." In *Third World Women and the Politics of Feminism.* Bloomington: Indiana University Press.

———. 1989–90. "On Race and Voice: Challenges for Liberal Education in the 1990s." *Cultural Critique* (Winter):179–208.

Mohanty, Chandra, Ann Russo, and Lourdes Torres. 1991. *Third World Women and the Politics of Feminism.* Bloomington: Indiana University Press.

Moraga, Cherrie, and Gloria Anzaldúa. 1983. *This Bridge Called My Back.* New York: Kitchen Table Women of Color Press.

Morgan, Alice. 1995. "Taking Responsibility: Working with Teasing and Bullying in Schools." *Dulwich Centre Newsletter* 2 (3): 16–28.

Morrison, Toni. 1970. *The Bluest Eye.* New York: Pocket Books.

———. 1992. *Playing in the Dark: Whiteness and the Literary Imagination.* Cambridge: Harvard University Press.

Mott Foundation, Charles Stewart 1994. *A Fine Line: Losing American Youth to Violence.* Annual Report.

Nava, Mica. 1995. "Discriminating or Duped? Young People as Consumers of Advertising/Art." In *The Media Studies Reader.* Ed. Paul Marris and Sue Thornham. Edinburgh: Edinburgh University Press.

Neu, Jerome. 1977. *Emotion, Thought, and Therapy.* Berkeley: University of California Press.

Nicholson, Linda. 1980. "Women and Schooling." In *Educational Theory* 30 (3)(summer).

Noddings, Nel. 1984. *Caring: A Feminine Approach to Ethics and Moral Education.* Berkeley: University of California Press.

Noriega, Jorge. 1992. "American Indian Education in the United States: Indoctrination for Subordination to Colonialism." In *The State of Native American: Genocide, Colonization and Resistance.* Ed. M. Annette Jaimes. Boston: South End Press.

———. 1995. *Poetic Justice.* Boston: Beacon Press.

Nussbaum, Martha. 1996. "Compassion: The Basic Social Emotion." *Social Philosophy and Policy.* (13)1

O'Brien, Tim. 1990. *The Things They Carried.* New York: Penguin Books.

Olsen, Tillie. 1965. *Silences*. New York: Dell Publishing Company.

Omi, M., and H. Winant. 1986. *Racial Formation in the United States: From the 1960s to the 1980s*. New York: Routledge.

Ong, Walter. 1977. *Interfaces of the Word*. Ithaca: Cornell University Press.

———. 1982. *Orality and Literacy*. New York: Methuen.

Orner, Mimi. 1992. "Interrupting the Calls for Student Voice in 'Liberatory' Education: A Feminist Poststructuralist Perspective." In *Feminisms and Critical Pedagogy*. Ed. Carmen Luke and Jennifer Gore. New York: Routledge.

O'Sullivan, Tim et al. 1994. *Key Concepts in Communication and Cultural Studies*. New York: Routledge.

Paley, Nicholas. Ed. 1995. "Tim Rollins and the K.O.S.," In *Finding Art's Place: Experiments in Contemporary Education and Culture*. New York: Routledge.

Parker, David, Rosamund Dalziell, and Lain Wright. 1996. *Shame and the Modern Self*. Victoria: Australian Scholarly Publishing.

Parmeter, Sarah-Hope, and Irene Reti, eds. 1988. *The Lesbian in Front of the Classroom*. Santa Cruz: HerBooks.

Pateman, Carol. 1989. *The Disorder of Women*. Stanford: Stanford University Press.

Patton, Paul. 1996. *Deleuze: A Critical Reader*. Cambridge: Blackwell Publishers.

Paulhan, Frederic. [1884] 1930. *The Laws of Feeling*. New York: Harcourt, Brace & Co.

Pearson, Carol, Donna Shavlik, and Judith Touchton, eds. 1989. *Educating the Majority: Women Challenge Tradition in Higher Education*. New York: MacMillan.

Penley, Constance. 1986. "Teaching in Your Sleep: Feminism and Psychoanalysis." In *Theory in the Classroom*. Ed. Cary Nelson. Chicago: University of Illinois Press.

Perry, Theresa and James Fraser. 1993. *Freedom's Plow: Teaching in the Multicultural Classroom*. New York: Routledge.

Peters, Michael A. 1996. *Poststructuralism, Politics and Education*. New York: Bergin & Garvey.

Peters, Michael and James Marshall. 1996. *Individualism and Community: Education and Social Policy in the Post-Modern Condition*. London: Falmer Press.

Piaget, Jean. 1981. *Intelligence and Affectivity*. Palo Alto, CA: Annual Reviews Inc.

Pihama, L., and D. Mara. 1994. "Gender Relations in Education." In *The Politics of Learning and Teaching in Aotearoa — New Zealand*. Ed. E. Coxon et al. Palmerston North: Dunmore.

Pinar, William, ed. 1975. *Curriculum Theorizing: The Reconceptualists*. Berkeley: McCutchan.

Pinar, William, and W. Reynolds, Eds. 1992. *Understanding Curriculum as Phenomenological and Deconstructed Text*. New York: Teachers' College Press.

Poovey, Mary. 1984. *The Proper Lady and the Woman Writer: Ideology as Style in the Works of Mary Wollstonecraft, Mary Shelley, and Jane Austen*. Chicago: University of Chicago Press.

———. 1988. *Uneven Developments*. Chicago. University of Chicago Press.

Popkewitz, Thomas. 1991. *A Political Sociology of Educational Reform*. New York: Teachers College Press.

Postman, Neil. 1988. "News." In *Conscientious Objections: Stirring Up Trouble About Language, Technology, and Education*. New York: Knopf.

———. 1995. "Some Gods that Fail." In *The End of Education*. New York: Knopf.

Postman, Neil, and Charles Weingartner. 1969. "Crap Detecting." In *Teaching as a Subversive Activity*. New York: Dell Publishing Co.

Pratt, Minnie Bruce. 1984. *Identity: Skin/Blood/Heart. In Yours in Struggle*. Ed. Bulkin et al. New York: Longhaul Press.

Prentice, A., and M. Theobald, Eds. 1991. *Women Who Taught*. Toronto: University of Toronto Press.

Prescott, Daniel. 1938. *Emotions and the Educative Process*. American Council of Education.

———. ed. 1957. *The Child in the Educative Process*. New York: McGraw-Hill Book Company, Inc.

Prudential Foundation. 1995. *Everyday Heroes: Rocks in the Community*. Annual Report.

Rabinow, Paul. Ed. 1984. *The Foucalt Reader*. New York: Pantheon Books

Rawls, John. 1972. *A Theory of Justice*. Cambridge: Harvard University Press.

Ray, Isaac. 1963. *Mental Hygiene*. New York: Hafner Publishing Co.

Raymond, Janice. 1985. "Women's Studies: A Knowledge of One's Own." In *Gendered Subjects*. Ed. Margo Culley and Catherine Portuges. Boston: Routledge and Kegan Paul.

RCCP National Center. "An Initiative of Educators for Social Responsibility." Brochure. (Handout A). New York.

Redl, Fritz, and William Wattenberg. 1951. *Mental Hygiene in Teaching*. New York: Harcourt, Brace & World, Inc.

Rich, Adrienne. 1985. "Taking Women Students Seriously." In *Gendered Subjects*. Ed. Margo Culley and Catherine Portuges. Boston: Routledge and Kegan Paul.

Riley, Denise. 1988. *Am I that Name?: Feminism and the Category of "Women" in History*. Minneapolis: University of Minnesota Press.

Roberts, Peter. 1996. "Rethinking Conscientisation." *Journal of Philosophy of Education*. 30(2). 179–196.

Roderick, Tom. 1997–98. "Johnny Can Learn to Negotiate." *Educational Leadership*. (December/January): 86–90.

Roman, Leslie. 1996. "Spectacle in the Dark." *Educational Theory* 46 (1).

Rorty, Amelie, ed. 1980. *Explaining Emotions*. Berkeley: University of California Press.

———. 1988. *Mind in Action: Essays in the Philosophy of Mind*. Boston: Beacon Press.

Rorty, Richard. 1979. *Philosophy and the Mirror of Nature*. Princeton: Princeton University Press.

Rosaldo, Michelle Z. 1974. *Women, Culture and Society*. Stanford: Stanford University Press.

———. 1984. "Toward an Anthropology of Self and Feeling." In *Culture Theory: Essays on Mind, Self, and Emotion*. Ed. Richard Shweder and Robert Levine. New York: Cambridge University Press.

Roscoe, Will. 1991. *The Zuni Man-Woman*. Albuquerque: University of New Mexico Press.

Rose, Steven, R. C. Lewontin, and L. Kamin. 1984. *Not in Our Genes: Biology, Ideology, and Human Nature*. London: Penguin Books.

Rosenblatt, Louise. 1938. *Literature as Exploration*. New York: Noble and Noble.

Rosenblatt, Roger. 1997. "The Year Emotions Ruled." *Time*. 22 December: 64–8.

Ross, Sir David. 1964. *Aristotle*. Albuquerque: Methuen & Co. Ltd.

Rousmaniere, Kate. 1994. "Losing Patience and Staying Professional: Women Teachers and the Problem of Classroom Discipline in New York City Schools in the 1920's." *History of Education Quarterly* 34. (1) (Spring): 49–68.

Rousmaniere, Kate. 1997. *City Teachers: Teaching and School Reform in Historical Perspective*. New York: Teachers' College Press.

Rousmaniere, Kate, K. Dehli, and N. de Coninkl-Smith, eds. 1997. *Discipline, Moral Regulation, and Schooling*. New York: Garland Publishers.

Rubin, Gayle. 1975. "The Traffic in Women." *Towards an Anthropology of Women*. Ed. R. Reiter. New York: Monthly Review Press.

Ruddick, Sarah. 1980. "Maternal Thinking." *Feminist Studies* 6 (2).

Ryan, W. Carson. 1939. "Review of Mental Conflicts and Personality." Mandel Sherman. *Harvard Educational Review* 9 (1) (January).

Salner, Marcia. 1985. "Women, Graduate Education, and Feminist Knowledge." *Journal of Education* 167 (3).

Sandoval, Chela. 1991. "Feminist Theory under Postmodern Conditions: Toward a Theory of Oppositional Consciousness." In *Sub/versions*. Santa Cruz: University of California.

Sarbin, Theodore R. 1989. "Emotions as Situated Actions." In *Emotions in Ideal Human Development*. Ed. Cirillo, et al. Princeton, NJ: Lawrence Erlbaum.

Sartre, Jean Paul. [1956] 1966. *Being and Nothingness*. Trans. Hazel Barnes. New York: Wash. Square Press.

Scarry, Elaine. 1985. *The Body in Pain*. New York: Oxford University Press.

Scheff, Thomas. J. 1979. *Catharsis in Healing, Ritual, and Drama*. Berkeley: University of California Press.

Scheffler, Israel. *In Praise of the Cognitive Emotions*. New York: Routledge.

Scheman, Naomi. [1980] 1993. "Anger and the Politics of Naming." In *Engenderings: Constructions of Knowledge, Authority, and Privilege*. New York: Routledge.

———. 1996. "Feeling Our Way Toward Moral Objectivity." In *Mind and Morals: Essays on Ethics and Cognitive Science*. Ed. L. May, M. Friedman, and A. Clark. Cambridge: MIT Press.

Schneir, Miriam. 1972. *Feminism: The Essential Historical Writings*. New York: Vintage.

Schniedewind, Nancy. 1987. "Feminist Values: Guidelines for Teaching Methodology in Women's Studies." In *Freire for the Classroom*. Ed. Ira Shor. Portsmouth, NH: Boynton/Cook.

Schrag, Francis. 1972. "Learning What One Feels and Enlarging the Range of One's Feelings." *Education Theory* 22 (4) (Fall): 382–94.

Schwager, Sally. 1997. "Foreward." *Harvard Educational Review* 67 (4) (Winter): ix–xiii.

Scott, Joan. 1991. "The Evidence of Experience." *Critical Inquiry* 17 (Summer): 773–97.

Sedgwick, Eve. 1990. *Epistemology of the Closet*. Berkeley: University of California Press.

Seeburger, Francis. *Emotional Literacy: Keeping Your Heart*. New York: Crossroad Publishing Company.

Sherman, Nancy. 1989. *The Fabric of Character*. Oxford: Clarendon Press.

————. 1997. *Making a Necessity of Virtue: Aristotle and Kant on Virtue*. Cambridge Cambridge University Press.

Showalter, Elaine. 1997. *Hystories*. New York: Columbia University Press.

Shreve, Anita. 1989. *Women Together, Women Alone: The Legacy of the Consciousness-Raising Movement*. New York: Viking.

Silverman, Kaja. 1983. *The Subject of Semiotics*. New York: Oxford University Press.

Simon, Judith, A. 1993. "State Schooling for Maori: The Control of Access to Knowledge." In *Creating Space in Institutional Settings for Maori*. Ed. G. Smith and M. Hohepa. University of Auckland.

Simon, Roger I. 1992. *Teaching Against the Grain*. New York: Bergin and Garvey.

———. 1994. "The Pedagogy of Commemoration and the Formation of Collective Pedagogies." *Educational Foundations* 8 (1): 5–24.

Smith, Barbara, ed. 1983. *Home Girls: A Black Feminist Anthology*. New York: Kitchen Table, Women of Color Press.

Smith, Dorothy. 1987. *The Everyday World as Problematic: A Feminist Sociology*. Boston: Northeastern University Press.

———. 1989. "Emotions, Philosophy, and the Self." In *Emotions in Ideal Human Development*. Ed. Cirillo, et al. Princeton: Lawrence Erlbaum.

Smith, Graham. 1997. *Kaupapa Maori Theory and Practice*. Unpublished dissertation, University of Auckland, New Zealand.

Smith, Linda Tuhiwai. 1992. "Maori Women: Discourses, Projects, and Mana Wahine." In *Women and Education in Aotearoa 2*. Ed. S. Middleton and A. Jones. Wellington: Bridget William Books.

——. 1998. *Decolonizing Methodologies: Indigenous Peoples and Research*. London: Zed

Books.

Snitow, Ann, Christine Stansell, and Sharon Thompson. 1983. *Powers of Desire, The Politics of Sexuality*. New York: Monthly Review Press.

Sofoulis, Zoe. 1996. *What Scholar Would Endorse Me? Transference, Counter-Transference and Postgraduate Pedagogy*. Jessica Benjamin Day Conference. 17 August.

Soja, Edward. 1996. *Thirdspace: Journeys to Los Angeles and Other Real and Imagined Places*. Cambridge: Blackwell.

Solomon, Barbara. 1985. *In the Company of Educated Women: A History of Women and Higher Education in America*. New Haven: Yale University Press.

Solomon, Daniel et al. 1992. "Creating a Caring Community: Educational Practices That Promote Children's Prosocial Development." In *Effective and Responsible Teaching: The New Synthesis*. Ed. F. K. Oser, A. Dick, and J. L. Patry. San Francisco: Jossey-Bass.

Solomon, Robert C. 1976. *The Passions*. New York: Anchor Press/Doubleday.

Spelman, Elizabeth V. 1988. *Inessential Woman: Problems of Exclusion in Feminist Thought*. Boston: Beacon Books.

———. 1989. "Anger and Insubordination." In *Women, Knowledge, and Reality*. Boston: Unnwin Hyman.

———. 1991. "The Virtue of Feeling and the Feeling of Virtue." In *Feminist Ethics*. Ed. Claudia Card. Lawrence: University Press of Kansas.

Spiegelman, Art. 1986. *MAUS*. New York: Pantheon Books.

Spivak, Gayatri Chakravorty. 1987. *In Other Worlds*. New York: Routledge.

———. 1990. *The Post-Colonial Critic*. Ed. Sarah Harasym. New York: Routledge.

———. 1993. *Outside in the Teaching Machine*. New York: Routledge.

Spring, Joel. 1986. *The American School, 1642–1985*. New York: Longman.

Stearns, P. and C. 1986. *Anger: The Struggle for Emotional Control in America's History*. Chicago: University of Chicago Press.

Steedman, Carolyn. 1985a. "'Listen, How the Caged Bird Sings': Amarjit's Song." In *Language, Gender, and Childhood*. Ed. Steedman et al. Boston: Routledge and Kegan Paul.

———. 1985b. "Prisonhouses." *Feminist Review* 20.

Steedman, Carolyn, Cathy Urwin, and Valerie Walkerdine. 1985. *Language, Gender, and Childhood*. Boston: Routledge and Kegan Paul.

Stern, Daniel N. 1985. *The Interpersonal World of the Infant: A View from Psychoanalysis and Developmental Psychology*. New York: Basic Books.

Stern, Fritz. [1956] 1970. "Introduction." In *The Varieties of History from Voltaire to the Present*. New York: World Publishing Company.

Stocker, Michael. 1996. *Valuing Emotions*. New York: Cambridge University Press.

Stodghill, Ron. 1997. "The Promise Keepers." *Time*. 13 October.

Stone, Allucque're.1995. *The War of Desire and Technology*. Cambridge: MIT Press.

Stone, Lynda, ed. 1994. *The Education Feminism Reader*. New York: Routledge.

Sweetser, William. [1850] 1973. "An Examination of the Intellect and Passions. New York." In *The Beginnings of Mental Hygiene in America*. Ed. Gerald Grob. New York: Arno Press.

Sykes, Christopher. 1991 [videorecording] *How to Tell A True War Story* (on Timothy O'Brien).

Treichler, Paula. 1986. "Teaching Feminist Theory." In *Theory in the Classroom*. Ed. Cary Nelson. Chicago: University of Illinois Press.

Tyack, David, and Elisabeth Hansot. 1982. *Managers of Virtue*. NY: Basic Books.

United States General Accounting Office. 1995. *School Safety: Promising Initiatives for Addressing School Violence*. Washington: General Accounting Office.

Unwin, Cathy. 1985. "Constructing Motherhood: The Persuasion of Normal Development." In *Language, Gender, and Childhood*. Ed. Steedman et al. Boston:

Routledge and Kegan Paul.

UTS Review. 1997. *The Postmodern University* 3 (1).

Vance, Carole. 1984. *Pleasure and Danger: Exploring Female Sexuality*. New York: Routledge.

Veysey, Lawrence 1965. *Emergence of the American University*. Chicago: University of Chicago Press.

Walkerdine, Valerie. 1981. "Sex, Power, and Pedagogy." *Screen Education* (Spring).

———. 1984. "Developmental Psychology and the Child-Centered Pedagogy: The Insertion of Piaget into Early Education." In *Changing the Subject*. Ed. Julian Henriques et al. New York: Methuen.

———. 1985. "On the Regulation of Speaking and Silence: Subjectivity, Class, and Gender in Contemporary Schooling." In *Language, Gender, and Childhood*. Ed. Steedman et al. Boston: Routledge and Kegan Paul.

Washington, Booker T. 1901. *Up From Slavery — An Autobiography*. New York: Doubleday.

Watt, J. 1989. *Individualism and Educational Theory*. The Netherlands: Kluwer Academic Publishers.

Welch, Lynne, ed. 1990. *Women in Higher Education*. New York: Praeger.

Weiler, Kathleen. 1997. "Reflections on Writing a History of Women Teachers." *Harvard Educational Review* 67 (4) (Winter): 635–57.

———. 1988. *Women Teaching for Change: Gender, Class, and Power*. Boston, MA: Bergin and Garvey.

Weiner, Gaby, ed. 1985. *Just a Bunch of Girls: Feminist Approaches to Schooling*. Philadelphia: Open University Press.

Weis, Lois. 1993. "White Male Working-Class Youth: An Exploration of Relative Priviledge and Loss." In *Beyond Silenced Voices*. Ed. Lois Weis and Michelle Fine. Albany: State University of New York Press.

West, Cornel. 1992. "The Postmodern Crisis of the Black Intellectual." In *Cultural Studies*. Ed. Lawrence Grossberg et al. New York: Routledge.

———. 1993. *Race Matters*. Boston: Beacon Press.

White, Hayden. 1978. "The Historical Text as Literary Artifact." In *Tropics of Discourse*, Baltimore: John Hopkins University Press.

Whitford, Margaret. 1988. "Luce Irigaray's Critique of Rationality." In *Feminist Perspectives in Philosophy*. Ed. Morwenna Griffiths and Margaret Whitford. London: Macmillan Press Ltd.

Williams, Patricia. 1991. *An Alchemy of Race and Rights*. Cambridge: Harvard University Press.

Williams, Raymond. 1961. *The Long Revolution*. New York: Columbia University Press.

———. 1977. *Marxism and Literature*. New York: Oxford University Press.

Williamson, Judith. 1988. *Consuming Passions — The Dynamics of Popular Culture*. New York: Marion Boyars.

Willis, Paul. 1977. *Learning to Labour*. Hampshire: Gower Publ. Co.

———. 1990. *Common Culture*. Buckingham, England: Open University Press.

Wirth, Arthur. [1972] 1980. *Education in the Technological Society: The Vocational-Liberal Studies Controversy in the Early Twentieth Century*. Wash. DC: University Press of America.

Witek, Joseph. 1989. *Comic Books as History*. Jackson: University of Mississippi Press.

Wolf, Stacy. 1993. "Trinh Minh-Ha's 'Difference' as a Pedagogical Metaphor." *Women and Performance: A Journal of Feminist Theory*. 6(1), 31–41.

Woodward, Kathleen. "Freud and Barthes: Theorizing Mourning, Sustaining Grief." *Discourse: Journal for Theoretical Studies in Media and Culture*. 13 (1): 93–110.

———. 1990–91. "Introduction." (special issue on Discourses of the Emotions.) *Discourse: Journal for Theoretical Studies in Media and Culture*. 13 (1): 3–11.

———. 1992–93. "Grief-Work in Contemporary American Cultural Criticism." (Special issue on the Emotions, Gender and the Politics of Subjectivity.) *Discourse: Journal for Theoretical Studies in Media and Culture.* (15) 2: 94–113.

Woodward, Samuel B. 1973. "Hints for the Young In Relation To the Health of Body and Mind." 4th ed. In *The Beginnings of Mental Hygiene in America.* Ed. Gerald Grob. New York: Arno Press.

Woolf, Virginia. 1937. *A Room of One's Own.* New York: Harcourt Brace & Co.

Worsham, Lynn. 1990–91. "Emotions and Pedagogic Violence." (Special issue on The Emotions, Gender and the Politics of Subjectivity.) *Discourse: Journal for Theoretical Studies in Media and Culture* (15) 2: 199–248.

Wub-E-Ke-Niew. 1995. "The Mission School." In *We Have the Right to Exist.* New York: Black Thistle Press.

Young, Iris. 1990. *Throwing Like a Girl and Other Essays in Feminist Philosophy and Social Theory.* Bloomington: Indiana University Press.

Young, Robert. 1990. *White Mythologies: Writing History and the West.* New York: Routledge.

Zinn, Howard. 1980. *A People's History of the United States.* New York: Harper Perennial.

Zuckermann, Mosche. 1988. "The Curse of Forgetting: Israel and the Holocaust." *Telos.* 78 (fall): 43–54.

AUTHOR INDEX

SUBJECT INDEX